The Emperor's
Old Groove

PETER LANG
New York • Washington, D.C./Baltimore • Bern
Frankfurt am Main • Berlin • Brussels • Vienna • Oxford

The Emperor's Old Groove

Decolonizing Disney's Magic Kingdom

EDITED BY
Brenda Ayres

PETER LANG
New York • Washington, D.C./Baltimore • Bern
Frankfurt am Main • Berlin • Brussels • Vienna • Oxford

Library of Congress Cataloging-in-Publication Data

The emperor's old groove: decolonizing Disney's Magic Kingdom /
edited by Brenda Ayres.
p. cm.
Includes bibliographical references and index.
1. Walt Disney Company. I. Ayres, Brenda.
PN1999.W27E48   384'.8'0979494—dc21   2002156041
ISBN 0-8204-6363-9

Bibliographic information published by **Die Deutsche Bibliothek.**
Die Deutsche Bibliothek lists this publication in the 'Deutsche Nationalbibliografie';
detailed bibliographic data is available on the Internet at http://dnb.ddb.de/.

Cover design by Joni Holst

The paper in this book meets the guidelines for permanence and durability
of the Committee on Production Guidelines for Book Longevity
of the Council of Library Resources.

© 2003 Peter Lang Publishing, Inc., New York
275 Seventh Avenue, 28th Floor, New York, NY 10001
www.peterlangusa.com

Printed in the United States of America

To

Brad, Sue, and Dave

CONTENTS

ACKNOWLEDGMENTS

The genesis of this project lies with Susan Hines. She invited several of her friends, including me, to submit abstracts for articles that would analyze Disney's film animation from postcolonial perspectives. Immediately the idea engaged me. I grew up on Disney. And, although many of my intellectual friends prefer movies that are cynical and dark, I am usually the first one at the box office to see the latest Disney animated film. Often I have to watch these movies alone, well, except for the little people who blurt their questions out loud, incessantly, and make the aisles run with sticky Coke. After the movie, I usually have to buy the soundtrack, which will go into my Walkman and keep my mind off the pain and drudgery that come with jogging. For Christmas, my relatives know to buy me T-shirts, sweatshirts, and earrings from Disneystore.com.

I can't help it; I love Disney's animation. I usually laugh and cry more and louder than anyone in the audience (another reason why my friends won't go with me). When I leave the theater, I am reassured that good always triumphs over evil, and a little bit of suffering produces character, and that is the only reason why people have to suffer. It must be the Victorian in me to like Disney so much.

That is not to say that I am not wise as to what Disney tries to sell. I came out of *The Lion King* livid at its gender and racial stereotypes. I do think that Disney does a good thing by teaching children through characters like Quasimodo to know people by what they have inside instead of by their outward appearance. I get goose bumps every time I hear Pocahontas' "Colors of the Wind," believing, surely, that its young hearers will be encouraged to celebrate diversity instead of be afraid of it and/or despise it. When I first saw *Mulan*, I thought, finally, a Disney film conveying that girls can become anything they want or need to be. Last summer, I was delighted with *The Emperor's New Groove* (the source of this manuscript's title), thinking that my two nieces and their generation would really hear an important message, that selfishness and self-centeredness make only unhappiness for all.

However, even though Disney promotes many highly virtuous ideals and socially desirable behavior, I agree with Susan; Disney is insidious. Under the guise of goodness and wholesomeness, these movies propagate Western notions and prejudices and Victorian ideologies that I find egregiously unacceptable and dangerous. Many of them sabotage whatever strides have been made in the recent decades to increase the world's understanding, tolerance, and validity of all of its inhabitants. Regardless of how painful it has been to disparage shows that have brought me such great joy, pleasure, and hope over the years, I have embraced this investigation of the colonizing efforts and effects of Disney's animated films, along with the other contributors, with a sense of necessity and urgency.

Early in the project, I volunteered to run a call for papers in the *PMLA* in order to attract more scholars who shared this mission. Abstracts came from all over the world and from scholars of various disciplines. After initially co-working with me in editing a few of the early articles, Susan had to bow out for the same reason that several other contributors did: pressing work on a dissertation. Susan graciously allowed me to take over, something for which I will always be grateful, because I came to adore the whole business of creating a collection of criticism and because I believed in the importance of this project.

So to Susan, this manuscript and I owe a huge debt.

As well as to the wonderful contributors: Mark Axelrod, Kellie Bean, Stephen Buhler, Richard Finkelstein, Sheng-mei Ma, Dianne Macleod, Pushpa Parekh, Christiane Staninger, Kathleen E. B. Manley, Brian Szumsky, and Christopher Wise. Along with brilliant insights, these people demonstrated great patience with my requests for revision, and were very committed to producing the best articles they could. For more than three years, some of them became my best e-mail buddies. Most of them world travelers, they continued to e-mail from Ouagadougou, Senegal, France, England, India, and elsewhere. Several of them sent words of encouragement and praise. All responded with such courtesy and professionalism, so that the Disney mailbox was a great source of happiness for me. I regret to see it close.

There were some scholars who could not deliver, though, because of busy schedules, and some of these unwritten papers I felt to be a tremendous loss to the project. Additionally there have been several scholars, including myself, who have much to say about non-Disney animated films, Disney nonanimated films, and Disney enterprises. Therefore, I look forward to the success of *The Emperor's Old Groove*, that it might generate more investigation. Much needs to be said about the film industry that forms children's minds.

In addition to these wonderful writers and fellow scholars, I want to express my appreciation to Middle Georgia College for its support of this project. At a two-year college (at least at this one, which prioritizes teaching), there is no such thing as release time of any sort or secretarial or student assistance to support research; nevertheless, through the state-of-the-art technology and other equipment at MGC and with the assistance of Paul Robards who ordered much material through interlibrary loan, this book developed into a reality.

Finally, to Walt Disney and The Walt Disney Company, I want to convey my gratitude for the positive messages that their films have transmitted to generation after generation of young people. The world has known much beauty because of the artistry and music of Disney. It is the purpose of this collection of criticism, however, to censure what is not beautiful, what is not wonderful, what is not colorful about the world of Disney. It is the hope of the scholars that *The Emperor's Old Groove* will promote a world that guarantees freedom for all cultures and individuals, for this world to know peace, not through hegemony, but through the "colors of the wind."

The author and publisher gratefully acknowledge permission for the use of the following material:

Brian E. Szumsky, "'All That Is Solid Melts into the Air': 'The Winds of Change' and Other Analogues of Colonialism in Disney's *Mary Poppins*," from an earlier version titled "'All That Is Solid Melts into the Air': Analogues of Change and Colonialism in Disney's *Mary Poppins*," *The Lion and the Unicorn* 24.1 Jan. 2000. Copyright © 2000 The Johns Hopkins University Press.

Sheng-mei Ma, "Mulan Disney, It's Like, Re-Orients: Consuming China and Animating Teen Dreams," from an earlier version titled "Mulan Disney—It's Like, Re-Orients: Consuming China and the Name of the Dish," *The Deathly Embrace: Orientalism and Asian American Ethnicity* (Minneapolis: University of Minnesota Press, 2000). Copyright © 2000 Sheng-mei Ma.

INTRODUCTION

(He)gemony Cricket!
Why in the World Are We Still
Watching Disney?

Susan Hines and Brenda Ayres

In the 1940 animated film *Pinocchio*, it is the tiny insect, Jiminy Cricket, who is, while genuinely willing, in part conscripted to be the conscience of kindly old Geppetto's wayward wooden boy. When given the freedom and opportunity, Pinocchio chooses the theater over education, and the fantasy of Pleasure Island—a kind of theme park that affords young boys absolute run of the place—over the more abstemious reality of the mainland. Despite the gold badge he wins from the Blue Fairy at the film's conclusion, Cricket proves a notoriously poor conscience. He allows Pinocchio to get away from him at the outset, arriving on the scene (again and again) only after a good deal of stupefyingly ingenuous and woodenheaded thinking has already taken place. Of course, without Pinocchio's unprincipled decision making, there would be little in the way of a story to tell. There would be no dark adventures, no dramatic tension between unconscionable behavior and conscientious thought.

And, arguably, there would be no Disney. Without the boyish zeal with which Walt Disney developed and marketed this particular brand of theater and fantasy, there would be no multinational company, no Disney Productions, Incorporated. It also stands to reason that now, one hundred years after Disney's birth, there would be but a modest corpus of dissenting criticism daring to challenge the wholesomeness of Disney film animation. Dorothy Clarke Sayers, a librarian in California, was one of the first to question Disney's work. That was in 1960, followed by Richard Schickel's analytical biography in 1968. However, Schickel seems loath to infer much of anything negative about Disney, his hero. Schickel's analysis focuses mainly on Disney's popularity as affirmation of middle-class American values with very little complaint. In the seventies, Bruno Bettelheim's *The Uses of Enchantment: The Meaning and Importance of Fairy Tales*, Roger Sale's *Fairy Tales and After*, Nicholas Tucker's *Suitable for Children?*, Jack Zipes' *Breaking the Magic Spell*, and Sandra Gilbert and Susan Gubar's *The Madwoman in the Attic*—all analyze the effect of fairy tales on children. These studies should have immediately spawned a host of criticism on Disney's films that appropriated such fairy tales and made them even more accessible and dele-terious to children. Instead, in the eighties came similar treatments of fairy tales: Ruth Bottigheimer's *Fairy Tales and Society* and Madonna Kol-benschlag's *Kiss Sleeping Beauty Good-bye*. Betsy Cohen's *The Snow White Syndrome* contained a repudiating analysis of Disney's *Snow White* but quickly abandoned it after page 14. In his criticism of those who are critical of fairy tales, Jack Zipes' introduction to *Don't Bet on the Prince* refers little to Disney's adaptations except for a brief mention of Kay Stone's 1975 arti-cle, "Things Disney Never Told Us" (6-7). In her 1993 introduction to a spe-cial issue of the *South Atlantic Quarterly*, Susan Willis had good reason to ask "why there is so little serious criticism of Walt Disney" (1). Since the *Quarterly*'s special issue, Marc Eliot has written a critical biography of Dis-ney, calling him "Hollywood's Dark Prince."[1] In the nineties, two notable collections of Disney criticism were published as well. Routledge's *Disney Discourse: Producing the Magic Kingdom* (1994) and Indiana University Press' *From Mouse to Mermaid: The Politics of Film, Gender, and Culture* (1995) are formidable volumes, building upon Dorfman and Mattelart's seminal postcolonial critique of Disney comic strips, *How to Read Donald Duck: Imperialist Ideology in the Disney Comic* (1975), and confirming to some extent Willis' premonition that "the floodgate of Disney criticism is about to open" (2). What this collection of essays does not confirm, however, is Willis' curiously somber speculation that critical approaches to Disney will be "dominated by postmodern discourse," the kind of analysis she de-scribes as indulging in that "game of mirrors...where history is erased and critical discourse...delights in the erasure" (2).

In fact, *The Emperor's Old Groove* has much to say about reality. It might even come across to some as terribly serious, for it takes little delight in the kind of "erasing" Disney has traditionally promulgated. While they may interrogate Disney's success at capturing and colonizing so many imaginations with some degree of enjoyment and even a certain awe, the crit-ics represented in this volume are nevertheless sincerely committed to setting the record straight. Unlike previous critical collections, this one focuses on the Disney feature films that target children almost exclusively; and, instead of those characteristically unwieldy Disney essays that offer sprawling dis-cussions of numerous films and film subsidiaries, television networks and productions, theme parks, consumer paraphernalia and merchandise, hotel chains, cruise lines, and Disney corporate politics, this volume includes, more simply, a series of close readings of individual animated films.

While such a project is now contextually possible because of the breadth of research and criticism that has already taken place, this deliberately narrow focus is also purposeful. That is, this volume of criticism intends a close, careful look at the very heart of Disney; it demonstrates, as other volumes have argued somewhat tangentially, that Disney's animated films for children are at the center of its ideological hegemony and capitalist expansion. Its theme parks (now in countries such as France and Japan), its "eleven billion dollars in annual sales" (Lewis 95), and its much diversified film, television, recording, and publishing industries are largely predicated on the "magic" that Walt Disney devised with the singular intent of selling to children.

Therefore it is especially important to note how calculated that "magic" has been. For Walt Disney hardly invented the likes of Mickey Mouse in some Coleridgean fit of pure imagination; he was responding to—even seizing upon—a very real cultural crisis in the United States. As Richard de Cordova has noted:

> During the late 1920s and early 1930s the cinema's address to children was contested ground and a matter of frenzied concern. Reformers denounced the movies' influence on children and mounted well-organized efforts across the country to regulate and control this aspect of children's leisure. One particularly important aspect of these efforts involved the creation and supervision of a canon of films for children. (203)

Not only did Walt Disney come along at the right time, he knew American audiences and knew what the majority of them wanted. He also knew that the quickest way to their hearts—as well as to their pocketbooks—would be through their children. While at once pacifying reform-minded adult moviegoers, Disney, who delivered his version of the fairy tale (always with the happy ending) to Depression-era audiences who sought escape and confirmation, gained in a relatively short period of time access to and approval from what is now the largest consumer group in the world: the American family.

That predominantly white, middle-class American audiences are still watching Disney makes plenty of sense; despite the U.S. economy's post-1930s reversal of fortune, the national character is slow to change. Today Americans have their elaborate film-rating system and government-mandated V-chip technology, and Disney is—with its recent barrage of animated films for children: *The Lion King* (1994), *Pocahontas* (1995), *The Hunchback of Notre Dame* (1996), *Hercules* (1997), *Mulan* (1998), *Tarzan* (1999). *The Emperor's New Groove* (2000), and *Atlantis: The Lost Empire* (200 popular and more fiscally hearty than ever. In fact, because there and still is so little in the way of motion picture entertainment s any and all children, Disney now attracts an even more diverse market. Americans of other, non-European racial and cultural groups are watching as well—and often with much of the same credulity.

As Disney brought white American children (and their parents) to the movie theaters to see its various appropriations of nineteenth-century European folktales, such as the Brothers Grimm's *Snow White* (1937), Carlo Collodi's *Pinocchio* (1940), and Hans Christian Andersen's and Charles Perrault's *Cinderella* (1950), it uses a similar strategy to effect a multicultural, even multinational, appeal. Disney's appropriations in the 1990s were especially daring and controversial; the cultural territories of Arab folklore in *Aladdin* (1992), African society in *The Lion King*, Native American history in *Pocahontas*, and French and Chinese canonical literature in *The Hunchback of Notre Dame* and *Mulan*, respectively, have been reconstituted and sanitized to draw in a much larger portion of the children's market. Disney's move in this direction might at first seem a worthy, even admirable, endeavor, no matter what the motivation (i.e., that a multicultural agenda is just good business). But all of the critics in this collection will demonstrate consistently that Disney is not about to abandon its original formula for success—or its mainstay audience—to do some great good in the world.[2]

The Disney company is going to continue to behave much like Pinocchio, doing what seems most attractive, divested of conscience—a kind of pure corporate id, with no strings attached. The moral obligation of educating children need not get in the way of the entertainment business, as the Disney corporation will continue to rely heavily upon the good fairies of its legal department and simply choose to ignore or silence the relatively tiny voices of its critics. As long as the general public is inclined to be amused by the likes of Pinocchio rather than informed (however belatedly) by the likes of Cricket—as long as elaborate, wooden lies go uncontested and are met with no real consequences—Disney, more than likely, will continue along its present course: the course it has always taken.

From the very beginning, children and their families have been the Disney market. The company has sold itself against a backdrop of violence (real and celluloid) in the guise of innocence, packaging itself for mass appeal and reinforcing the status quo of American family values. In contrast to the how-to-make-bombs and cyberporn Web sites on the Internet, for example, emerged Disney.com: The Web Site for Families (not "a" Web site but "the" Web site). The Disney formula, which idealizes states of childhood and adolescence, nevertheless underscores the absolute necessity of the traditional, nuclear family. Thus, child and parent consumer groups are assuaged; despite the independence that Disney child or adolescent animated characters seem to have, they inevitably desire (more than anything else) a family.

Introduction

Of course, independence is usually conferred upon boys in wonderful world: Pinocchio and Mowgli in *The Jungle Book* (1967) tend to do as they please, while Snow White and Cinderella just do more than their share of housework. It is a traditional and, for many, comfortable gender stereotype, but it is one that makes sense to perpetuate if the Disney children's canon is going to be resilient. Characters, such as Ariel in *The Little Mermaid* (1989) and Pocahontas, shouldn't be too different in terms of their limitless spunk and generosity and their limited cultural enfranchisement, or other Disney "masterpieces" might risk losing their conventional appeal. Children, especially, relate to what they know. Radical differences can be bewildering and, in the context of children's entertainment, would require too much in the way of critical or contentious thinking. Disney, instead, feeds the play instinct, disseminating its message not only via film to child but via child to child. Part of the reason even the most politically and culturally aware parents cannot say "no" to Disney is that their children are likely to know about the canon already. The likely scenario is that some of their friends at school will watch and talk about Disney videos; and it is highly likely that they will see their first Disney film at school. In the United States, Disney has emerged not only as an important form of entertainment but as an important form of socialization, a process that Stephen Buhler, one of this book's contributors, calls "Disneyfication" (more fully explained in Part I, in Ayres' chapter, "The Wonderful World of Disney: The World That Made the Man and the Man That Made the World").

The ambivalent position of Disney in the lives of a few of this volume's contributors is worth noting. Stephen Buhler ("Shakespeare and Company: *The Lion King* and the Disneyfication of *Hamlet*"), who admits somewhat reluctantly that he was a devoted Mickey Mouse Club fan during much of his childhood, found the idea of evading or circumventing Disney very tempting when his daughter Tess was born. However, for all his professorial concern about gender stereotypes and cultural misinformation, he acknowledges, "We're subsidizing Eisner....For all the problems with Disney, there hasn't been much competition until recently. It remains to be seen whether competition will encourage greater responsibility and whether external criticisms can foster more constructive self-critique" (Buhler 1997). Pushpa Parekh ("*Pocahontas*: The Disney Imaginary") agrees. Her daughter Shruti has also grown up with Disney. Like Buhler, Parekh has been careful to attend movies with her child and to contest ever so gently—"I don't want to push too much of what we [cultural critics] do on her." Parekh doesn't worry about her daughter too much though, as Shruti sees much of Disney as an outsider anyway; the tropes of sexism and racism are, after all, everywhere. While Parekh herself finds the Disney depiction of Pocahontas to be historically and politically malicious, she can still understand Shruti's enthusiasm. Although it is both inaccurate and unethical to represent and valorize this beautiful brown woman for what (in the simplified Disney view) amounts to selling out her culture to Europeans, Parekh explains that Shruti was very enthusiastic about seeing someone who looks like herself in the movies: "She is so happy at the difference that she doesn't worry so much about the other representations" (Parekh 1997).

Yes, Disney promotes family togetherness in more ways than it may be aware. Cultural materialists and postcolonial critics can kick back and enjoy (however subversively) Disney with their own children, and point out from time to time the irony of the situation. Here they are: full-fledged members of Disney's most revered institution—only they will rarely, if ever, get to see that institution played out in Disney movies. From *Snow White* to *Atlantis*, Disney's animated films tend to focus on the absence or dissolution of families. While courting family viewer empathy, the Disney impetus is to confirm status quo family values by depicting most nontraditional families, most nonnuclear families, as painfully lacking or wholly dysfunctional. The message is clear: In traditional families, threats are always external. Cruella De Vil probably did more than puppy love to foster all that doggy solidarity in *101 Dalmatians* (1961). Nontraditional families, however, are usually plagued with internal, domestic troubles. In *Pinocchio*, Geppetto, who is literally a single parent overnight, makes the kind of error that no stereotypical mother figure could make: He sends his son out into the world to find his way to school, alone, on the first day of his life. Triton, Ariel's father and King of the Sea in *The Little Mermaid*, has no wifely assistance either. The result is that his youngest daughter gets away from him all too readily, in part to create her own more traditional family: a family in which she can be the mother.

Because the American family is central to the Disney enterprise, this collection of essays continues with "Disney Family" and progresses to issues that are linked inextricably to the problematic Disney concept of family. The third and fourth parts of the book, "Disney Women" and "Disney Culture," respectively, build upon these analyses, demonstrating how "traditional" family roles are reflected in society at large as well as projected onto society's big screen. The fifth part of the book, "Disney Literature," observes how Disney has, by affiliating itself with literary texts of high culture, managed to consecrate its own ground while usurping the ground of its literary fathers. Part VI, titled "Disney History," examines how Disney rewrites significant historical events to advance its company ethos. Nowadays when young Americans hear the name Pocahontas, for example, they are inclined nk of the reductive cartoon, not the woman of North and Native American history. When people hear the name Pinocchio, they hardly remember Carlo Collodi's book. They remember the familiar celluloid image of the lederhosen-clad wooden boy and the lyrical tune: "When you wish upon a star / Makes no difference who you are." The average moviegoer might be shocked to learn that Jiminy Cricket, who sings this song in the movie, is squashed like the insect he is in the original Collodi tale—killed by a Pinocchio who is, quite literally, haunted by his conscience.

But always conscious and suspicious of Disney's "happy endings" is Mark Axelrod, the author of the first essay in Part II, "Disney Family." In "Beauties and Their Beasts & Other Motherless Tales from the Wonderful World of Walt Disney," Axelrod exposes Disney's "creative" retellings of classic children's literature, such as Mme. de Beaumont's *Beauty and the Beast* and Andersen's/Perrault's *Cinderella*. His focus is Disney's representation of the family, and in particular its representation of the traditional family's central figure: the mother. In addition to his critique of the general absence of mother figures in Disney, Axelrod examines the paradoxical (mis)treatment of mother figures in animated films that are marketed as "family entertainment." These women, when they do appear, he argues, are generally "reconstituted in the figure of the 'cruel' stepmother." That female authority figures are, more often than not, cast as villains in Disney is also a theme played out in Brenda Ayres' analysis of *Snow White*, "The Poisonous Apple in *Snow White*: Disney's Kingdom of Gender." The stepmother, asserts Ayres, is wicked because "she is not part of a family enclosure....[She is] a power-woman who defies the traditional role as wife and mother."

The opposite of the "power-woman" is, of course, the powerless-woman, the Snow Whites of Disney's world, the tropes of animated wives-and-mothers-to-be. These women are characterized generally as pure, modest, and beautiful; their true natures are often submissive and dependent, inclined toward domestic tasks rather than vocations. The idea that Disney's heroines (if they are not already powerless) tend to abnegate what power they might possess is a thesis common to the essays that make up Part III, "Disney Women." In "Stripping Beauty: Disney's 'Feminist' Seduction," for example, Kellie Bean calls *The Hunchback of Notre Dame* another iteration of the long-standing Disney project of "transforming women into acceptable marriage partners." In order to market the old (successful) formula of patriarchy and misogyny to a modern audience, however, Disney has been careful, Bean notes, to choose or re-create tales that, while they seem more palatably feminist on the surface, actually reinforce the stereotypes of patriarchy and misogyny by turning even mildly defiant women into willing models of female passivity by emphasizing their physical beauty and marriageability.

Like Esmeralda, the sensuously drawn and ethnically "othered" gypsy woman of *The Hunchback of Notre Dame*, the Arab princess Jasmine is, according to Christiane Staninger's "Disney's Magic Carpet Ride: *Aladdin* and Women in Islam," yet another servant of the Disney formula. Jasmine is attractive to a young, American audience because she "wants independence, rejects the suitors who approach her—and does so for reasons of personal dislikes." The moral of her story, however, is that in order to extricate herself from an apparently antifeminist Arabian law and Islamic culture, she must buy into the Westernisms of (a less apparent) individualist patriarchy. For Staninger, who contests thoroughly and systematically Disney's assumed antifeminism of Arab culture, *Aladdin* is deceptively more than a children's story that "the (conservative) Disney Studios could advance without fear." It is, she writes, a "propaganda movie for Western Imperialism" that "shows the supposed unworkability of Middle Eastern traditions and the need for American intervention." Like other authors in this volume, Staninger is not the only critic to note the strange juxtaposition of the Gulf War in 1991 and *Aladdin*'s release in 1992. That gender stereotypes are often played out in the context of cultural stereotypes in Disney is also the subject of Kathleen Manley's essay. For Manley, though, Disney's *Beauty and the Beast* reinforces the stereotype of "Woman As Civilizing Force," an intriguing reading of the typically colonized figure of mother turned colonizer.

Yet, as Brian Szumsky argues in the first of the essays in Part IV, "Disney Culture," mothering (in reality) is far more postcolonial an activity than colonial. "'All That Is Solid Melts into the Air': 'The Winds of Change' and Other Analogues of Colonialism in Disney's *Mary Poppins*" explores Disney's promotion of English ideology, based on a culture that both revels in and struggles with the implications of its imperialist past. It deals with an American film whose subject is, more or less, Great Britain's imperialist decline, representing yet another interesting variation on a theme: colonizer turned colonized. In Szumsky's reading of *Mary Poppins*, the cultural and social fabric of England is depicted as highly unstable. The empire that was nineteenth-century England is at odds with its twentieth-century self: "counter groups...question the preconceptions of the earlier age; suffragettes looking for the vote and voicing opinions regarding the place of women, the anti-imperialist opposition to the Boer War, the rise of Germany and America as world powers and its effect on Britain as a Western leader." Played out against such a backdrop is the story of the Bankses, a white, well-to-do family who are, as the film implies, the emotional victims of their Victorian heritage. The Banks family is, until the arrival of the singing interloper, Mary Poppins, represented as emotionally dysfunctional although extremely well ordered and prosperous. That the family crisis is resolved and that happiness is restored when Mr. Banks in fact quits his allegiance to the bank (literally his employer) is, for Disney, an unusual critique of capitalist expansion but one that, Szumsky argues, allows Disney to "sidestep issues and criticism of America's own imperialist endeavors." That these issues are indeed side-stepped (for Disney fun and profit) is the main point of Christopher Wise's "Notes from the *Aladdin* Industry: Or, Middle Eastern Folklore in the Era of Multinational Capitalism." For Wise, "*Aladdin* represents a 'First World' attempt to creatively resolve the 'problem' (or ongoing crisis) of an 'archaic' Middle Eastern economy or 'mode of production' that refuses easy penetration by multinational capitalism, largely because of Islamic religion, custom, and tradition."

That creative resolutions to problems of culture often begin with crafty revisions of the literature, history, and religion of particular cultures is not only one of the realities of colonial expansion but a Disney trademark. In Part V, "Disney Literature," Stephen Buhler deconstructs the manner in which Shakespearean quotations and analogues are deployed in the presumably African tale of *The Lion King*. His essay, "Shakespeare and Company: *The Lion King* and the Disneyfication of *Hamlet*," critiques the film's appropriation of the Bard in such a way that the effect, argues Buhler, endows the film with a "striking lack of cultural awareness." In Richard Finkelstein's "Disney's *Tempest*: Colonizing Desire in *The Little Mermaid*," a similar conclusion is drawn. However, Finkelstein is much less appreciative (or protective) of the Bard and Western literature in general. By appropriating such literature, Disney, he asserts, "is not desecrating a purer, more appealing version" of any given canonical work but creatively "substituting signs for experiences using an earlier fictional system which did the same."

When Disney borrows from Eastern rather than Western literary canons, however, the view is often a world of difference. Feelings of desecration tend to be more pronounced, and perhaps rightly so. According to Sheng-mei Ma's "Mulan Disney, It's Like, Re-Orients: Consuming China and Animating Teen Dreams," Disney takes on the sixth-century Chinese folk legend of Hua Mu Lan not for the sake of popular dissemination so much as for the sake of popular consumption. The legend is made as palatable (and pronounceable) to an American audience as possible. And the result is the worst kind of stereotyping. So laden is the film with "clichéd notions of the East" and "tired Orientalist objects" that its purpose seems as utterly transparent as Mushu, the dragon, a character in *Mulan* named for the familiar Chinese dish Mooshu Pork. Taking the form of China's most powerful, grandiloquent symbol (the dragon), Mushu in his concluding line, Ma notes, shouts, "Call out for eggrolls!" The imperative, last words of "the Other" are thus familiar and consoling to the average American filmgoer.

In fact, representing the Other as familiar and consoling is one of the more seductive features of Disney's "multicultural" strategy of late—and as Pushpa Parekh argues in "*Pocahontas*: The Disney Imaginary" (the first of the essays in Part VI, "Disney History"), one of its more pernicious features. While the film would appear to pander to an increasingly multicultural America in "an age of 'political correctness,'" Parekh sees the Other figures in *Pocahontas*—the Native Americans—as culturally subsumed. "Disturbingly," she explains, "this rewrite is merely a reinscription of an old colonial practice: utilizing the Other in the business of the spiritual awakening of the European who still dominates the American continent." The practice, however, is less usual for Disney, for it is generally inclined to represent the European American as a kind of missionary or catalyst for the "spiritual awakening" of distant cultures, of foreign peoples. What the film *Aladdin* demonstrates is that Disney will have it both ways.

Not only is *Aladdin* a rather brazen cultural critique of a stereotyped Arab culture, contends Dianne Macleod in "The Politics of Vision: Disney, *Aladdin*, and the Gulf War," but, in the context of recent history, it is rapacious propaganda—or the Disney fairy tale (come true) of how to make "over $500 million" and support American interests in the Persian Gulf. The heroes of the film are young Aladdin and Jasmine, the un-Arabed Arabs who inhabit Disney's fictional city of Agrabah (an obviously jumbled Baghdad) but who become heroes by contesting (and changing) Arabian law and Islamic religious tradition. That the un-Arabed Arabs actually look American (Aladdin was reportedly modeled after actor Tom Cruise) and the stereotyped Arabs look like Saddam Hussein or Ayatollah Khomeini is much more than coincidence. It's entertainment. "Both phases of the Gulf War were presented to the American public as media events," writes Macleod, "but Desert Storm, in particular, was a carefully constructed photomontage of sound bites and media clips designed to rivet viewers with short attention spans by simplifying the difference between good and evil and by keeping them entertained with nocturnal close-ups of exotic locales, terrifying scenes of destruction, and a dazzling display of technology. So did *Aladdin*."

The ethos of oversimplification and subjectivity, this force of Disneyfication, is a major concern shared by the authors of this collection. A child's experience of the world *is* oversimplified and subjective, and to some degree, that is the pure, idyllic beauty of childhood egoism. But it is egoism nonetheless: a regard only for the self—the Other can be acknowledged but only in relation to the self. It is the egoist who resists the worlds of Others and constructs his or her own.

Needless to say, Americans have always privileged the independent spirit, the entrepreneurial endeavor, but it is imminently grown-up (and real people are born, after all, to grow up) to understand the necessary limits of independence and entrepreneurship—otherwise life turns solipsistic and greedy, and adulthood becomes childish. There is indeed a point at which to question Disney's solipsism and greed, especially when it affects children. Needless to say, this collection of criticism has its limits; it cannot critique every Disney film. Nor has every contributor agreed upon the hegemonic strategies at work in each film, as demonstrated by the three chapters in this study that analyze *Aladdin*. Actually, none of the contributors were privy to what the others wrote for the manuscript. This ensured the multiple perspectives that were desired for this project. Further, more can be said about more recent film animation and Pixar films. However, the goal of this project has never been to be comprehensive. We wish only to pose questions and challenges to ideals of past, present, and future Disney films that we feel are urgent. We argue that Disney ideology is a form of empire building, that its emperor constantly reaches a new audience with an old groove of noxious ethos. "The first movie I ever saw was Disney's *Snow White*," Ayres recalls. "Like the perfect American nuclear family, my stay-at-home Mom, my 'breadwinning' Dad, my brother, baby sister, and I packed into the Oldsmobile and then parked at the Stony Brook Drive-in. While munching on hot dogs, my family watched family entertainment at its finest.

Or was it?

Notes

1. This biography follows several sanctioned by the Disney company: Diane Disney Miller's *The Story of Walt Disney*, Richard Schickel's *The Disney Version: The Life, Times, Art, and Commerce of Walt Disney*, Bob *Thomas' Walt Disney: An American Original*, and Leonard Mosley's *Disney's World*. Eliot's, however, provides a candid portrayal of the man although it does not often document sources with any credibility. Nevertheless, Eliot refused to sign an agreement that if granted access to Disney archives, he would print only that text approved by the company. Hence his book differs from earlier Disney biographies that read like sanctioned, sanctimonious propaganda spun by the public relations desks at Walt Disney Productions.
2. Disney is fiercely protective and one of the most litigious of the Hollywood film production companies. It put up a tenacious fight with Marc Eliot and Bantam in 1991 over the publication of Walt Disney: *Hollywood's Dark Prince* and prevented the editors of *From Mouse to Mermaid: The Politics of Film, Gender, and Culture* (1995) from using the name "Disney" in the title of their book. See Jon Lewis' essay "Disney After Disney: Family Business and the Business of the Family" in *Smoodin's Disney Discourse* (1994) and Elizabeth Bell, Lynda Haas, and Laura Sells' "Introduction: Walt's In the Movies" in *From Mouse to Mermaid*.

Works Cited

Bell, Elizabeth, Lynda Haas, and Laura Sells, eds. *From Mouse to Mermaid: The Politics of Film, Gender, and Culture*. Bloomington: Indiana UP, 1995.

Bettelheim, Bruno. *The Uses of Enchantment: The Meaning and Importance of Fairy Tales*. New York: Knopf, 1976.

Bottigheimer, Ruth B. *Fairy Tales and Society: Illusion, Allusion, and Paradigm*. Philadelphia: U of Pennsylvania P, 1986.

———. "From Gold to Guilt: The Forces Which Reshaped Grimms' Tales." *The Brothers Grimm and Folktale*. Ed. James M. McGlathery, with Larry W. Danielson, Ruth E. Lorbe, and Selma K. Richardson. Urbana: U of Illinois P, 1988. 192–204.

Buhler, Stephen. Personal interview. 11 March 1997.

Cohen, Betsy. *The Snow White Syndrome: All About Envy*. New York: Macmillan, 1986.

de Cordova, Richard. "The Mickey in Macy's Window: Childhood, Consumerism, and Disney Animation." Smoodin 203–213.

Dorfman, Ariel, and Armand Mattelart. *How to Read Donald Duck: Imperialist Ideology in the Disney Comic*. Trans. and Introd. David Kunzle. New York: International General, 1975.

Eliot, Marc. *Walt Disney: Hollywood's Dark Prince*. New York: Birch Lane, 1993.

Gilbert, Sandra M., and Susan Gubar. *The Madwoman in the Attic: The Woman Writer and the Nineteenth-Century Literary Imagination*. New Haven: Yale UP, 1979.

Kolbenschlag, Madonna. *Kiss Sleeping Beauty Good-bye: Breaking the Spell of Feminine Myths and Models*. Garden City, NY: Doubleday, 1979.

Lewis, John. "Disney After Disney: Family Business and the Business of Family." Smoodin 87–105.

Miller, Diane Disney, as told to Pete Martin. *The Story of Walt Disney*. New York: Dell, 1957.

Mosley, Leonard. *Disney's World*. New York: Stein and Day, 1985.

Parekh, Pushpa N. Personal interview. 10 March 1997.

Pinocchio. Dirs. Hamilton Luske and Ben Sharpsteen. Walt Disney Productions, 1940.

Sale, Roger. *Fairy Tales and After: From Snow White to E. B. White*. Cambridge, MA: Harvard UP, 1978.

Schickel, Richard. *The Disney Version: The Life Times, Art, and Commerce of Walt Disney*. New York: Simon & Schuster, 1968.

Smoodin, Eric, ed. *Disney Discourse: Producing the Magic Kingdom*. New York: Routledge, 1994.

Stone, Kay. "Things Disney Never Told Us." *Journal of American Folklore* 88 (1975): 42–50.

Thomas, Bob. *Walt Disney: An American Original*. New York: Simon & Schuster, 1976.

Tucker, Nicholas, ed. and introd. *Suitable for Children? Controversies in Children's Literature*. Berkeley and Los Angeles, U of California P, 1976.

Willis, Susan. "Critical Vantage Points on Disney's World." *South Atlantic Quarterly* 92.1 (1993): 1–6.

Zipes, Jack. *Breaking the Magic Spell: Radical Theories of Folk and Fairy Tales*. Austin: U of Texas P, 1979.

———, ed. and introd. *Don't Bet on the Prince: Contemporary Feminist Fairy Tales in North America and England*. New York: Methuen, 1986.

Part I
Disneyfication

CHAPTER 1

The Wonderful World of Disney: The World That Made the Man and the Man That Made the World

Brenda Ayres

The world was not a happy place in 1937 when the first full-length, talking, animated feature in the history of the movies was released. Nearly every country was staggering under war loss and erratic economies. The terms of the Versailles Treaty left the world in anything but peace. Propelled by rising nationalism and fascism, countries aggressively vied with each other to expand their borders and markets. At the same time, Soviet Russia grappled with reconstruction after its devastating involvement in the First World War and after its cataclysmic revolution. Elsewhere, powerful conservative parties pressed to restore moral, social, and political stability, not only throughout Europe, but also in the United States.

World War I was a near suicide for most Western civilizations. They could not come that close to extermination without also coming to a realization of their vulnerability. Excess followed in the wake: excessive paranoia, excessive restrictions of liberty, excessive malaise, excessive solutions—and excessive efforts to attain hegemony, whether in returning to the prewar status quo or in gaining postwar domination. Even though the war trenches had never reached America, the fissures in the American sociopolitical structure were just as perilous, and the struggle for hegemonic ideology just as acute.

Walt Disney did not serve in the trenches. Not yet at the age of seventeen and therefore too young to be accepted into the navy, Disney did join the Red Cross Ambulance Corps and saw firsthand the devastation of war-torn France (Schickel 63–64 and Eliot 13). One must not underestimate how that experience must have shaped Disney's political consciousness which, in turn affected his production of political text, especially in his animated films, which, in turn shaped the political consciousness of his viewers, especially millions of children "weaned" on Disney.

Yet, according to biographer Richard Schickel, Disney denied deliberate attempts to convey political messages in his films. He demurred from inferences of his being intellectual enough to create double meanings and metaphors, publicly expressing surprise when so many reviewers and viewers found symbolic messages in the 1933 *The Three Little Pigs* (Schickel 154–57, Sinyard 23, and Eliot 72–75). And Neil Sinyard has concluded that *The Three Little Pigs* is the only film that Disney made of "such immediate social relevance," describing the cartoon as an "old-fashioned moral tract about the virtues of industriousness, self-reliance, and preparedness" (23). With apparently the same myopic vision as Sinyard, Schickel stated that Disney was not interested in politics (157). The biographer interpreted the cartoon as reflecting a growing economic sentiment during the Depression: Only those who built their houses conservatively would be able to keep out the big bad wolf of hunger and disaster (154–57).

Disney was not apolitical. He served J. Edgar Hoover as a domestic spy, reporting on "red" movements in the movie industry and through his testimony to the House Un-American Activities Committee. In 1959 Disney reportedly coerced his employees to contribute to Nixon's campaign (Dorfman and Mattelart 19). According to Allen Woll, Nelson Rockefeller, then the director of the Office of the Coordinator of Inter-American Affairs, hired Disney to produce "a message of democracy and friendship below the Rio Grande." The result was *The Three Caballeros*, designed to reassure South American governments that the United States had no agenda to aggressively colonize it (qtd. in Burton 25). Evidence of religious, racial, and gender biases in Disney's business dealings and creative production attests to the man's political involvement. He knew how to use the power gained from his studios to "Disneyfy" others, that is, to impose his own values on those within the reach of his power.

To all such and similar comments made by other observers about his works throughout his career, Disney most humbly pleaded innocence: "We make the pictures and let the professors tell us what they mean" (qtd. in Schickel 156). Time and time again during interviews and in front of the camera, Disney projected himself as a simple, down-on-the-farm, Midwestern commonsensical, and Yankee-know-how kind of fellow who had nothing to do with deeper intellectual sensibilities or a political agenda. In an attempt to define Disney's philosophy, a reporter for *The New York Times Magazine* deduced that the creator of *Snow White* was not going to talk about such things because it would give him "highfalutin importance" (Churchill 9). It is that Midwestern image—white, middle class, all-American, apple pie, Bible on the coffee table, anti-intellectual, heterosexual nuclear family—that has come to form the Disney ideal. Disney products colonize generations of chil-

dren and parents to embrace this ideal and to regard divergence as inferior or
evil. The Disneyfication of our children, then, is empire building, complete
with an imperialistic colonizing force that effects either conformity to the
ideal or denigration of the Other.

This process has been accomplished through Disney's frequent appropriation of fairy tales, effectively so in that fairy tales have often been used to
indoctrinate the young. Jessica Yates argues that Soviet Russia did this. She
and Ruth Bottigheimer discuss (separately) Hitler's use of Grimms' fairy
tales, with their promotion of German virtues ("industry, cleanliness, and
order" [Zipes, "Dreams" 216]) and German culture as Nazi propaganda (49;
"From" 194, respectively). By 1850, so Bottigheimer theorizes, when Germany was still divided but developing into a powerful and united Prussian
empire, Grimms' tales entered the Prussian elementary school system
("From" 199). From 1912 to 1934, sales of Grimms' increased to 250 print-
ings, and to 600 by 1940 ("Publishing"). In 1945, occupation forces banned
the fairy tales in Germany, blaming them for having taught Nazi children
how to be brutal (Zipes, "Struggle" 167; Langfeldt 56).

Disney's sphere of influence is readily apparent in these statistics, re-
corded by Schickel in 1968:

> 240,000,000 people saw a Disney movie, 100,000,000 watched a Disney television
> show every week, 800,000,000 read a Disney book or magazine, 50,000,000 lis-
> tened or danced to Disney music or records, 80,000,000 bought Disney-licensed
> merchandise, 150,000,000 read a Disney comic strip, 80,000,000 saw a Disney edu-
> cational film....

And over 6.7 million visited the Magic Kingdom (19). In 1988, the turnstiles
registered more than 26 million people at Walt Disney World. According to
Kay Stone, this is the most visited tourist site in the world, other than Spain
(395). Walt Disney World sees more than 100,000 people per day. That is
more than 30 million per year (Sorkin 205). The 43-square-mile swamp in
Florida has been compared to the size of San Francisco and is twice the size
of Manhattan (Fjellman 185). Marc Eliot estimated that by 1993, more than
one billion people had paid to see one of 657 Disney films (224).

What is especially important about all of these statistics is that the audience consisted mostly of children. As Schickel noted, one-third of all American citizens were under the age of fourteen in 1966; these were the baby
boomers (19). Disney exerted more power to promote an American ideal
than anyone else alive at the time. What American child, regardless of religion, sex, culture, language, economic class, or geography, did not watch a
Disney cartoon? What baby boomer did not know the Mouseketeers by
name?[1] This particular audience of children are now parents and grandpar-

ents who have passed on the values that they derived—albeit probably un-consciously—from Walt Disney.

I was one of those demographics. The first movie I ever saw was Disney's *Snow White*. Like the perfect American nuclear family, my stay-at-home Mom, my "breadwinning" Dad, my brother, baby sister, and I packed into the Oldsmobile and then parked at the Stony Brook Drive-in. While munching on hot dogs, my family watched family entertainment at its finest.

Or was it?

Years later, Roy E. Disney's introduction of the home video release of *Snow White* billed the animation as safe: "It's time for your family to enjoy one of my family's proudest achievements." In response to such implied colonizing statements intended to ensure preservation of the middle-class family, the purpose of this essay as well as the others in this collection is to explore the "counter-discursive,"[2] to explore Disney's concept of family—whence it came and into what historical soil it was received—to identify in what ways Disney's version of children's fairy tales reinforce a mythological notion of American "beauty, joy, and truth," to borrow Lyndon B. Johnson's praise of Disney's work. These are qualities that the U.S. president deemed immortal.[3] However, a system of values—with its signifiers of beauty, joy, and truth—is neither fixed nor immutable, but is determined by those who have the power to define and propagate it. Ashcroft, Griffiths, and Tiffin's significant work on postcolonial theory places truth in its most truthful cor-relative:

> Truth is what counts as true within the system of rules for a particular discourse; power is that which annexes, determines, and verifies truth. Truth is never outside power or deprived of power, the production of truth is a function of power, as Foucault says, "we cannot exercise power except through the production of truth." (167)

Disney's version of truth is the message of a colonizer: Mine is the only acceptable culture and you will assimilate. At the center of my culture is the white, middle-class, American, Protestant, conservative nuclear family, with clearly defined and separate gender roles performed by a heterosexual couple, committed to raising their children in the same mold. Deviant behavior will be construed as truly evil. Stephen Buhler in his chapter calls this process of propagandizing this ideology, Disneyfication. Beginning with its activation in films of the 1930s and continuing into the present, Disney's ideological dynamics beg to be deconstructed.

Schickel gave this warning about Disney's charms:

> If you have a child, you cannot escape a Disney character or story even if you loathe it. And if you happen to like it, you cannot guide or participate in your child's dis-

covery of its charms. The machine's voice is so pervasive and persuasive that it forces first the child, then the parent to pay it heed—and money. In essence, Disney's machine was designed to shatter the two most valuable things about childhood—its secrets and its silences—thus forcing everyone to share the same formative dreams. It has placed a Mickey Mouse hat on every little developing personality in America. As capitalism, it is a work of genius; as culture, it is mostly a horror. (80)

Throughout his analytical biography, Schickel considered Disney another Horatio Alger (11): another rags-to-riches story. However, Schickel seemed mostly concerned about Disney's promotion of the Protestant work ethic. The worst that he pronounced about the Disney industry was that it instilled in America's children a craving for the almighty dollar.[4]

Disney's films effect much greater myth with broader implications and farther-reaching detriment than just their political and cultural influence. They also doggedly reinforce traditional notions of gender behavior, villainizing any who do not conform, like the evil stepmothers, Ursula the Sea Witch, Madame Medusa, Cruella De Vil, Judge Claude Frollo, Jafar, Governor Ratcliffe, and Shan Yu. Keisha Hoerrner analyzed Disney's full-length animated films, arriving at some shocking statistics. She borrowed four categories of antisocial behavior created by Bradley S. Greenberg in a 1980 study of television drama. They include: physical aggression, verbal aggression, deceit, and theft. Hoerrner studied a total of 864 behaviors modeled on the Disney screen and estimated that 66% of them were antisocial. Of those, 84% were performed by white males. Out of 864 behaviors, 570 were enacted by males, and most of this activity was rewarded. Females were taught that they were not significant actors: They didn't have presence and they should keep quiet and invisible (213–28). These are the stereotypes that are being passed on to our children as proper behavior types. Consider Disney's infamous female miscreants: Are they not burlesques of women, grotesque because they do not comply with gender expectations? This is another form of Disneyfication.

For decades, audiences have allowed Disney to dictate gender norms, and they have also entrusted him and his company to dictate cultural norms, accepting that "Made in America" is best.

The Disney company has always portrayed "Uncle Walt" as the quintessential American. His family can be traced to the Norman Invasion, when the name had been D'Isigny (Thomas 3, Eliot 3, Miller 5) and then became De Disney (Schickel 45). It is very "American" to trace some ancestor back to service to William the Conqueror, and Disney could. Then his clan participated in a revolt against King James II (in good anti-aristocracy American fashion) which, once foiled, cost the loss of its land. Following a stay in Ireland (Eliot 3), his great grandfather, Elias, immigrated to New York in 1834, but settled in the Canadian frontier in an area first "graced" by a European only nine years before (Thomas 2). Elias' son married another Irish immigrant, and smitten by gold fever, the couple relocated to California (3). His eldest son, another Elias, married the first generation of a Scottish-English family to be born in America. This was Walt Disney's father. He lived in many states during his own pursuit of the American Dream. Disney's heritage, therefore, shares the same history as do many Americans, the immigrant who long ago left the British Isles in search of El Dorado. Disney's movies promise reward for "wishing upon a star." Regardless of setting or origin of fairy tale or folklore upon which they are based, Disney's films convey the American "inalienable right" of life, liberty, and the pursuit of happiness.

Walt Elias Disney was born in Chicago, but the father, wanting his children to avoid the evils of urban life and exercising his liberty to pursue happiness for his own, moved to a farm in Missouri. Later they settled in Kansas City, Missouri, which, as Schickel remarked, is the geographic center of the United States (72). His growing up there might be reason alone to warrant the image of Disney as the consummate American whose films could be trusted to be as wholesome as apple pie. Presumably the Midwest, the heartland, is as American as America gets. Ironically, the Disney family resided in a city that was a hotbed of racism.

It would not be fair to assume that just because Kansas City was notorious for racial bigotry, Disney was likewise. However, Disney's perpetuation of unflattering black stereotypes throughout his cartoons is equally as notorious. In fact, the Interracial Film and Racial Guild attacked just such racism in *Song of the South* (Eliot 183–84). Later, critics had much to say about racial stereotypes in *The Lion King* and *Aladdin*, two Walt Disney Productions animations that postdate Disney but very much adhere to the spirit of Disney.

Another childhood influence that would cast the political convictions of the adult Disney was his father. Elias Disney apparently was sympathetic to the Socialist Party,[5] a problem for Walt, who had to live in a right-wing area of the country. His peers often beat him up because of his father's work on forming a farmers' union (Schickel 58). Most of Disney's pictures refute his father's politics (72).

As much as his films politicize the American family, they also reflect Disney's psychological makeup. His father was a severe man who literally wielded the strap freely and cruelly. In addition, he exploited his sons as free labor. The biographers tend to agree that Disney felt a lack of love and acceptance from his father, and that this is the reason that in such films as *Pinocchio, Peter Pan,* and *Mary Poppins,* children search for an effective father.

Not much is said about Disney's mother, but the absence of mothers or failure of mothers to act like mothers throughout his animated films is striking.[6] Skeptical of his parentage, Disney was driven by a lifetime preoccupation with his possible illegitimacy, an obsession which was reflected in his work. The earliest reason that Disney probably questioned whether Elias was his real father was due to the excessive beatings that he received. Most children find solace in hoping that a cold or abusive parent is not really a true parent at all, which would explain (to the child) the lack of natural love for the adopted child. They rationalize the parent's cruelty as anger over possibly having to raise a bastard.

Besides that and a lack of family resemblance, Disney was unable to secure a birth certificate from the Hall of Records. He finally found a record of a Walter Disney born to Elias and Flora Disney on January 8, 1891, but Walt was really born ten years later (Eliot 12). The discrepancy motivated Walt to accept what was to become a seventeen-year appointment as an official informant on "communist" activity in Hollywood in exchange for the FBI's search for his identity (124). Hoover's people either discovered or fabricated a story of a woman in Mojacar, Spain, who gave illegitimate birth to a child and then immigrated to California. Supposedly she was Walt's mother (Eliot ch. 11).

Driven by his own hunger for familial security, Disney's recurrent theme was "the sanctity of family and the tragic consequences when that sanctity was broken." Most heroes in the animated films share the same conflict; they are missing effective parent figures. They must reconcile this conflict before they can achieve wholesomeness and before the film's plot will be resolved (Eliot xx).

Striving for the ideal family and prioritizing family seemed to be Disney's impetus throughout his life. Separation anxiety, Bruno Bettelheim reasons, is one of the major childhood concerns that fairy tales address. Oedipally, children are jealous of the love that one parent has for the other and intuit that they must detach from the parent. The fairy tale encourages children to believe that they will survive the loss of a parent or parents. Not only that, they will grow up and marry and have children of their own. The typical fairy tale reassures children that familial relationships are something upon which they can always depend, even if the identity of the family members change (199–215). One of the reasons why Grimms' fairy tales form the bases of many of his animations may be due to Disney's own search for family identity. Surely, most of these films do follow the paradigm of orphans' forming their own family structures.

The Grimms' father died when the older brother, Jacob, was only eleven.

Two years later he and Wilhelm lost their grandfather. The deaths effected serious repercussions: The Grimms lost their large house and social standing. The brothers faced an uphill battle to excel academically and to recoup financial and social stability. Then when they were young men, their mother died. Jack Zipes suggests that their rendition of fairy tales reflects a fear of separation and a quest for an ideal family life ("Dreams" 206–16).

One can argue the differences between the experiences, culture, and history of the Brothers Grimm and Walt Disney. One can argue the difference between Walt Disney's life and politics and his film animations. One can find differences between Grimms' fairy tales and Disney's film animations. Apparently from their texts and films, however, anxiety about identity impelled both of them.

A quest to secure familial security draws the storyboard for most of Disney's film animation, and at its summit has always been Disney, in the flesh and later in the spirit. The only person that the older Disney was close to and trusted was his brother Roy (Schickel 62). He did not allow anyone else to supervise the upbringing of his own children (Thomas 204). Biographies sanctioned by Walt Disney Productions placed the family as paramount, as it became increasingly so to people whose lives had been disrupted by wars and the Depression. However, Eliot's biography, an unadulterated version that escaped Disney's public relations department, revealed a man who was more often than not an absentee parent who could not handle the role of father.[7] Nevertheless, the nuclear family prevailed as the ideal in his movies, and Disney aggressively and conscientiously promoted that ideal. After all, he was one of the founders and vice president of the Motion Picture Alliance for the Preservation of American Ideals (Eliot 171). This component of Americanism, as such, relegated people to outside the American periphery if they were not a part of a nuclear family.

Another telling detail about Disney's life that indexed his adherence to radical right-wing fundamentalism was the public ridicule he directed at one of his most talented staffers, Art Babbitt. This animator was working on *Fantasia* and decided to take piano lessons at his own expense to help better understand the integration of music with art in this film. When Disney learned of this, according to Eliot, he said to the employee, "Well, what the hell's the matter with you; are you some kind of faggot?" (138) and "fag," according to Schickel (250). This is a revealing signifier of a value system held by a man who powerfully defined the value system for America.

Many people do not want to know that there was a dark side to the man who lionized childhood. They want to take their children to a Disney movie with the unquestioning assurance that Disney values are just what the world needs in order to better all lives. If Disney became an indisputable success during the Depression by packaging hope, truth, and the American way, the package is vastly more successful today as putting to rights all of the wrongs under which our society staggers. In Disney, everyone should want and love a child; he or she who does not is clearly evil. In Disney, unloved, unwanted children may begin with lives in abject misery, but to these come new lives complete with a lifetime warranty: "happily ever after."

In Disney, the good girl gets to marry the good boy, and the audience knows that their formation into a nuclear family will endure and flourish with familial bliss. Besides, in Disney's world, divorced people get back together because they should never have divorced in the first place. Boys and girls and men and women who are bad get punished; they often repent their ways to become the most benevolent contributors to their community. Good always triumphs over evil. Misfits are gathered into the bosom of some family, so that no one will be alone or ever suffer another identity crisis.

This is the wonderful world that Disney fantasizes for viewers. It is what most viewers want to believe. But just like the real world, fantasy is riddled with anxieties. How could it be otherwise, considering its creator? When one turns on the Disney Channel, Tinkerbell, as she has for decades, taps the castle with her magic wand, and then the world explodes into color. Looking at only the pretty colors in a Disney animated film can be deceptive. The colors of a troubled world are also there, without touch-up, without erasure, without filtering, and without blocking. Without them, the fantasy perpetuates a hoax. According to Bruno Bettelheim, fairy tales "suggest images to the child by which he can structure his daydreams and with them give better direction to his life" (7). If Bettelheim is correct, or, more to the point, if Disney does have a colonizing agenda to use fairy tales as ideological machinery to impose one set of cultural values on another—and of course, Disney does—then why would we want our children to be colonized by an ideology that does not tolerate difference? What appears to be full of color, in reality (or in the realest of fantasies) is drawn in only black and white.

Notes

1. Bob Thomas estimated that three-fourths of the nation's television sets were tuned in to *The Mickey Mouse Club* every weekday from 5 to 6 (290). This show, by the way, was the first program that I, a baby boomer, watched on my parents' very first television set. By virtue of the novelty of television, this program probably had even greater impact on the children of the fifties.
2. A useful term from Ashcroft et al., *The Empire Writes Back* (193).
3. President Lyndon B. Johnson's encomium at Disney's death (Thomas 382).
4. Insofar as Disney did adapt a number of Grimms' fairy tales to film animation, Jack

Zipes' argument that Grimms' reinforced the value of hard work ("Dreams" 207–16) adds weight to Schickel's observation.

5. Elias was an active supporter of Eugene V. Debs and fought against the exploitation of the working class. Even though this sentiment was a part of the son's upbringing, as Eliot showed, Disney was not very sensitive to his own exploitation of the working class, and he was adamantly opposed to unions throughout his career. However, what he did share with his father was a hostile anti-Semitic attitude, blaming most of his problems on an un-definable conspiracy of the Jews (Eliot 6).

6. A point developed in my chapter on *Snow White* and in the chapter by Axelrod.

7. Eliot told several stories of Disney's staying away from home for weeks at a time, especially when his daughter Sharon was adopted as a baby and he could not bear her crying. Other accounts indicated that Disney had as little self-control as did his father in dealing with his children. He slapped his first child, Diane, so hard that his wife threatened to leave him and take the children so far away that he would never find them (165). It was not the last time that his wife made such a threat. As Eliot showed, Disney was not very sensitive to his own exploitation of the working class, and he was adamantly opposed to unions throughout his career. However, what he did share with his father was a hostile anti-Semitic attitude, blaming most of his problems on an undefinable conspiracy of the Jews (Eliot 6).

Works Cited

Ashcroft, Bill, Gareth Griffiths, and Helen Tiffin. *The Empire Writes Back: Theory and Practice in Post-colonial Literatures*. London: Routledge, 1987.

Bettelheim, Bruno. *The Uses of Enchantment: The Meaning and Importance of Fairy Tales*. New York: Knopf, 1976.

Bottigheimer, Ruth B. "From Gold to Guilt: The Forces Which Reshaped Grimms' Tales." *The Brothers Grimm and Folktale*. Ed. James M. McGlathery, with Larry W. Danielson, Ruth E. Lorbe, and Selma K. Richardson. Urbana: U of Illinois P, 1988. 192–204.

——. "The Publishing History of Grimms' Tales: Reception at the Cash Register." Haase 78–101.

Burton, Julia. "Don (Juanito) Duck and the Imperial-Patriarchal Unconscious: Disney Studios, the Good Neighbor Policy, and the Packaging of Latin America." *Nationalisms and Sexualities*. Ed. Andrew Parker, et al. New York: Routledge, 1992. 21–41.

Churchill, Douglas. "Disney's Philosophy." *The New York Times Magazine*. 6 March 1938: 9.

Dorfman, Ariel, and Armand Mattelart. *How to Read Donald Duck: Imperialist Ideology in the Disney Comic*. Trans. and Introd. David Kunzle. New York: International General, 1975.

Eliot, Marc. *Walt Disney: Hollywood's Dark Prince*. New York: Birch Lane, 1993.

Fjellman, Stephen M. *Vinyl Leaves: Walt Disney World and America*. Boulder, CO: Westview, 1992.

Haase, Donald, ed. *The Reception of Grimm's Fairy Tales: Responses, Reactions, Revisions*. Detroit: Wayne State UP, 1993.

Hoerrner, Keisha L. "Gender Roles in Disney Films: Analyzing Behaviors from Snow White to Simba." *Women's Studies in Communication* 19.2. Summer 1996: 213–28.

Langfeldt, Dr. J. "The Educational and Moral Values of Folk and Fairy Tales." *Suitable for Children? Controversies in Children's Literature*. Ed. and introd. Nicholas Tucker.

Berkeley and Los Angeles: U of California P, 1976. 56–63.

McGlathery, James M., et al., eds. *The Brothers Grimm and Folktale*. Urbana: U of Illinois P, 1988.

Miller, Diane Disney. *The Story of Walt Disney, As Told to Pete Martin*. New York: Holt, 1956.

Schickel, Richard. *The Disney Version; The Life Times, Art, and Commerce of Walt Disney*. New York: Simon & Schuster, 1968.

Sinyard, Neil. *The Best of Disney*. New York: Portland House, 1988.

Sorkin, Michael. "See You in Disneyland." *Variations on a Theme Park: The New American City and the End of Public Space*. New York: Hill and Wang, 1992.

Stone, Kay. "Things Walt Disney Never Told Us." *Journal of American Folklore* 88 (1975): 42–50.

Thomas, Bob. *Walt Disney: An American Original*. New York: Pocket Books, 1976.

Yates, Jessica. "The Other 50th Anniversary." *Mythlore* 61. Spring 1990: 47–50.

Zipes, Jack. "Dreams of a Better Bourgeois Life: The Psychosocial Origins of the Grimms Tales." McGlathery 205–19.

——. "The Struggle for the Grimms' Throne: The Legacy of the Grimm's Tales in the FRG and GDR since 1945." Haase 167–206.

Part II
Disney Family

CHAPTER 2

Beauties and Their Beasts
& Other Motherless Tales
from the Wonderful World of Walt Disney

Mark Axelrod

One can clearly find commonalities in Disney's *Snow White, Sleeping Beauty, Cinderella, The Little Mermaid*, and *Beauty and the Beast*. On one level they are all Disney appropriations of works by nineteenth- and eighteenth-century writers such as the Grimms and Andersen, Perrault and Mme. Leprince de Beaumont. But they have another very interesting phenomenon in common: There are no mothers. Some of them have stepmothers, though they are evil and far removed from the matronly sacredness of a June Cleaver or a Harriet Nelson. However, none of the films have "real" mothers, that is, biological or genetic mothers. To think of the Disney phenomenon as predicated on the legitimacy of the "nuclear family," or on the notion Dan Quayle delivered at the 1992 Republican National Convention that "family comes first," would merely be an illusion, like the "reality" imposed on celluloid itself. In a curious state of social allegiances, Quayle's admiration of family values, and, by extension, of a mother's role within the family, would be totally at odds with the rather perverted and divisive vision offered by Disney. The vision has become, for the current Disney "family," a phenomenon that approaches the role of mother in rather disparaging ways, and ultimately begs the question: How is it that some of Disney's greatest animated achievements are, if not misogynistic, works that have devalued motherhood and the role of the mother within the nuclear family?

One might think that Disney would be at the vanguard of motion picture filmmakers who produce adulating films about mothers and motherhood, since Disney is and has been clearly associated with the family, with "good, old-fashioned" family entertainment. One need not go into depth here about how important the role of mother is in the psychological development of the child. One could argue about the role of mother in terms of economics and the family, and where she has been classified in a sex-gender system which is and has been dominated by white males. One could also argue about the roles of mothers and fathers in terms of their ability or lack of ability to be nurturing. Certainly there are some men who are more nurturing than some women, and some women who are far more nurturing than other women, but clearly the role of mother is profound in the creation and maintenance of a child's self-esteem, of a child's sense of self, and of feelings about his/her mother and women. So where, then, does Disney (the company) fit into this archetypal system of mothers and mothering and nurturance? In fact, it does not.

One concern here is the issue of "adaptation" and how those works chosen by Disney and/or the Disney corporation have been adapted. There are and have been two main approaches to adaptation: fidelity to the target text and ability to manipulate the target text. In his article "The Well Worn Muse," Dudley Andrew writes that the distinctive feature related to adaptation is "the matching of the cinematic sign system to a prior achievement in some other system" and that "every representational film adapts a prior conception." But "adaptation delimits representation by insisting on the cultural status of the model" and "in a strong sense adaptation is the appropriation of a meaning from a prior text" (qtd. in McFarlane 21). Brian McFarlane goes on to say that "the stress on fidelity to the original undervalues other aspects of the film's intertextuality. By this, I mean those non-literary, non-novelistic influences that work on any film, whether or not it is based on a novel" (21). Certainly, McFarlane alludes to the notions of cinematic content or storyline, since the great majority of adaptations are not that concerned with the stylistic integrity generated by the target text. But McFarlane makes an extremely critical comment when he states, "It is equally clear, however, that many adaptations shave chosen paths other than that of the literal-minded visualization of the original or even of 'spiritual fidelity,' making quite obvious departures from the original. Such departures may be seen in the light of offering a *commentary* on or, in more extreme cases, a *deconstruction*...of the original" (22). Disney, or the corporation that bears his name—past, present, and presumably future—has chosen certain texts for adaptation. Additionally, how it has decided to adapt those texts is critical, because, as McFarlane has argued, the Disney filmmakers make a decision on whether or not issues of "fidelity" to the target text are important. In other words, in the adaptation process, someone must make a decision as to whether the final project will adhere to or veer from the integrity of the target text. In that case, Disney has the option of "adapting" the "mothers" from those target texts as being nurturing, abusive, or absent.

Invariably, from *Snow White* to *Beauty and the Beast*, one sees in Disney "products" a clear vision of motherhood (if not the feminine) which tends to deal with matronly and/or womanly figures in one of three significant ways:

(1) the role of mother is totally neglected or eliminated (*Sleeping Beauty, Beauty and the Beast*, even *Aladdin*); (2) the role of mother is reconstituted in the figure of the "cruel" stepmother (*Snow White, Cinderella*); or (3) the role of a leading female authority figure, where no mother or stepmother exists, is transformed into an evil character (*The Little Mermaid*). There is, of course, Cinderella's "fairy godmother," who, like Disney's stepmothers, is not a blood relative. She is neither mundane nor motherly, but ethereal and self-serving, since she exists not only as a mediating device between the "horrors" of living with an "evil" stepmother and the "joys" of living with a handsome and economically privileged prince, but exacts a price for her "matronly" consideration by reminding Cinderella that "the magic only lasts till midnight." When the clock strikes twelve, the fairy godmother's best little girl is once again in rags. The godmother does not act as a mother might, but as a mitigating medium between the sanctions of poverty and wealth. As for the good fairies in *Sleeping Beauty*, their magic acts only as a kind of "vaccine" against the "evil witch Maleficent." Yet throughout the story, the Queen, Sleeping Beauty's mother, plays no role at all in attempting to subvert Maleficent's evil intentions. It is only through the good graces of the fairies, Flora, Fauna and Merryweather, who sequester Sleeping Beauty in the woods, that she is protected at all. Once again, a mother is impotent to action and, by virtue of another woman's evil intentions, essentially abandons her child.

Examples from Disney's films are replete. There is no mention of Snow White's mother, nor of her father for that matter. From *Cinderella*: "Once upon a time a wealthy widower lived in a fine house with his daughter, Cinderella....Sadly the gentleman died soon after [remarriage] and Cinderella discovered that her stepmother was a cold and cruel woman." Once again there is no mention of the biological mother and the influence of her on Cinderella. Finally, from *Beauty and the Beast*:

> In a nearby village, there lived a young woman named Belle. She was the kindest and most beautiful girl in the village. Although she spent most of her time taking care of her father, Maurice, a hardworking but unsuccessful inventor, she loved to read more than anything else.

There is no mention of Belle's mother at all. As a matter of fact, there is no clear indication that any of the mothers alluded to or ignored were, in fact, the main character's biological mother, which raises some interesting questions about the biological legitimacy of the main character. It would not be out of the question to imagine Disney's vision of motherhood as the vision of a child who was either abandoned by his parents or who questioned his own birthright, an issue that has been dealt with before (see Ayres' chapter, "The Wonderful World of Disney: The World That Made the Man and the Man That Made the World").

What is curious about the Disney phenomenon of motherless children (primarily daughters) is that the same storyline has continued for over fifty years. From *Snow White* (1937) to *Beauty and the Beast* (1991), it is as if Walt Disney's predilection for commodifying virtue by selling products that either ignore or dehumanize the role of woman and/or mother has become a kind of Disney trademark, if not company policy, which has been carefully nurtured. Even mothers of nonhuman characters in animated features such as *Bambi*, *Dumbo*, and the most profitable of Disney's films, *The Lion King*, are either exterminated or are somehow ineffectual. In the "classic" Disney version, Bambi's mother is shot to death by a hunter. Dumbo's mother is physically restrained and can do nothing to safeguard her baby. Simba has little relation with his mother and is dependent on Timon, Pumbaa, and Rafiki. These erasures beg yet another question: Why did Walt Disney choose to reconstitute the mother figure as either absent or evil, as a creature who either abandons or abuses her young through birth or marriage, and why has The Walt Disney Company perpetuated the role?

In the biography *Walt Disney: Hollywood's Dark Prince*, Marc Eliot pays critical attention to Disney's relationship with his own mother: "Other times, during the day, Walt would sneak into his mother's bedroom and put her clothes on and her makeup. Afterward, he would stand in front of her full-length mirror to admire his reflection. He knew this version of his mother, unlike the real one, would always be there when he needed her" (7). To say Disney was a cross-dresser would be missing the point; he apparently experienced a sense of abandonment over and over again. Apparently he was plagued by doubts of his true parentage. "This infection of doubt," according to Eliot, "would eat at Walt the rest of his days, infusing his future films with a feverish passion that would deepen their dramatic themes" (12). These themes have been played out over and again in Disney as those of the *abandoned child* and the *nonexistent mother*. The culmination, at least for Disney, reached its peak with the adaptation of Carlo Lorenzini's (aka Carlo Collodi) *Pinocchio*, which was in production at the time of the death of Disney's own mother, a death which many believe to have been a suicide (Eliot 111–12). When Disney was finally able to return to production, the first thing he did was to rework the studio's plot of *Pinocchio*, eliminating almost all of the completed footage and rewriting a new script that eliminated a puppetmaker's wife (who would, of course, have become Pinocchio's mother) implied in an earlier script in favor of emphasizing the puppet's desire to become a human. The Eisnerian parallel here is, of course, the Little

Mermaid, who also yearns to become a human being and in whose film one cannot overlook the role that free will presumably plays, especially in relation to capital conquest. After all, the man she loves is a prince, not a pauper.

For some unclear reason, however, the Disney magic, fabricated to engage the imagination of the ideal and not the recognition of the real, subsumes any notion of the role of mother. In speaking of *Snow White*, for example, the brilliant Russian filmmaker Sergei Eisenstein was overwhelmed by the *medium* and overlooked the *message* when he wrote, "Disney's works themselves strike me as the same kind of drop of comfort, an instant of relief, a fleeting touch of lips in the hell of social burdens, injustices, torments, in which the circle of his American viewers is forever trapped" (qtd. in Leyda 7). Though on some preadolescent level, perhaps Eisenstein was too infatuated with the techniques of Disney's animation to recognize the flaws in the subtext on an adult level. As Ariel Dorfman and Armand Mattelart have written in their brilliant analysis, *How to Read Donald Duck,*

> There are automagic antibodies in Disney. They tend to neutralize criticism because they are the same values already instilled into people, in the tastes, reflexes and attitudes which inform everyday experience at all levels. Disney manages to subject these values to the extremist degree of commercial exploitation. The potential assailer is thus condemned in advance by what is known as "public opinion," that is, the thinking of people who have already been conditioned by the Disney message and have based their social and family life on it. (28)

Animation genius aside, *Snow White* was just the point of departure for a collection of animated films which, regardless of their animation value or the brilliance of their scores or their sizable worth in commodified objects sold in Disney stores, clearly eliminate the role of mother as a nurturing, comforting hedge against the evils in the world. Certainly Eisenstein, whose works were so preeminently humane, should have recognized that flaw. In contrast, the image of the mother is reconstituted such that the feminine is "raised" to a level in which stepparental child abuse is often an acceptable mode of behavior (*Snow White* and *Cinderella*) or in which motherhood exists only as something that may be implicitly nostalgic, but never uttered (*The Little Mermaid* and *Beauty and the Beast*).

One could make the argument that the stories Disney chose to animate were not his stories to begin with and the apparently negative role of mother is something for which Disney need not take responsibility. Accurate reproduction of details seemingly has not been a priority for Disney (the company). In the original story of *Snow White* which Disney adapted, the Grimm brothers create a mother who dies, an evil stepmother who eventually also dies, seven dwarfs (none of whom had names), and a prince who takes pity on Snow-White and takes her coffin with him:

> The prince ordered his servants to carry the coffin on their shoulders [perhaps not to soil his own], but they stumbled over some shrubs, and the jolt caused the poisoned piece of apple that Snow-White had bitten off to be released from her throat. It was not long before she opened her eyes, lifted the lid of the coffin, sat up, and was alive again. (Grimms 204)

Such an ending was not in keeping with the romantic way Disney stories should end. Regardless of how the tale is told, the fact still remains that it was Disney who, out of dozens of Grimms' tales to be told, ultimately chose both *Snow White* and *Cinderella* to adapt to the Disney formula. In both originals, the mothers are kindly and caring, even though they die while their daughters are very young. In *Cinderella* the dying mother says, "Dear child, be good and pious. Then the dear Lord shall always assist you and I shall look down from heaven and take care of you" (Grimms 86). Disney's version not only omits a mother—more strikingly—it omits a pious mother, as if no such creature could exist.

All of this psychodrama accounts for why Disney himself may have preferred to create a motherless universe for his adolescent female characters, but what of the new Disney? What of the Disney after Walt, where the board of directors do not have to ask themselves the hand-wringing question "What would Walt have done?" to get something accomplished? Hans Christian Andersen's *The Little Mermaid* is an excellent example of how a work can be "Disneyfied" (in the best Disney tradition) beyond reasonable recognition and without the authority of Disney the man. In Andersen's story, "for many years the king of the sea had been a widower, and his old mother kept house for him. She was a wise woman and proud of her royal birth....she deserved much praise, especially because she was so fond of the little princesses, her grandchildren" (39). Clearly the role of mother has not been relegated to an inferior position, and the figure of the Little Mermaid's grandmother plays a prominent role in the story, as do the Little Mermaid's five sisters (none having any significant role in the film). Granted, the Sea Witch is present in Andersen's tale, but she mediates between the world of the sea and the world of the humans. Though she exacts a price from the Little Mermaid (the appropriation of the Mermaid's voice), she is not destroyed in the end to exact a happy ending. To the contrary, the Little Mermaid dies. The fact that this film is a post-Walt production only accents the notion that the Disney company, at least when it comes to animation, has been and will continue to be an advocate of a motherless universe. Apparently it is proud of that accomplishment if one is to believe in the economic viability of such projects.

After Walt Disney's death in 1966, the Disney empire appeared on the verge of being swallowed by itself. According to Mark Potts and Peter Behr in their book *The Leading Edge* (1987),

> the company's decline was traced to a group of managers that seemed bent on not of-fending the memory of Walt Disney. Under the leadership of long-time Disney em-ployee Cardon Walker and then Ronald W. Miller—Walt Disney's son-in-law—the company meandered through the two decades after the founder's death with its output reflecting anything but the vastly changing culture of those years....At Walt Disney Productions, it seemed, projects were being judged not so much on creative or artistic merits, but rather by one criterion: "What would Walt have done?" (153)

Though Eisner has accomplished a major economic overhaul of Disney Pro-ductions, certain components of the Walt Disney vision are still viable. Quoting Eisner, Potts writes that "the basic fabric of the company hopefully will remain, and on that fabric we will build a different company. It's clearly a different company, but at the same time, the same company" (153). It has been Eisner who has pushed the rereleasing of a number of Disney's older animated features which are also older animated visions of "mother" (or lack of her), such as *Snow White, Bambi, Dumbo,* and *Pinocchio*, violating the Disney Commandment, "Thou Shalt Not Overexpose." It is also Eisner who has promoted the new animated features which are also the new visions of mother (or the lack of her) in *The Little Mermaid, Aladdin*, and *Beauty and the Beast*. As Richard Schickel writes in *The Disney Version*,

> Before his first month in office had passed, Michael Eisner was saying things that no one at Disney had ever dared to say before. For example, he was looking at video in a new way, speculating that carefully controlled exposure in these markets could per-haps enhance the value of some of the studio's classics, teasing the public into a new awareness of their virtues—while contributing mightily to cash flow. He was propos-ing, as well, that there might be valid ways for the studio to use the less costly and long-eschewed techniques of limited animation to penetrate the Saturday-morning television cartoon market, which Disney had abandoned to competitors less caring about what was said and shown. (425)

The notion that Disney was "more caring" than its competitors regarding "what was said and shown" is, apparently, no longer a consideration at least in terms of the family. One of Disney's later television dalliances, *Goof Troop*, has, presumably, rendered Goofy divorced at best, a widower at worst; and Max, his son, motherless. The entire show, if not promoting the virtues of capitalism, clearly extols the apparent virtues of dysfunctional families. It is certainly too late to blame Uncle Walt for that, though the method and manner is certainly in keeping with the Disney tradition of motherless families led by Mickey and Minnie, Donald and Daisy, and all of Donald's nephews. Actually, even Pluto is without a mom to call his own.

One could argue that Walt Disney was ahead of his time, that he was prescient and foresaw the inevitable disintegration of the nuclear family into a family of "familial foreigners" controlled by "heartless stepmothers." In a way, he predated the Reagan-Bush years, in which, as Barbara Kruger maintains, there was "the substitution of an idyllic image of family life for the real life material struggles of a dissolving American family" (qtd. in Bassin 199). Supposing that Disney's vision of children in America was the correct one and that perhaps Snow White's evil stepmother (who wanted Snow White killed and her heart returned in a box) was merely reflective of the real American attitude toward children, an attitude that W.C. Fields made a part of Americana and that no V-chip could ever eliminate—one could make that argument, but it would be a feckless one, if not a cynical one, for Disney's choice in creating a motherless and faithless universe is much different than Eisner's choice in creating a motherless and faithless universe. For Disney, it seems, the choice arose out of a psychological void contingent on a family life seemingly filled less with joy and nurturance than with confusion and abuse. Eisner's perpetuation of the devalued role of mother seems to be based upon a position of profitability; and that, ironically, is "what Walt would have wanted."

Since Eisner's "coronation," Disney has gone from economically susceptible to economically resplendent. Its films have garnered billions of dollars, not only from animated features, but through ancillary spin-offs such as videos, CDs, dolls, puppets, trinkets, key chains *ad nauseum ad astra*—the stuff which Italians call "Americanata" and which Nabokov would have called "poshlost." For example, as Leonard Maltin has written,

> In 1938 it was estimated that *Snow White* had earned $4.2 million in the United States and Canada alone. After its eighth reissue in 1993 that total had swelled to more than $80 million. In 1989, *USA Today* computed that if one adjusted for inflation and changing box-office prices, *Snow White*'s theatrical earnings up to that time would exceed six billion dollars! When the film made its long-awaited video debut in 1994, it outsold *Jurassic Park* (its contemporary "rival" for release that fall) to become the biggest-selling video of all time. (32)

Huge profits indeed for the animated versions of child abuse and attempted murder.

In terms of economic viability, Eisner's decisions have put the magic kingdom back in the darkest recesses of the black. But at what cost? For some, like Eisenstein, the subtext of a motherless universe seems to be un-important. Why create an animated feature in which parents (especially mothers) play a vital role when one can do without them so effectively? So cost effectively? Certainly, to consider doing the obverse would not cost Disney anything extra in dollars, since motherhood (like the Notre Dame hunchback, who is yet another motherless character) is public domain and, therefore, free of any cost for Disney to adapt. But in an era when notions of the family from El Ché to Dan Quayle to Rush Limbaugh can actually have something in common, is it possible that the Disney company stands alone as some kind of ultra-reactionary monolith, durable in its fidelity to eliminating motherhood? The great irony in all of this is that the entire notion of "family entertainment" is brought into question. John Taylor, in *Storming the Magic Kingdom,* has written that besides the rather false image which Disney gave to others, relative to the way "good family men" are supposed to be (he swore, smoked, and drank routinely),

> it was true that a gap existed between the social standards Disney upheld and the per-sonal behavior of many of the men who set them. But Disney's executives fussed and fretted over the company's image precisely because Disney was in the family enter-tainment business. More than that, Disney did market a value system....The experience offered by the parks and by Disney films could be intermittently frightening or sad, but it was not designed to challenge the assumptions of customers or assault middle-class values. (25–26)

Not designed to assault middle-class values? If one assumes that demeaning the role of mother is not assaulting middle-class values, then certainly Dis-ney had, and Eisner has, his finger on the pulse of American values.

And to that end, and to the Disney company's "credit," for over five dec-ades (if not longer) it has been able to maintain the image of a family-oriented family company (albeit transnational) while at the same time pro-ducing a product that if not demeaning to mothers, then totally ignores them in the grand scheme of child rearing and in the extended name of "family values." In a way, there is something unconscionable about all of that; about that illusory image the Disney company has conceived, exploited, and main-tained; about the hypocrisy which was Disney in his own fashion and which he fashioned in that image and about the commodification of that image.

Curiously, "film critics," such as Maltin and Michael Medved, seem somehow oblivious to this commodifying image. In Medved's book *Holly-wood vs. America,* a work presumably "taking on" the film and television industry because of its negative attitude toward family values (and a book endorsed by Limbaugh), the chapter titled "Maligning Marriage" says prac-tically nothing about motherhood per se, and nowhere in the book does

38   THE EMPEROR'S OLD GROOVE

Medved "take on" the pervasive "Disney attitude" about the family. Perhaps Medved, like Maltin, like so many others "in the business," are oblivious to what Disney does and has done. Perhaps, like Eisenstein, they merely "see" what they want to see and disregard the rest. Perhaps it is the fact that the films are really cartoons with cartoon characters and as such remove us from those daily tragedies in which the same stories filmed with humans would render us outraged at the abuse and the violence and the indifference. Perhaps that is the greatest of Disney's achievements: to render harmless that which is harmful. In a way, each time one pays a Disney price for a Disney product, one is contributing to the exploitation of that "family image" which somehow flies in the face of any genuine notion of family and is not only disingenuous, but deceitful. In large measure, it truly validates the Disney company's monopoly on the "fiction of family" and renders large the meagerness of motherhood.

Works Cited

Andersen, H. C. *Andersen's Fairy Tales*. Trans. Pat Shaw Iversen. New York: Penguin, 1987.
Bassin, Donna, Margaret Honey, and Meryle Mahrer Kaplan, eds. *Representations of Motherhood*. New Haven:Yale UP, 1994.
Dorfman, Ariel, and Armand Mattelart. *How to Read Donald Duck: Imperialist Ideology in the Disney Comic*. Trans. and introd. David Kunzle. New York: International General, 1975.
Eliot, Marc. *Walt Disney: Hollywood's Dark Prince*. New York: Carol Publishing Group, 1993.
Grimms. *The Complete Fairy Tales of the Brothers Grimm*. Trans. Jack Zipes. New York: Bantam, 1987
Leyda, Jay, ed. *Eisenstein on Disney*. London: Methuen, 1988.
Maltin, Leonard. *The Disney Films*. New York: Hyperion Books, 1995.
McFarlane, Brian. *Novel to Film: An Introduction to the Theory of Adaptation*. Oxford: Clarendon P, 1996.
Medved, Michael. *Hollywood vs. America*. New York: HarperCollins, 1993.
Potts, Mark, and Peter Behr. *The Leading Edge: CEOs Who Turned Their Companies Around: What They Did and How They Did It*. New York: McGraw-Hill, 1987.
Schickel, Richard. *The Disney Version: The Life, Times, Art and Commerce of Walt Disney*. New York: Simon and Schuster, 1985.
Snow White and the Seven Dwarfs. Dir. David Hand. Animated. Voices: Adriana Caselotti and Harry Stockwell. The Walt Disney Company. 1937.
Taylor, John. *Storming the Magic Kingdom: Wall Street, the Raiders and the Battle for Disney*. New York: Knopf, 1987.

CHAPTER 3

The Poisonous Apple in *Snow White:* Disney's Kingdom of Gender

Brenda Ayres

Once upon a time a queen "had a daughter, with a skin as white as snow, lips as red as blood, and hair as black as ebony, and she was named Snow-White. And when she was born the Queen died" (Grimm 162).[1] The 1937 Disney-fied *Snow White* begins as does the fairy tale, in that Snow White is not to have a mother.[2] The girl child is separated from her so that the former can immediately begin a process of being defined by patriarchy. Then once she becomes a woman, she must leave home and make a family of her own. Kay Stone has mapped the psychological plot points thus so: A girl blossoms, she dies, and then she is born again (54). When Snow White reaches puberty, she dies to childhood, and through a kiss, is born again a woman. This is necessary so that she can mate, reproduce, and then die, so that her child can repeat the cycle, hence, propagate the species.

Snow White's second mother fails to provide a proper role model because she seems to be independent, self-assertive, resourceful, and free of male domination and influence. Thus Snow White must be removed to a home where she can learn how to take care of a house and meet the needs of not only one man, but seven. This is precisely the paradigm for many Victorian domestic novels, particularly those written by women writers in Britain and America. The young heroine becomes parentless, is forced to face the cold world alone, matures through suffering, learns to perform good deeds, and as a reward, becomes a suitable mate for a good man. Marriage is the end of her maturation, with the understanding that marriage will result in propagation that, in turn, continues the cycle; marriage typically ends the story.

That Disney mirrors a Victorian tale is to say that Disney also perpetuates a nineteenth-century notion of domestic ideology: Women are to be submissive, self-denying, modest, childlike, innocent, industrious, maternal, and angelic—all traits that perfectly describe Snow White. They are descriptors in contrast to men, who are their own nominatives. Men are the explorers, inventors, and negotiators of the world "out there." In nineteenth-century domestic novels, as well as in *Snow White*, the audience does not get to know the men very well because they are off riding their steeds, spearing whales, racing to reach the North Pole first, shooting savages and buffaloes, or searching for the origin of the Nile. Like nineteenth-century domestic novels, Disney's fairy tale seems to be a female *bildungsroman*. Snow White is definitely the protagonist, with her appearance in all but seven of the film's twenty sequences (Allan 161). The story is not about a prince on a quest with dragons to slay. However, as Sandra Gilbert and Susan Gubar have pointed out, Snow White and her mothers, including the villainous stepmother, are androcentrically defined, constrained, and objectified. Even though the focus of the story is a woman's coming into maturity, she matures in order to be someone's wife, and later, a mother. The purpose of both Grimms' and Disney's fairy tales is to frame females into a patriarchally acceptable portrait of a womanly ideal.

The first two Disney scenes are framed pages of a book. Its gothic font and ornate design are typical of children's stories from the Victorian period, like Grimms', seventeen editions of which were published from 1810 to 1856 (Stone 57). Patriarchal values are instantly established: "There lived a lovely little Princess named Snow White. Her vain and Wicked stepmother the Queen feared that some day Snow White's beauty would surpass her own"—the beauty of two women is pitted against each other for male approval (more on this later). Then the magic mirror forms the next frame, shortly followed by the containment of the stepmother's image in the mirror. She asks the famous question: "Who is the fairest one of all?" The mirror now reflects a disembodied mask with a clear masculine voice that answers that question. Similarly, Snow White becomes framed by the mirror image of the wishing well. She sings about her wish for the one she loves to find her. Finding *him* is not an option; she is to *be* found, passive voice. And then of course, the prince appears, as he will near the end of the story. The prince's castle completes the patriarchal frame. From the book to the magic mirror to the castle, even if the story is about Snow White and her mothers, all three women are framed and objectified by patriarchal circumscription.

The mother appears in the Grimms' tale framed by a window, pricks her finger, bleeds "and is thereby assumed into the cycle of sexuality" (Gilbert and Gubar 37). Mothers experience their own separation anxiety when they bring a child into the world. "And when she was born the Queen died"—the birth of a child and the death of a parent go hand in hand. It has often been said that giving birth makes a mother aware of her own mortality. Actually death was a reality to many women who did lose their lives giving birth during the nineteenth century, when the Grimms wrote their version of "Snow-White." Death is also a subconscious anxiety of giving birth because a child is a replacement of the adult. This anxiety is clearly evident in the replacement of not only the mother but also the stepmother, who, in both Grimms and Disney, continually asks the looking glass who is the fairest, that is, who is the woman who is sexually significant and attractive to men to justify her existence. The magic mirror, whose voice is patriarchal (Gilbert and Gubar 42), frames the next mother. It is a voice that determines her worth, and she allows its rules to rule her. Once the mirror decides she is no longer young and desirable enough compared with her daughter, she accepts this verdict and determines to eliminate her mortal competition. As Gilbert and Gubar note, later Snow White will be similarly locked in and objectified by her beauty, placed not inside a looking glass, but inside a glass coffin (36).

The looking glass defines the stepmother and Snow White with its masculine criteria for beauty and usefulness. The picture inside the frame is that of a queen, portrayed as another stereotype from the nineteenth century, a villainous woman found in the melodrama of the Victorian stage (Allan 159). More to the point, the Queen and Snow White are just as polarized as black and white, just as most Victorians expected fictional characters to be. In the first Disney scene, when the Queen fails to get the answer that she has wished from the mirror, her reflection turns to flames. A creature surrounded by the flames of hell, she is obviously an evil woman. Immediately the scene changes to the flawless face of Snow White. With the transparent complexion of a Victorian who has nothing to hide (Halttunen 52), and with her prepubescent state, Snow White is the Victorian feminine ideal. Also like a good Victorian girl, she is busy with domestic tasks: washing the steps near the wishing well.

One might deduce that a 1937[3] audience desired such simplicity, not just for their children to learn right from wrong, but for adults' own peace of mind. Theirs was a year of world chaos, and people wanted to believe that good would triumph over evil. Not only is this a prevalent theme in Victorian literature, so is it in Disney's films. And both media attempted to colonize their readers into believing that one cannot find self-identity and happiness outside of the nuclear family. Another prevalent quest of Victorian and other WW II cultures was order—meaning some benevolent force ensuring that good vanquishes evil, possible only through raising children within the nuclear family structure. This promised a countermeasure to a world gone mad with evil and dissolution of social systems. More specifically, it was the job of a mother to bring order, as Snow White demonstrates in bringing order to the dwarfs' cottage.

The stepmother seems wicked for this very reason; she is not part of a family enclosure; and her own house, a castle full of skeletons, spider webs, and rats, represents a home deprived of domesticity. The film does not mention anything about a husband, an additional indictment that the Queen is acting independently, but when does she act independently of the mirror? Gilbert and Gubar consider the mirror as the ever-present voice of the king (37–38). Regardless, the stepmother is portrayed as a power-woman who defies the traditional role as wife and mother. She is far from maternal, not only in her behavior but also in her body shape. It is not the rotund body of a woman designed to bear and comfort children. The audience is to reject her as a role model also because she worries about her appearance instead of being a self-abnegating woman. Bruno Bettelheim charges the Queen with being narcissistic, which he construes as negative behavior, and he charges Snow White with the same (201–3). Actually, the witch is able to trick Snow White into wanting to become more beautiful because the maiden is thinking not of herself but of the prince. Snow White is persuaded to taste the wishing apple in order to win him through her beauty (Yates 48). She is as much a victim of patriarchal design as is the stepmother. "Fairy tales are not just entertaining fantasies," Karen Rowe surmises, "but powerful transmitters of romantic myths which encourage women to internalize on aspirations deemed appropriate to our 'real' sexual functions within a patriarchy" (211). Yet, even though Snow White desires a heterosexual relationship that will ensure a new family unit, the wish nearly kills her, and it does kill her mother.

Snow White's wish-fulfillment is delayed when she rebels against patriarchal authority. The dwarfs, "stunted men," ergo phallic symbols (Bettelheim 210), warn her not to open the door to any stranger. Just like her prototype, the biblical Eve, Snow White is deceived into disobeying, with the enticement of receiving her heart's desire. Bettelheim supposes that she would not have been so easily tempted if her inner desires were not so akin to the temptations (211). What could have possibly enticed her to break out of a Victorian mode of obedience to patriarchy, to the warnings by the dwarfs to not allow entrance to strangers? Bettelheim and Shuli Barzilai argue that the apple represents a mother's breast and that Snow White needs to be reunited with a mother (212–13 and 532–34, respectively), but Barzilai also sees this as a need of the stepmother to resist separation from her daughter. Barzilai considers "Snow White" as an illustration of separation anxiety that both mother and daughter experience. Regardless, when Snow White bites the apple, she dies.

Similarly the Queen is not purely narcissistic. She relies on a "masculine" mirror to signify her identity; it is the male voice that determines when the Queen is or is not the fairest in the land. By Lacanian standards, the Queen can never be content with herself, nor be secure in her own power as long as she sees her image only as the Other. According to Lacan, children come to an understanding of themselves as separate beings from their mothers when they succeed in the mirror phase of development, that is, they see themselves, not as part of a mother, not attached to her breast, but as separate and complete individuals (1–7). When the Queen no longer sees her entire self in the mirror but sees Snow White as the Other who is displacing her, he is suddenly thrown into a reverse mirror stage, where she has been separated from herself. This notion is in line with Gilbert and Gubar's deduction that the stepmother and Snow White are one and the same woman: The stepmother is the assertive self; and Snow White, the passive (36–40). Likewise, Roger Sale considers Snow White and stepmother as the same self, only in different stages of development (43). Betsy Cohen reasons that every mother acts like the wicked queen at certain times in her life while dealing with daughter envy (8). Regardless of signification, these women are not individuals; they are types, cast in a morality play designed to frame and contain readers and viewers by expecting them to accept the values stipulated by the looking glass. The result is certain death to the female self, symbolized by the glass coffin.

Snow White overtly attempts to Disneyfy its viewers into gender conformity through indictments against rebellious women. When the Queen resorts to witchcraft, the audience is supposed to understand her behavior and her practice as evil. Actually, the film promotes any source of female empowerment as evil. Little girls must grow up to be like Snow White, who uses her beauty to attract a man so that she can serve him and serve her children. Beauty is not to be a source of self-liberating power. However, without beauty, the woman has very little currency to barter her own worth. Then she perceives herself and is perceived exactly as the hag the Queen becomes. If indeed the Queen has any other source of power, like magic, the question follows, why did she fear the little men so much as she fled from the cottage? Why did she not resort to magic to defend herself on top of a perilous cliff? Besides, where were her knights? The answer is simple: Without being the fairest one, she had no power whatsoever of her own and there was no knight, prince, king, or other male to come to her rescue. The Queen was not evil; she merely hated Snow White's power, which came from her beauty of youth (Hyman 296).

Further, if the stepmother cannot be happy because she does not tend to a husband and his children, then, in turn, Snow White cannot be happy because she does not have a mother and father; Snow White's song has to be "I'm wishing for the one I love to find me." If she cannot have a father, the next best thing is to marry a prince and have children. Once this is done, the nuclear family is restored, and harmony will reign in fairyland. In 1937, most Americans, at the brink of another world war, wanted to count on at least the stability of the family.

Disney depicted nature as epitomizing this order. The animals in this film are clearly mommies, daddies, and babies. Consequently, their existence is strikingly harmonious and peaceful. Significantly, as the huntsman gets ready to kill Snow White, she picks up a baby bird and asks where its mama and papa are. When she restores the bird to its family unit, then the huntsman refuses to obey the Queen's command to murder her. He chooses to honor instead Snow White's protection of family. Throughout the film Snow White is portrayed as both the daughter and the mother of nature. Of course she would trust that an apple, a natural product, would not harm her, just as she should trust her "natural" wish for the prince. Perhaps in the fairy tale and in Disney's film lies a subversive message: Being in love can kill you. You might get married, have children, and then die, just as did Snow White's biological mother. Perhaps such gender expectations—that a girl is supposed to grow up to become a wife and a mother—*are* the poisonous apples. After all, according to the biblical account, Eve came to know both childbirth and death only after she ate the apple. Overtly the emphasis of Disney's message is different. Performing one's traditional gender role within the family is the only way to live happily ever after. Covertly, the poisoned apple (shared, by the way, in Grimms' by both Snow-White and her stepmother) is, as Madonna Kolbenschlag puts it, "psychic bondage to men" (42) and results in sure death to the woman. In Disney's account, the apple's poison is to bring a sleeping death to the woman who partakes, with the only antidote possible being the kiss, being her union with a man.

This ideology is personified in the dwarfs. They are not "real" men like the prince, because, or as a result, their family is dysfunctional. When Snow White enters the cottage, she thinks that it must be the residence of seven children. The house must be in disorder and filth because there is no mother. Snow White is clearly the virgin adolescent entering womanhood. The dwarfs treat her as daughter, mother, and sexual object all in one, determined and defined by their need of her. After Snow White and the prince marry, they will act as parents to these little men. The dwarfs can hold down grown-up jobs, like working in a mine, but they are never to be valorized as a healthy family or as grown, happy men as long as they do not have parents or do not have wives of their own. And Snow White is not allowed to continue to function in the cottage without a husband. And the cottagers are not safe from wicked, autonomous women like the Queen. But nature makes things right by making sure that when the Queen tries to launch a boulder on top of them, lightning severs the cliff, causing her to fall and die.[4]

The dwarfish state of the seven men signifies their stunted growth as human beings who cannot grow up properly because they have not been nurtured by a caring mother. The motherless Snow White has to assume this role. Yet, there is something amiss when grown men are not allowed to "outgrow" the family unit; after Snow White and the prince marry, they will serve as parents to little men who will always be children. If the Disney ideal is for parents to raise their children into adulthood so that they, in turn, can reproduce healthy people and are positive contributors to society, then how is the portrayal of the dwarfs, within the family structure of Mother Snow White and Father Prince, an ideal? The dwarfs will always be dwarfs as a result, with an understanding that to be a dwarf is to be a freak. At least this was the message conveyed in the 1930s.[5]

Snow White attempts to Disneyfy its audience with Victorian ideology of family. Insofar as the fairy tale did originate in the nineteenth century, an adaptation with patriarchally defined gender ideology did not need to undergo very much alteration. Disney's film animation adopts these ideological codes even though it deviates from the fairy tale in significant ways. According to the Grimms' original rendition of this story, the wicked queen tries three times to murder Snow-White. Her first attempt is by lacing the girl's corset too tightly. Many women did indeed die because of corsets during the Victorian period. Perhaps the Queen does try to kill her, or perhaps the corset does it itself. This restraint was created to accentuate artificially a woman's bosom and derriere. The corset objectified a woman according to her sexual usefulness. The fairy tale might be construed as gender subversive, a covert attack on the corset as a symbol of many possible female constrictions.

The second attempt is with a poisoned comb. Even though Snow-White has been warned by the dwarfs to let no one into the cottage, and even though she has been tricked once, she still succumbs to vanity by allowing the crone to comb her hair. What almost kills her here? The crone or Snow-White's need to stay physically attractive in order to have worth as a woman? Subversively, these female signifiers, the corset and the comb, become emblems of death. Even if one accepts Barzilai's interpretation that the stepmother is simply performing maternal functions by dressing, combing, and feeding her child (532) and Cohen's explanation that the young woman fails to heed the advice of the dwarfs by allowing in an old peddler woman because she needs a mother (4–9), then one must also recall the looking glass and its male signifier of female worth. These instruments—the corset, the comb, and later the apple—do not feed female vanity as supposed by Bettelheim (202–3). These women are not allowed to develop their own ideals of beauty and self-worth. To be the fairest in the land is female competition for male validation. However, if the Disney ideological apparatus were consistently promoting family, then it would have been "natural" for Snow White to fall to temptation and then be rewarded for it. Instead, subversively wanting to be ideologically correct (to desire a heterosexual relationship and form a family of her own) nearly kills her!

The real temptation is as it has always been: the apple. Significantly, the apple is described as being "beautiful to look upon, being white with red cheeks, so that anyone who should see it must long for it, but whoever ate even a little bit of it must die" (Grimm 169). The apple, being white and red, is a reminder of the opening description of Snow-White as a baby in Grimms' and as an American, healthy beauty (Allan 161) in Disney's. The young woman's willingness to bite into the apple, with its sensual qualities and coloring of estrus, indicates her maturing into sexual desire (Sale 42–43). If she enjoys herself instead of existing only to bring pleasure to others, her narcissism must be punished. The ritualistic passing of Snow White's identity (signified by the apple) through matriarchy is poisonous. Or another way to read this denouement is the exchange of death, not from daughter to mother as occurred at the beginning of the story, but from mother to daughter as passing on the duty of the daughter, now as woman, to become a mother herself, which means death.

Like the biblical Eve, Snow-White does not physically die. The dwarfs, assuming her dead, cannot bear to bury her because she is still so beautiful. They place her in a glass coffin in order to always enjoy her beauty. Symbolically the woman is enclosed as one who is dead and as one who has no power to live her own life.

Although loving and domestic, alone without a husband, Snow-White has failed as a mother to the dwarfs and is poisoned because she is without a husband to protect her from the evils of the gender-rebellious world. Even though that is the message being conveyed, the fact that she does not really die and that she is enclosed within a glass coffin can be read to suggest that such women are dead in life, entombed but looking as if still alive.

The Grimm brothers do not have the prince kiss Snow-White. Actually, he is not referred to as the prince in the original fairy tale but as the king's son. His identification does not come from an autonomous self, but from a familial connection, as a king's son. He is part of the cycle that perpetuates nuclear families. He persuades the dwarfs to let him have the glass coffin. His servants stumble over a bush while carrying the fragile, glass coffin. Fortunately, this mishap shakes loose the bit of poisoned apple lodged in Snow-White's throat. She awakens, and the prince invites her to come with him to his father's castle to be his bride. The Victorian account rights things by maintaining patriarchal dominion. The bride and groom go to the father's castle. They invite the stepmother to the wedding and force her to dance in "red-hot iron shoes" until she falls down dead. The text warns that women who want to wear such shoes (travel their own path) will suffer a demise.

However, she would have died anyway, once displaced by Snow-White.

Disney's prince kisses Snow White, and she is miraculously resurrected. Just like the Victorian fairy tale, she has not really lived until united with a man: After that, she forms a proper family unit. The film portrays the ideal relationship for men and women as falling in love and setting up housekeeping. This is where truth, joy, and beauty reside. Overtly, anything that departs from this paradigm is false, deadly, and ugly. Covertly, the opposite is true.

In the early 90s, Filmation released a sequel to *Snow White*, titled *Happily Ever After*. The storyline continues, but this animated film greatly subverts the myth in the Disney version.

Fifty years after Disney's release, the nuclear family is no longer an essential absolute. *Happily Ever After* and postmodern renditions of *Snow White* mirror a different world than Disney's. In the 1988 film, instead of an evil stepmother, a man does evil. Lord Maliss comes to avenge his sister's death. Whereas in *Snow White*, women can be seducers and eaters of forbidden apples, in this film, a man acts as the evil agent. The prince and Snow White are on their way to the dwarfs' cottage to invite them to the wedding. Lord Maliss abducts the prince and turns him into a helpless, leprous troll. The prince is no longer in a position to save the day. Fortunately, in this version, Snow White is capable of saving herself.

A half-century later, Snow White has breasts. And she meets up with a snake, who with perfectly good phallic subtleties, scares her nearly to death. Sexual signifiers are key dynamics in these gender politics. What this film wants to do is oust the patriarchal colonizer and reestablish a new empire of gender.

Now the dwarfs have opened a mine in the next kingdom, and the cottage is filled with dwarfelles. These are females that have been empowered to control the world. Muddy is in charge of the earth; Marina, the lakes and rivers. Critterina takes care of the animals; Blossom, the plants. Sunburn operates the sun; Moonbeam, the night. Then there is Thunderella, who will become the mightiest of them all, once she can get the knack of controlling lightning.

These women are quite different from Doc, Happy, Sneezy, Dopey, Grumpy, Bashful, and Sleepy. These women are not missing their parents; they are content with who they are and what they do. They are a community of women who do not lack anything despite the apparent absence of parents, husbands, and children. There is Mother Nature, but she is not maternal; she is not a nurturer. She is busily creating, doing her own thing, and audiences are encouraged to approve of her.

The dwarfelles decide to leave the safety of the hollow to help Snow White rescue the prince. Unbeknownst to them, the prince follows like a shadow, a patriarchal presence but impotent and unable to provide help.

Lord Maliss' eyes have the power to change objects into anything he desires; he is a signifier. But Thunderella is able to thwart signification by forcing that power back to him, which is how he is destroyed. At the same time, the prince returns to his former self, now free from the signification of the evil man. The prince then says to Snow White, "Are you ready to live happily ever after?" The camera pans above the evil castle to a sunrise and clouds. The Disney film ends with a castle off in the distance—a symbol of Snow White's destination as home with her prince. In the later movie, the prince and Snow White will venture off into nature, a landscape defined not necessarily by heterosexual relationships where the mother and the father form the core, but by an organic, metamorphic existence that is constantly, naturally redefining itself without being defined patriarchally.

This is a radical departure from 1937. *Happily Ever After* and other postmodern fairy tales are a reaction to *Snow White*, written by people who are aware of the colonizing efforts to make universal that which can never be universal. The latest revision of fairy tales is a computer animation, *Shrek* by PDI/DreamWorks. It begins the same as Disney's *Snow White*, with a book and a similar tale: "Once upon a time there was a lovely princess. But she had an enchantment upon her of a fearful sort which could only be broken by love's first kiss."After that, the similarities vanish. The princess Fiona is a classic beauty with tiny waist, but she's under a spell. When the sun sets, she turns into an ogress, a short, chubby girl. However, her true love is an ogre, not Prince Charming. And the two live happily ever after. It is a new once-upon-a-time that hails a non-Victorian, non-Disneyfied version of Snow White, a new Eve who can take a bite out of the apple and make good use of the knowledge of good and evil, instead of ending up just baking apple pie.

Despite noble efforts by productions other than Disney's, film animation by the Disney company still dominates the children's market for entertainment. And ever since Mickey Mouse came squeaking onto the scene in the 1930s and getting himself out of scrapes through his relationship with Minnie, Disney films continue to reinforce hegemony of gender ideology in America. Jasmine is expected to give up royalty in order to marry. Belle, Nala, and Esmeralda are females who are obviously superior in character to their male counterparts. Yet they are to invest all of their resources toward making their men successful. Pocahontas is supposed to give herself to a man who represents a race who will wipe out her own race. Mulan is prepared to give up her life in order to save the life of her father and later the life of her lover. Ultimately, her demonstrated feats of bravery, fighting skill, and intelligence serve to bring honor to her father and prove her worthy of the captain's love. Kida must not be queen over Atlantis without a sweet, male nerd by her side. These are the latest sexist and xenophobic messages churned out by the Disney apparatus for the purpose of swaying children to conform to Victorian Western notions of gender behavior. Andrew Blake once reasoned that ideologies "exert fundamental control over the boundaries of cultural practice" (38). Disney's ideology of gender embowers cultures that fall under its spell. *Snow White* has been rereleased more often than any film in history (Forgacs 367–68) and keeps us taking a bite out of that same apple.

Notes

1. In the original 1810 unpublished version, The Grimms had the Queen be Snow-White's natural mother. Although she had wished for a beautiful daughter, after she had one who grew only more beautiful, the mother became so jealous that she took the daughter into the forest to pick flowers and abandoned her there (Stone 57).
2. This is as it should be, according to Bruno Bettelheim, who speculates that fairy tales help children work through the fear of losing their parents. "Only by going out into the world," so Bettelheim's theory goes, "can the fairy-tale hero (child) find himself there; and as he does, he will also find the other with whom he will be able to live happily ever after; that is, without ever again having to experience separation anxiety" (11).
3. Disney began the project as early as August 1934 (Allan 157). The first full-length, talking animated cartoon ever released, it premiered in Los Angeles on December 21, 1937 (Yates 47).
4. The bad are punished through an act of God; none of the good people have to do bad things to them (Yates 48). This is usually the same sort of fate in store for the bad people in most Victorian novels.
5. Useful here is an article by David Forgacs on attitudes toward adults with chondroplasia in his article (370–71).

Works Cited

Allan, Robin. "50 Years of *Snow White*." *The Journal of Popular Film and Television* 15.4. Winter 1998: 157–63.

Barzilai, Shuli. "Reading 'Snow White': The Mother's Story." *Signs: Journal of Women in Culture and Society* 15.3. Spring 1990: 515–34.

Bettelheim, Bruno. *The Uses of Enchantment: The Meaning and Importance of Fairy Tales.* New York: Knopf, 1977.

Blake, Andrew. *Reading Victorian Fiction: The Cultural Context and Ideological Content of the Nineteenth-Century Novel.* New York: St. Martin's, 1989.

Cohen, Betsy. *The Snow White Syndrome: All About Envy.* New York: Macmillan, 1986.

Forgacs, David. "Disney Animation and the Business of Childhood." *Screen* 33.4. Winter 1992: 361–74.

Gilbert, Sandra M., and Susan Gubar. *The Madwoman in the Attic: The Woman Writer and the Nineteenth-Century Literary Imagination.* New Haven: Yale UP, 1979.

Grimm, Brothers. "Snow-White and the Seven Dwarfs." *Grimms' Fairy Tales*. Trans. Mrs. E. V. Lucas, Lucy Crane, and Marian Edwardes. New York: Grosset, 1945. 162–73.

Halttunen, Karen. *Confidence Men and Painted Women: A Study of Middle-class Culture in America, 1830–1870*. New Haven: Yale UP, 1982.

Happily Ever After. Dir. John Howley. Animated. Voices: Irena Cara, Tracy Ullman, Phyllis Diller, Zsa Zsa Gabor. Filmation. 1993.

Hyman, Trina Schart. "Cut It Down and You Will Find Something at the Roots." *The Reception of Grimms' Fairy Tales: Responses, Reactions, Revisions*. Ed. Donald Haase. Detroit: Wayne State UP, 1993. 293–300.

Kolbenschlag, Madonna. *Kiss Sleeping Beauty Good-bye: Breaking the Spell of Feminine Myths and Models*. Garden City, NY: Doubleday, 1979.

Lacan, Jacque. "The Mirror Stage as Formative of the Junction of the I as Revealed in Psychoanalytic Experience." *Ecrits: A Selection*. Trans. Alan Sheridan. New York: Norton, 1977.

Rowe, Karen. "Feminism and Fairy Tales." *Don't Bet on the Prince: Contemporary Feminist Fairy Tales in North America and England*. Ed. Jack Zipes. New York: Methuen, 1986. 209–26.

Sale, Roger. *Fairy Tales and After: From Snow White to E. B. White*. Cambridge, MA: Harvard UP, 1978.

Shrek. Dir. Vicky Jenson and Andrew Adamson. Voices: Mike Myers, Eddie Murphy, Cameron Diaz, John Lithgow. PDI/DreamWorks, 2001.

Snow White and the Seven Dwarfs. Dir. David Hand. Animated. Voices: Adriana Caselotti and Harry Stockwell. The Walt Disney Company. 1937.

Stone, Kay. "Three Transformation of Snow White." *The Brothers Grimm and Folktale*. Ed. James M. McGlathery, with Larry W. Danielson, Ruth E. Lorbe, and Selma K. Richardson. Urbana: U of Illinois P, 1988. 52–65.

Yates, Jessica. "The Other 50th Anniversary." *Mythlore* 61. Spring 1990: 47–50.

Zipes, Jack. "Breaking the Disney Spell." *Mouse to Mermaid: The Politics of Film, Gender, and Culture*. Eds. Elizabeth Bell, Lynda Haas, and Laura Sells. Bloomington: Indiana UP. 21–42.

Part III
Disney Women

CHAPTER 4

Stripping Beauty: Disney's "Feminist" Seduction

Kellie Bean

The Walt Disney Company enjoys a long-standing and disturbingly immobile reputation as a dispenser of benign, even edifying, children's and family entertainment. The company successfully isolates its corporate image (troubled in the past decade by, say, accusations of unfair labor policy or cannibalistic business practices) from its cultural role as a producer of good, clean fun for the whole family. Framing itself as a promoter of tolerance and inclusion, Disney has convinced at least one reviewer that "[d]espite the right-wing reputation Walt Disney himself had, the studio's films have long honored a version of melting-pot liberalism. The outsider is welcomed, the tramp civilized, the beast turned human, the mainstream transformed" (Rothstein). A telling review, Rothstein's comment reiterates the terms so glibly defined in Disney films and roundly criticized by feminist, multicultural, and cultural theorists for about two decades. Rothstein exposes the race, gender, and class prejudices that drive nearly every Disney film when he lays down these dichotomous terms, the first of which must be ideologically transformed into the second: tramp/civilized, beast/human. Recalling essentialist binaries of evil/good, woman/man, passive/active, such an argument quickly undoes itself and introduces the terms for criticizing Disney's ideological position as it appears in animated films of the late twentieth century.

Of course, I am not the first to underscore the race, gender, and class problematic at the heart of the Disney message: Whiteness and wealth signify authority and goodness; dark skin indicates evil; marriage represents the inevitable reward of the righteous and properly catechized woman. My concern here will be with gender issues and, specifically, the feminist implications of Disney's regressive courtship narratives. When moving a female character into marriage, Disney first establishes her unfitness for that revered (in the land of Disney) institution, then transforms her into the standard, deserving Disney wife—that is, a voluptuously modest, submissive partner to a rescuing, dominant prince. This essay considers the Disney project of transforming female characters into acceptable marriage partners, and will read Esmeralda from *The Hunchback of Notre Dame* (1996) as both a representative and an extreme example. Lately, female autonomy precipitates this transformation; whereas earlier heroines required only the rescuing hand of a princely man through whom they achieved the proper class status, these later women require a different kind of rescue from the same kind of man. No longer merely poor and discarded by an uncaring family that fails to recognize her interior goodness, this heroine is now herself inherently in need, not just of physical rescue, but of ideological reform.

What interests me here is that Disney dresses this regressive argument in feminist clothes. That is, like two of her sisters, Belle of *Beauty and the Beast* and Jasmine of *Aladdin*, Esmeralda outwardly rejects the gender stereotypes embedded in the traditional courtship narrative and self-consciously characterizes herself as independent, unconventional, even feminist. Unfortunately, in the Disneyfied world, independence functions not as an indication of female power or self-determination, but rather as a strategy for seduction: Reluctance functions in a Disneyfied courtship as the lure with which the chosen woman finally attracts a husband. In a disturbing pattern of titillating resistance, from *The Little Mermaid* to *Mulan*, too many animated Disney films enact a no-means-yes scenario. For example, Belle, Jasmine, and Esmeralda are all the more sought after for being hesitant lovers. Indeed, these three don't actually reject marriage at all: Belle dreams of meeting the handsome prince she reads about, Jasmine falls in love easily when she is allowed to choose a husband for herself, and Esmeralda is swept off her feet by Phoebus. Embodiments of the male fantasy of strong, beautiful women turned weak by the approach of marriageable men, Disney's ostensibly "politically correct" female characters in fact reproduce the standard Disney version of female identity: the unconscious beauty who must inevitably be awoken into marriage.

Moreover, highly eroticized images of women accompany this regressive diegesis. Now, it may at first seem paradoxical to speak of Disney's female characters as highly sexual or of Disney's depictions of women as eroticized. Such hesitation testifies to the success of the organization's campaign to portray itself as dedicated to children; certainly Mickey Mouse appears committed to making children happy. Picture here achingly telegenic children, backlit, gazing wide-eyed at the fuzzy wonders of The Walt Disney Company. But Disney runs competing messages: Mickey Mouse and Esmeralda. Mickey and his friend Minnie are sexless mouse figures designed to be read as friends of children. Although David Forgacs disagrees (along with several critics he cites; see 365), they are themselves childlike and emphatically not erotic, exotic, or sexualized in any way. Conversely, Esmeralda and her Disney sisters (Snow White, Ariel of *The Little Mermaid*, Belle, Jasmine, Mulan, et al.) are male-defined fantasies of female biological perfection. Drawn according to the same impossible dimensions as the Barbie doll—or any number of surgically altered Hollywood actresses—Disney's heroines all feature tiny waists, large breasts, curvy hips, and sensuous hair.

Rather than any testament to female empowerment, these characters seem almost deliberate illustrations of Laura Mulvey's thesis of "woman as image, man as bearer of the look" (19). One could mistake the following well-known passage for a description of not only mainstream Hollywood film, but also of productions of The Walt Disney Company:

> The determining male gaze projects its fantasy onto the female figure, which is styled accordingly. In their traditional exhibitionist role women are simultaneously looked at and displayed, with their appearance coded for strong visual and erotic impact so that they can be said to connote *to-be-looked-at-ness*. (19)

Disney's animated works unfailingly reiterate this gender paradigm and defy more nuanced readings of the female image. Others have made similar observations. Constance Penley reminds us that it is critical for feminists reading film to acknowledge "the *determinism* of the classical system and its seemingly perfect fit with the mechanisms of male fantasy" (15; emphasis added). And even as feminist film theory/criticism builds on Mulvey's landmark essay, isolating and interrogating cinematic moments where "those mechanisms" of rigid binary gender coding "necessarily founder" (Penley 15), Disney's animated works remain insusceptible to this kind of interrogation. As Jack Zipes pointedly notes, nuance seems systematically removed from Disney's products: "The diversion of the Disney fairy tale is geared toward nonreflective viewing. Everything is on the surface, one-dimensional, and we are to delight in one-dimensional portrayal and thinking" (40). Disney's gender ideology is strongly self-conscious; Elizabeth Bell describes "the exacting, communally created images of women by men": "Disney animation is not an innocent art form: nothing accidental or serendipitous occurs in animation as each *second* of action on screen is rendered in twenty-four different still paintings" (108). Disney's "overwhelmingly male" production staff has historically emphasized the biological features that define heroines as female (Bell 107). Like Minnie, Disney women wear dresses. Unlike Minnie, their dresses simply serve to expose—and make available to the paying viewer—a hyper-idealized, highly sexualized female form beneath.

Disney's overriding concern for masculine libidinal investment in the female body is surprisingly explicit in the depiction of Esmeralda. *Hunchback* transforms the spunky Disney heroine—like Belle and Jasmine, whose innocent strength stirs man's desire to marry—into a fallen woman, the frankly sexual gypsy Esmeralda. The film insists on visually defining Esmeralda as the sum of her sexual parts: breasts, stomach, hair, and (new for Disney characters) pubic area. When she dances for a Paris crowd (an event to which we will return shortly), her dress falls against the curve of her abdomen and pubic bone, and the contours of her body are clearly delineated through shading and shadow. This libidinal progress falls into greater relief when considering the women who came before her. For example, during the early moments of Disney's *Beauty and the Beast*, Belle, a beautiful, bookish young woman, walks through a town square as neighbors and shopkeepers sing regretfully of her failure of (conventional) womanhood: too much interest in books, not enough in men. ("But beneath that fair facade, I'm afraid she's very odd," they croon.) Her gown reveals shoulders and cleavage. In *Aladdin*, Jasmine disappoints her community in a similar fashion, for she refuses every suitor her father solicits on her behalf and runs away to (temporarily) experience life on her own. She wears a costume that reveals her abdomen as well as shoulders and cleavage. During these moments, both women are displayed to their communities, which include the film audience, and their mildly independent characterizations dissolve into strictly visual depictions. Belle walks under the attentive gaze of her neighbors, who lean curiously out of doors and windows, and Jasmine wanders into an unfamiliar marketplace where vendors accost, startle, and confuse her. As with Victoria's Secret models and striptease artists, visual interest in Belle and Jasmine derives from their presentation as gendered performers. They are female bodies in a sea of staring eyes and masculine aggressors.

Indeed, one might be tempted to suggest that Disney self-consciously seeks to prove Laura Mulvey's theory of masculine spectatorship, to embrace almost exclusively a masculinist point of view regarding images of women. Esmeralda et al. are depicted as the "(passive) raw material for the (active) gaze of man" (25). We see this clearly enacted, for instance, in the street scenes in *Beauty*, *Aladdin*, and *Hunchback* described above and in the figures of the Disney heroines. The undeniable deliberateness of an image cast in such minute detail (twenty-four frames/second) highlights male prerogative and point of view beyond even what Mulvey identifies in her argument. That is, inside the Disney studios the "determining male gaze projects its fantasy onto the female figure, which is styled accordingly" (19). To paraphrase Jessica Rabbit of *Who Framed Roger Rabbit?*, Disney's heroines can't help that they are seductive ideals; they are "just drawn that way."

Esmeralda does inspire a wild response from the citizens of Paris. During the annual Feast of Fools celebration (another scene organized around the performance of the female body as commodity), Esmeralda is introduced as "the finest girl in France," who will "make an entrance to en*trance*." Present in the crowd are the mayor of Paris, Judge Frollo, who has called Phoebus home to rid Paris of the gypsy presence; Phoebus, captain of the guard and handsome prince stand-in; and Quasimodo, the hunchback. Esmeralda thrills the crowd with a provocative dance and irreverent behavior. For example, she flies into Frollo's lap, playfully kissing him on his pointed nose. The dance she performs alludes unmistakably to striptease: She wears seductive clothing that becomes increasingly revealing as the dance progresses, and she consistently teases her audience by approaching the edge of the stage and backing away. Her simultaneously flowing and clinging dress emphasizes her very 1990s body: trim, athletic, and voluptuous—an Olympic runner in a Wonder Bra. At certain moments of the dance, Esmeralda is as good as naked: Rather than a woman in a dress, she looks like a colorful sculpture of the naked female form. In one shot, she leans backward over the stage into the audience, and her cleavage dominates the frame in a close-up, not of her face, but of her breasts. When she pauses on stage, her dress falls across her body, clinging like wet tissue paper to her thighs, stomach, and pubic area. Finally, in that well-worn trope of Hollywood films, Esmeralda laces her limbs seductively around a pole (actually, a spear she snatches from a nearby soldier) and swings herself into the air.

Employing the phallic weapon as a prop in her general seduction of the ardent crowd, Esmeralda is, not insignificantly, rewarded with money. The crowd tosses coins at the conclusion of the dance. Like the filmmakers who prostitute this character, Esmeralda understands the power of her body over her audience and the money it will earn. Prostituting the female form comes easily to The Walt Disney Company. Witness the Victoria's Secret Fashion Show, aired on the Disney-owned ABC television network for the first time during prime time in the fall of 2001 (the other two broadcasts, 1999 and 2000, were limited to Webcasts on the Internet). According to Jack Trout, of Trout & Partners, a marketing consultancy firm, "Usually the networks [are] above anything like this," but "it's a sign of the times that these guys are looking for some extra dough" (*ABC News*).

Visually, strolls taken by Belle and Jasmine from one end of town to the other and Esmeralda's Feast of Fools dance mirror the televised performances of strutting Victoria's Secret models. The lingerie models practice a stylized indifference to the gaze they solicit, and their no-means-yes availability reveals and relies upon the same masculine desire we see in the Disney fairy tales under consideration here. According to the plot described in the street scenes' songs, the attention Belle and Jasmine receive is for the ostensible reason of their bold behavior—unescorted women openly eschewing masculine attention and support. Images of leering crowds, combined with the women's Barbie doll–inspired forms (according to Bell, the model for Belle's figure stands 5′2″ and weighs just ninety-two pounds), undermine their defiant characterizations (113). These scenes conflate two conflicting messages in both films: the potential political power contained in the women's indifference to convention and the genre's requirement for erotic female display. So, despite Belle's showing more interest in books than in the boorish suitor Gaston, and Jasmine's ending up in the marketplace after escaping her father's palace, these scenes construct Belle and Jasmine as little more than objects of desire. Both films insist from the start upon this contradictory message and finally elide the contradiction with plots that move into conventional marriage scenarios. Once coupled, the women lose their mildly feminist attributes and become merely blushing brides.

No longer one of the "helpless ornaments" (Zipes 37) of the *Snow White*-to-*Little Mermaid* era, Esmeralda comes to us as a partially unwrapped package, a seductive woman whose behavior and dress seem to promise further revelations. While clinging loyally to the company standard of womanhood, Disney's *Hunchback* embraces female sexuality more aggressively, handling Esmeralda's image with even less subtlety than it does the images of her sisters. The film marginalizes Esmeralda through her status as a gypsy and ties that status to her open sexuality. For example, we first see Esmeralda after a mother passes with her young son and warns, "Stay away, child. They're gypsies. They'll steal us blind." The tracking shot moves from the mother and child to Esmeralda's small camp, where she dances for coins in the street. Dressed to draw attention to her physical form, she plays the tambourine and holds the gaze of Phoebus, a mounted soldier, whose status and staring fail to intimidate her. He offers a coin, as the mother proceeds in her proper role of instructing her male child to avoid women like Esmeralda. Just as the street scenes in the earlier films do, this scene absorbs the question of Esmeralda's individual character within the film's visual argument about female sexuality by forcing her to embody the alleged truth of that argument. Indeed, the plot will eventually play out the supposed dangers of Esmeralda's material existence: She horrifies a good mother, distracts Frollo from proper worship, beguiles Phoebus (the leering soldier) from his job, and causes Quasimodo to neglect his master.

As I have said, the display of Esmeralda in *Hunchback* differs significantly from earlier depictions of Disney women in its sophisticated salaciousness. While she never dons the sequined corsets and thongs featured on the Victoria's Secret Fashion Show, Disney's new daring is revealed in *Hunchback* toys with the notorious striptease pay-off: exposing the female sex organ. Despite our cultural landscape's inarguable saturation with images of women's bodies, these images rarely include the pubic area. For that reason, of course, we find its revelation all the more stunning. (Remember Sharon Stone's meteoric rise in fame when she crossed her legs a bit too languorously in *Basic Instinct*.) Naked models in Calvin Klein ads and on PETA billboards, for example, assume positions designed to portray female nudity but conceal the vagina; models modestly raise a leg or lounge on their stomachs. Meanwhile, *Hunchback*, while resisting strict anatomical accuracy, denies such modesty to its model, and boldly includes her vagina as part of the visual offering. Just as her breasts are exposed, or highlighted as areas of visual interest, by the clothing that conceals them, so is her pubic area.

Moreover, the film encourages an (admittedly) ambivalent sympathy for the obsessive man who menaces Esmeralda and the rest of the gypsy population by depicting his fixation—erotic, vaginal—as dangerous to him. Esmeralda's material presence, her body itself, visibly terrifies even as it seduces Frollo, and he prays for her destruction. In this scene, Frollo sings of his tormented desire before a cavernous hearth as images of Esmeralda envelope him in the form of flame and clinging, sinuous smoke. Ensnared in her teasing, diaphanous body, Frollo struggles to free himself in a surprisingly erotic scene. This portion of the film calls on the horror film tradition; through ominous light and shadows, the room becomes a haunted house, Esmeralda the evil spirit, and Frollo the endangered occupant. Perversely, Frollo prays for protection against the woman he has been hunting and whose people he systematically oppresses. Drawn in a transparent gown that calls attention to the curves of hips, thighs, buttocks, and (especially) breasts, Esmeralda represents the evil haunting the space and the male character—that is, unchecked female sexuality. In the intersection of the haunted space, the horror film tropes, and Frollo's apparent suffering, the film reveals the depth of its misogyny. While the film stops short of rendering Frollo as unambiguously sympathetic, it situates the woman as the cause of his terror. This scene in particular portrays not just Esmeralda but, more explicitly, the female sexual function as the true source of the violence threatening the beloved cathedral of Notre Dame and the city itself.

These renderings make feminist psychoanalytic interpretation difficult to resist. Frollo (and Disney animators) fairly performs the "scopic economy" within this film's diegesis, and especially in this scene. The fact of the animated female image being drawn, visually brought to life, by a masculine team of creators adds sinister nuance to Irigaray's observation:

[Woman's] entry into a dominant scopic economy signifies, again, her consignment to passivity: she is to be the beautiful object of contemplation. While her body finds itself thus eroticized, and called to a double movement of exhibition and of chaste retreat in order to stimulate the drives of the "subject," her sexual organ represents *the horror of nothing to see*. (26)

Frollo's prayer for Esmeralda's destruction perpetuates his—and the film's—vaginal preoccupations. During the scene in which he prays, the Palace of Justice transforms into a devouring vagina the size of the building, literally embodying the real source of his fear and his repressive regime, conveniently enacting the projection motivating patriarchy's anxiety of "nothing to see." At first he stands before a large hearth, a hot, gaping opening from which the body of Esmeralda issues. Then the passage stretches out behind him and is lined on both sides with towering images of faceless, hooded robes, not unlike familiar images of the Ghost of Christmas past. But these robes are red, with black open hoods, and the color contrast creates a sensation of bottomless depth beyond the dark openings. These figures overwhelm Frollo, swirl around him, and finally completely encircle him. As they move, the black openings elongate, enfolded by labial red hoods; when they finally fly off and away, the faces of the hoods are now just narrow black slits (think here of Georgia O'Keeffe flowers). When Phoebus interrupts this masturbatory reverie, Frollo is visibly shaken and embarrassed.

For Frollo, Esmeralda is so bad, she's good. In the face of his own fantasy his behavior resembles that of a patron in a strip bar. In other words, he fantasizes that the woman's seductive dance is in fact a genuine response to his presence. As Dahlia Schweitzer argues, "What we understand as the stripper is as much a construction of the male mind as a role played by women. [...] They become a feminine ideal in which natural sentience and vitality have been replaced with a monolithic eroticism serving male fantasy" (68). The no-means-yes scenario embedded within nearly all of Disney's romance narratives suggests a kind of emotional striptease, in which a woman lures her suitor with the possibility of sexual acquiescence through a hesitant refusal, what we might also imagine as an insentient slumber from which she must finally be awoken. Disney introduced the notion of titillating courtship in its earliest full-length feature, *Snow White*, in which the object of the prince's desire is unavailable yet tantalizingly visible: a beautiful woman encased in a glass coffin. Narratives of sleeping beauties argue that remaining unattainable (either through direct refusal or deep sleep) functions as a kind of modesty, and insist on this modesty as a term of appropriate female behavior. Remaining unattainable is, therefore, the equivalent of being chaste. Esmeralda's role as provocative dancer answers this requirement for modesty in a new way. Like other handsome princes, when Phoebus first sees his love, he responds with romantic/erotic interest: He moans, "What a woman!" *Hunchback* replaces the glass coffin with a Feast of Fools striptease. The dance functions as the initiating moment in the story of their coupling, when Esmeralda literally teases Phoebus with an apparent hesitation to reveal herself or remove her clothes, by drawing attention to that possibility. *Hunchback* turns the notion of modesty mentioned above inside out, then. Esmeralda does not passively await the arrival of her prince, but actively courts the libidinal attention of the entire town. She has been drawn to occupy the opposite extreme of the polarities embedded in any courtship narrative that relies upon feminine chastity. If she's not an obedient sleeping beauty, then she's a transgressive sex object.

The film resolves the paradox of a "stripping beauty" through an extended and rehabilitating courtship between Esmeralda and Phoebus—and, significantly, by having Esmeralda censure her own behavior. For example, she begins a prayer to the Virgin Mary with an apology, "I shouldn't even speak to you." She also apologizes for what she does for a living when she admits to Quasimodo, "If I could do this [sculpt like him], you wouldn't find me dancing in the street for coins." And the plot of the film reiterates this visual argument throughout. As a gypsy, Esmeralda exists on the margins of Paris society. Frollo makes this point explicitly when he tells Phoebus how gypsies exist "outside the normal order." Additionally, her beauty sets her apart (no other women in Paris look like her, as the many crowd scenes demonstrate), as does her affiliation with the hunchback, whom she befriends, and interestingly, seems not to find the least bit ugly. Moreover, her survival, like Quasimodo's, depends upon the mercy of the patriarchal institutions of the church and the captain of the guard. Through the convention of sanctuary, both characters find protection from a hostile community in the bell tower of Notre Dame, and an alliance with Phoebus finally releases both from the terror of Frollo's clutches.

Significantly, Esmeralda speaks in the voice of Demi Moore, whose celebrity escalated dramatically in the period after she appeared naked twice on the cover of *Vanity Fair*, and who has appeared topless six times on-screen. Starring in Andrew Bergman's film *Striptease*, released within a week of *Hunchback* in June 1996, Moore manages to finish the dance begun in the children's film. Almost unbelievably, her character takes her clothes off in a bar called The Eager Beaver. As one of the most powerful actors in Hollywood, as one of the first women to be paid on a par with men, Demi Moore enjoyed at this time visible authority in the American film industry. However, we cannot ignore that she earned this power through a disproportionate concern with her physical appearance. For example, according to *People* magazine:

> While the movie [*Striptease*] was in production, Moore's daily exercise encompassed a long predawn run on the beach, as many as three hours of dance rehearsal, a session

with her personal trainer in a special trailer outfitted with $15,000 worth of gym equipment and 2½ hours of yoga. (Cerio and Ramsay 90)

Obviously, she has earned her professional cache by removing her clothes to reveal a body like Esmeralda's, a fiction of patriarchy, a female ideal disconnected from actual female biology and obtainable only through such extreme measures as tortuous exercise, plastic surgery, or the art of animation.

Andrew Bergman's film and Disney's children's story contain essentially the same female character. Both display an arrogant disregard for received notions of appropriate female behavior by consciously trading on their most visible commodity, their bodies. However, both also privately express regret and shame over that decision. These characters inhabit, then, oppositional identity positions in their own minds; they see themselves as good girls gone bad. Their putative feminist arguments, like the films' ostensible political positions, are all show, easily stripped away. Although Esmeralda dances/strips only briefly, this is apparently her profession, as it is for Moore's character, Erin Grant. Both women find themselves in desperate situations, on the margins of society as defined by the films, and so turn reluctantly to dancing/stripping for a living. Grant commiserates with her strip-bar sisters that stripping is the only way she can make enough money to fight for custody of her daughter, despite her character's having previously been employed by the FBI. Perhaps being a beautiful woman working as a clerk for the Federal Bureau of Investigation proved no less difficult than stripping—and she asserts that the FBI paid less well. The film locks Grant between two pillars of patriarchal ideology, then: a law enforcement agency and a strip bar. Serving men within the macho walls of the former phallocratic institution, an institution defined by its devotion to the law, or serving men's desire more directly in the latter may be virtually the same thing. At best, either role forces the character to act ideologically against herself; that is, as either FBI clerk or stripper, she services the patriarchal system that creates these institutions and her subordinate role within them.

Moreover, the plot of the children's film mirrors the plot of the R-rated one. Both stories are fueled by the sexual obsession of a man for a woman, an obsession that puts the woman in direct physical danger. Frollo has Esmeralda arrested in the army's roundup of gypsies, ties her to a stake, and then offers her the following reprieve: "Choose me or the fire." In other words surrender sexually to him or be burned at the stake. In *Striptease*, Grant faces a similarly appalling choice: surrender to a man she finds repellent, the corrupt politician David Dillbeck, played by Burt Reynolds, who insists upon private dances, or lose her seven-year-old daughter. Both women struggle on their own behalf, but their films' plots force them finally to passively await rescue. In an interesting twist, Erin Grant's rescuing prince appears in the form of a large, black bodyguard played by Ving Rhames. Hunchback ends with Phoebus as the hero. He arrives as fire threatens Notre Dame, and the talking gargoyles sigh with relief: "I think the cavalry's here." The resolution of the plot obviates any successful struggle Esmeralda may have enacted on her own, and reiterates her marginal position. Further, her alliance with Phoebus draws her into the patriarchal fold, for in the final moments of the film she emerges from the cathedral on his arm to the cheers of delighted Parisian citizens. (All the scene lacks is a white dress and flying rice.)

Like Frollo, Disney is clearly ambivalent about the value and function of the female body. The full-length animated features produced by Disney in the late twentieth century suggest a preoccupation with this body's role in the courtship tradition—to say nothing of a straightforward fascination with the female form. While Disney artists obviously delight in drawing female characters, those drawings betray a deeper misogynist conviction and simply continue the fairy tale tradition embraced by the company since *Snow White*. Hesitant refusal, the no-means-yes drama of seduction, necessarily sympathizes with the masculine desirer (no can only mean yes from the desirer's point of view). Female point of view does not exist in the Disney erotic fantasy; female characters enact the misogynist and paradoxical fantasy of the available stripper: in other words, a sex toy that can be animated into service, whether that be in marriage or in movies.

Works Cited

ABC News. "Victoria's Secret Fashion Show a Hit." 16 November 2001. <http:\\abc. go.com/entertainment/news/2001/11/VictoriasSecret>.

Bell, Elizabeth. "Somatexts at the Disney Shop: Constructing the Pentimentos of Women's Animated Bodies." Bell, Haas, and Sells 107–124.

Bell, Elizabeth, Lynda Haas, and Laura Sells, eds. *From Mouse to Mermaid: The Politics of Film, Gender, and Culture*. Bloomington: Indiana UP, 1995.

Cerio, Gregory, and Carolyn Ramsay. "The Eye of the Tiger." *People* 24 June 96: 88–94.

Forgacs, David. "Disney Animation and the Business of Childhood." *Screen* 33.4. Winter 1992: 361–74.

The Hunchback of Notre Dame. Dirs. Gary Trousdale, Kirk Wise. Animated. Voices: Tom Hulce, Demi Moore, Tony Jay, Kevin Kline. The Walt Disney Company, 1996.

Irigaray, Luce. *This Sex Which Is Not One*. Trans. Catherine Porter. Ithaca: Cornell UP, 1985.

Mulvey, Laura. *Visual and Other Pleasures*. Bloomington: Indiana UP, 1989.

Penley, Constance. *Feminism and Film Theory*. New York: Routledge, 1988.

Rothstein, Edward. "From Darwinian to Disneyesque; In *Tarzan's* Evolution, A New Theory: The Survival of Nearly Everything." *New York Times* 15 July 1999.

Schweitzer, Dahlia. "Striptease: The Art of Spectacle and Transgression." *Journal of Popular Culture* 34.1 (2000): 65–75.

Striptease. Dir. Andrew Bergman. Castle Rock Entertainment, 1996.

Zipes, Jack. "Breaking the Disney Spell." Bell, Haas, and Sells. 107–124.

CHAPTER 5

Disney's Magic Carpet Ride: *Aladdin* and Women in Islam

Christiane Staninger

Aladdin (1992) became the biggest moneymaker for Disney since the founding of the company. This charming romance, coupled with the mystique of Arabic locale, the wit of Robin Williams, and the appeal of Broadway music, pushed sales past Disney's last success, *Beauty and the Beast,* as Buena Vista Productions reports. Despite or because of the movie's success, some critics questioned Disney's description of Middle Eastern life in general and the description of women in particular, voicing their concern that Disney did nothing to help destroy the West's stereotypical view of the East as a country of violence and oppression of women's rights.

Academics hesitantly admitted to their fondness for the movie while squirming uncomfortably when questioned about its political insensitivity. When *Aladdin* was released by Disney Productions, I was initially amazed at this movie's popularity in academic circles, which are usually critical of such rather stereotypical representations of ethnicity. I marveled at their (and my own) ability to push aside the then current events—by which I mean the "Allied" offensive in Iraq—in order to enjoy "escapist" entertainment. Regardless, while any number of intrigues involving the reception of *Aladdin* could be the subject of inquiry, I centered my analysis on the nature and implications of the co-protagonist, Princess Jasmine, the Valley Girl in veils.

My questions about this character have been grouped into three categories. Each called for a different theoretical approach. The first category of questions focused on the character of Princess Jasmine as such, which is to ask, "Why has this character been so appealing to American teenagers for a decade?" particularly given the political climate, before and after the events of September 11, 2001. My speculations in this area will argue that Princess Jasmine represents a pseudo–feminist, pseudo-cross-cultural model—a most tame model, for sure, but one which the (conservative) Disney Studios could advance presumably without fear.

The second category of questions concerned Princess Jasmine's representation as a prototypical Middle Eastern woman and her reception by non–Middle Eastern audiences. Obviously Disney was eschewing most facts in drawing this character. Yet the fact remains that the movie claims her to be generically Middle Eastern. To what degree did an American audience fix in on Jasmine's ethnicity? Or perhaps the question is better phrased in the negative: What textual cues allow the audience to forget her ethnicity? After all, when the movie opened to huge audiences, the United States was at the same time actually bombing in and around its fictional location. Disney claims that it is by accident that the release of *Aladdin* coincided with the then current American affairs in the Middle East (the idea for the movie was conceived years before the Gulf War) (Nelson).

This second question was framed by Edward Said's theory of Orientalism, in which Said argues that to the Occident, the Orient is almost a European invention (1). If Jasmine is a Westernized model of an Oriental princess, which already is a (by now historically grounded) Western invention, then Princess Jasmine is thrice removed from any "adequate" representation of an Islamic woman.

The third category strays from the *Aladdin* movie to question "Women in Islam." Both locally and nationally, attention has increased on the "role" of Islamic women, especially with respect to the "role" of Western women. Fictions about the Middle East are most provocative when it comes to the "veiled" woman. She (the Islamic woman) appears to offer solace to the Western woman and man, who can content themselves with the claim that "well, things aren't that bad here." But a number of ethnographic studies—most prominently those of Elizabeth Warnock Fernea and, more recently, Fatima Mernissi—expose Islamic feminism in a light which actually turns the critique upon Western feminism.

***

Why is the character of Jasmine so appealing to American audiences? Why did (and does) her picture grace bedspreads and towels? Why was the part of Jasmine the most sought after solo at a local eighth-grade music production? Because she is, by all accounts, one of the most popular fictional California teenagers of the 1990s. She was created to embody the strong, independent young woman, the new ideal of young girls. This new strength desired in female heroines explains why Disney not only deviated from the original description in "Ala Al-Din and the Wonderful Lamp," where the princess is no more than a passive object of desire, but also from recent animations. Disney animator and creator of Jasmine Mark Henn says of his character: "Jasmine is very different from the rest [of the group of recent Disney heroines]; a lot more feisty than Belle (from *Beauty and the Beast*), and not as naive as Ariel (from *The Little Mermaid*)." Jasmine is a typical teenager in the trappings of an Arab princess, beginning with her clothing (*Aladdin*; Production Information 22). The similarity between her garb and see-through dresses, baggy pants, halter tops, and long hair held in "scrunchies," part of the year's Southern California dress code at the time the film was released, is staggering. Her speech as well resembles that of an American teenager: While most of the characters in *Aladdin* speak with a Middle Eastern accent, she (with Aladdin and the Genie) does not. Her values are the ones of a Western young woman. Nowhere is her faith addressed. She wants independence, rejects the suitors who approach her—and does so for reasons of personal dislikes—and runs away from home and its boredom. Aladdin and the market of Agrabah can offer excitement, and she finds interest in the street-smart daredevil from the "wrong" side of the tracks, who is as clearly un-Arabic as she. This innovative teenager, in whom Disney animator Glen Keane combined "the confidence, likeability and physical traits of Tom Cruise, certain personality elements of Michael J. Fox, the fluid movements and style of rapper M. C. Hammer, along with his own sensibilities" ("Disney Presents" 20), can offer excitement and adventure. What then develops is a typical "uptown girl" story set to Broadway tunes: Boy loves girl, boy is not worthy of girl, boy becomes worthy and marries girl. But girl is independent, one has to remember: When Aladdin poses as a prince and acts macho, she recoils and refuses to become his "trophy wife." When she informs Aladdin, the Sultan, and Jafar, the evil vizier, of her decision to not marry anybody, she leaves all three of them speechless, and only hypnosis brings the Sultan to order her to marry the vizier, for it is understood that one does not "boss" Jasmine around, and simple orders do not work on her. When finally Aladdin uses his third wish to free the Genie and therefore relinquishes his hopes to become a prince once more, it seems that he has lost Jasmine forever. But the Sultan cannot stand to be in the way of "true love" and changes the law: Now Jasmine can marry whom she chooses. Jasmine's strong will and determination convinces her dad to change century-old laws.

It is this determination (and her animated beauty, of course) that the group of eighth-grade girls, whom I questioned on these matters, liked the most. Jasmine stands up to Aladdin, her father, and the vizier. She knows what she wants. She does not let her father make her decision, and she does not allow him to treat her like a little kid. These are traits that my informants admired. One could assume then that Disney has done feminism a favor, by creating such a clearly identifiable and strong role model.

***

While this Americanization of *Aladdin*'s Jasmine could have been benevolently interpreted as Disney's attempt to make the movie inviting to a large American audience and to fledgling American feminists in particular, Americans of Arab descent did not see it this way. They suspected a more sinister reasoning behind this popularization and spoke of the unfortunate underlying messages that this movie projects: Colonialism works, and the Middle East is to be mistrusted.

Leila Gorchev of the *Washington Post* believed that movies like these stereotypings of Middle Eastern violence keep alive the animosity between Americans and Arab countries. Gorchev asks years before the tragedy of September 11, 2001: "When will it be okay to be an Arab?" She believes that this movie could have been the perfect opportunity to change the stereotypical hostile American opinion of the Arab world, exemplified in the movie's opening song: "Oh I come from a land / From a faraway place / Where the caravan camels roam. / Where they cut off your ear / If they don't like your face. / It's barbaric, but hey, it's home," describing Islamic law as violent and arbitrary. Disney could have used the movie, Gorchev argued, to show that the Arabic world is not violent and can produce its own role models and heroes, but it completely Americanized them: "Aladdin and Jasmine's cultural values are...presented as American, representing innocence, subversion of social tradition, freedom of choice and courage."

In defense of Disney, one could argue that at least this time Disney's heroes are not white. Donna Britt, who writes for the *Washington Post*, praises *Aladdin* as one of "Disney's few animated films featuring people of color." The term "people of color" is generally used for Americans of African (and Mexican?) descent, as distinguished from and by white people. To consider the cast of a movie set in a Middle Eastern country "of color" is a clear tautology, because everybody is "of color." In another sense, the only "person of color" in the movie is Robin Williams' blue genie.

But if one wants to insist that Disney features "people of color," then it is painfully obvious that the protagonists—Jasmine, Aladdin, and the Genie— are not. Their features are decidedly white/European. The others have large noses, sinister eyes, and violence on the mind. Aladdin and Jasmine have none of these. They are dark-haired Ken and Barbie. While common stereotypes force images of Middle Eastern violence, harems for polygamist husbands, and bearded terrorists, Aladdin and Jasmine break that stereotype, it is true, but in a distinctly Western, not Middle Eastern, fashion, and are therefore not useful in improving the Arab American or Arabic image.

On the contrary, *Aladdin* could be called a propaganda movie for Western imperialism, because it shows the supposed unworkability of Middle Eastern traditions and the need for American intervention. Who indeed is the young man who is worthy of the lamp? Aladdin, with his Bugs Bunny brazenness. Who is the fairest of the fair? Jasmine, feisty feminist. Even her name, Jasmine, a far cry from the original, Badr al-Budur, in "Ala Al-Din and the Wonderful Lamp," is as mainstream American as are Jennifer and Joshua. The goals of Aladdin are the stuff that the American dream is made of: Live long and prosper, and liberate your indentured servants. Freedom is what everyone is after. Jasmine wants freedom from prearranged husbands and lifestyles; Aladdin wants freedom from poverty. The Sultan wants freedom from his evil-angular vizier Jafar (Erte meets Nancy Reagan), and the Genie wants freedom from the lamp. By pursuing their American dreams of prosperity and freedom, Jasmine and Aladdin circumvent the entire structure of Islamic culture (but how do I know that these values are not Islamic?), replacing it with a "better" system of values, one that American audiences can identify with.

Gorchev challenged Disney to use its influence to dispel stereotypes, and not help solidify them. Why, Gorchev asks, invent the fictitious city of Agrabah, when the original Aladdin story shows reference to Baghdad?—because it would ennoble the Iraqis, and "we" dislike them too much to grant them a place in Disney history? Or because Disney wanted to prevent criticism from those condoning the United States' aggression against Baghdad and Iraq?

Disney tried to defend itself. Charles S. Nelson, PR mensch of Buena Vista Productions, told me of the company's collective surprise when the movie reaped criticism instead of rewards. Nelson believed that Disney should be given credit for its achievement of offering American girls a strong feminist role model. And Howard Green, another spokesman for Disney, is quoted in the *Washington Post*: "[The criticism] is certainly coming from a small minority, because most people are very happy with it. All the characters are Arabs, the good guys and the bad guys, and the accents don't really connote anything" (qtd. in Scheinin). Buena Vista took painstaking measures to present a somewhat authentic Arab town. The animation was influenced by Arab calligraphy, primarily the S-curves, and by Persian miniature paintings from A.D. 1000 to 1500, from which the authentic shades of colors were taken. Artistic supervisor Rasoul Azadani, a native Iranian, flew to his hometown of Isfahan in 1991 to photograph buildings and interiors in order to authentically capture the Islamic world of the fifteenth century. Disney states that Azadani's over eighteen hundred pictures which he took during the trip became the basis for many of the layouts and backgrounds of the *Aladdin* movie (*Aladdin*; Production Information 24).

But the fact remains that the protagonists are not Middle Eastern if they are modeled after Tom Cruise, Ed Sullivan, and the like. The Genie, Robin Williams, is purposely and undeniably Robin Williams. Only a small minority was bothered by the tautology in movie, further proving Gorchev's point: Mainstream America does not recognize the prejudice and stereotyping as such. That is why it is not bothered by them. Exactly because only a few cried wolf, more Americans need to be educated about the reality of Islam, because most obviously they do not recognize the characterizations of Aladdin and Jasmine as incorrect.

The relationship between the Middle East and the West has always been based on a narrative, says Edward Said in *Orientalism*. Said has concluded that the West, particularly England and France, less so the United States, has traditionally fabricated a history of mythical lands: "In any instance of at least written language, there is no such thing as a delivered presence, but a re-presence, or a representation" (21). This representation describes the Western image of a culture, not the culture itself (if that is indeed possible) or the Middle East's understanding of its own culture. The term "Orientalism" has become for Said the manipulation by Europe (and the United States) of the Orient.

Colonialism in the Middle East in this century has provided Western countries—England and France at the forefront—with power over a different culture and religion. Aside from the financial gain, colonization allowed for the creation of a developmental playground, provided difference, and offered the opportunity to learn about oneself by setting oneself off with somebody one is not, along the lines of the tired cliché that one does not know how good home is unless one travels abroad. This phenomenon Said describes when he argues that the "Orient is...one of [the] deepest and most recurring images of the Other" (1). Being the Other is an unequal relationship, for one is not allowed to be oneself in one's own right, but is reduced to a reflecting pond, with offsetting function. In this function as the Other, the West's view of the Orient has swung from the familiar (which is nonthreatening) to the alien: "The Orient at large, therefore, vacillates between the West's contempt for what is familiar and its shivers of delight in—or fear of—novelty" (59).

If one dominates the Other, and if one possesses something as indefinable as "scruples" and "morals," dominance requires the invention of a guilt-freeing narrative. The West's historical narrative describing the East as a violent culture of fanatics has survived with the help of the media. Anti-Arab and anti-Islamic prejudice has been reinforced by the electronic, postmodern world (Said 27). Especially since "the Middle East is now so identified with

Great Power politics, oil economics, and the simple-minded dichotomy of freedom-loving, democratic Israel and evil, totalitarian, and terrorist Arabs, the chances of anything like a clear view of what one talks about in talking about the Near East are depressingly small" (27). After the events of September 11, the chances are even less than that.

***

Jasmine's feminist ambitions are American ambitions. She is a typical American teenager, and perhaps presumably that Disney did not care to show the true characteristics of a Middle Eastern woman. But is that so? Middle Eastern scholar Vali Nasr points out that—ironically—Disney's description of Jasmine as a Middle Eastern woman is not that far from the truth. While her behavior might be stereotypically American teenager, her desires are not. Nasr points out that Jasmine's particular speech and behavior patterns would not be atypical for a Middle Eastern princess, but her desires and goals would otherwise. A true Middle Eastern princess would have probably not been as direct as Jasmine, he argues. Middle Eastern women have had much more power than Westerners give them credit for, and not just recently. It is the West's prejudiced perception that Middle Eastern women are submissive, passive, and quiet. In the past, men ruled their homes, having direct influence over the succession of the throne or the family rank, making economic and local political decisions. While it might not appear so to a foreigner, Middle Eastern women have been immensely powerful since the age of Muhammad, though interest groups have been trying to suppress that power. The Western world, which needs to experience strength in a more outward expression in order to recognize it, has traditionally failed to see women's power. In the present, Nasr says, Middle Eastern women are striving for the same rights that American women are, but for the West it is not always fast enough.

The anthropologist Elizabeth Fernea describes this power of the Middle Eastern woman in her book *Guests of the Sheik*. While the book is forty years old, it is a powerful account of Islamic family life, which compares favorably to that of the (albeit mythical) June Cleavers of nearly forty years ago in America. When Fernea lived in a rural Iraqi village, she witnessed strength and power in these women, and she found herself surprised that "in spite of the relative obscurity in which these women lived, I came to realize how much they influenced men, their husbands and especially their sons..." (65). Mothers had the final say in the lives of their sons, especially when choosing a wife. Fernea speaks of strong companionship among women, who would help one another and be respected and taken care of in old age.

She suggests: "The idea of old people's homes must have been particularly reprehensible to these women whose lives of toil and childbearing were rewarded in old age, when they enjoyed repose and respect as members of their children's household" (189). In this village, women did not hesitate to discuss the joys of sex with their female friends. While the American woman of the 1960s raised her children in relative isolation and needed to depend primarily on her husband (working, therefore absent) for companionship, Fernea watched her newfound friends in the village share companionship, personal tragedies, joys, and husbands, for this was still a world of polygamy (for males). And while this world has definitely been a patriarchial world, Fernea believes that it is not as bad as the West makes it sound: "I could tell my friends in America again and again that the veiling and seclusion of Eastern women didn't mean necessarily that they were forced against their will to live lives of submission and near-serfdom" (316). She considered these women to be happy.

A 1988 documentation of Middle Eastern women's lives is Bouthaina Shaaban's text *Both Right and Left Handed*. She, too, wants to break the stereotypical image that we see on television, and instead introduce us to the real Arab woman, the one whose image is not allowed in our living rooms. This woman is strong and struggles to become an equal partner in her world. I was struck by similarities between her story and the struggle of Western women for equality. Shaaban describes the conflicting messages her parents sent, by encouraging her to go to school and by cheering on her achievements, but then banishing her from their lives when she selected her own husband. In our society it is still very common to encourage daughters to go to school and get a good education, but not so much in order to have a challenging, fulfilling career, but for an emergency, "in case something happens to your husband and you would have to support yourself." The conflicting message in both cultures is that everything a woman does is in reference to a husband.

The double standard of sexual "purity" is alive and well in both cultures, too. Shaaban writes:

> According to our law her husband would have the right to hand her divorce paper immediately [if he found evidence during the wedding night that his bride was not a virgin] and she would have been the object of social disgrace. Today, young men's attitude to virginity is changing (though no man would openly admit this), and is becoming quite relaxed and understanding; nevertheless, the Article in the law is still there in case any male chauvinist would like to make use of it. (10)

About domestic issues, Shaaban writes: "Although women have become professionals and politicians and have excelled in many fields, at home they are still considered the weaker sex, and are expected to act as servants" (27). The same phenomenon exists in the United States, and I find it distressing to see that a lot of women participate in this behavior. While there are certainly a lot of men who enjoy passing off housework and childcare onto women, a lot of women I know actively and insistently encourage and demand their own presence in that traditional role, denying fathers the experience of being a responsible caretaker, feeling satisfied only when the house remains their domain.

Shaaban, while pointing out that there is much work to be done, is delighted by the changes that have been made in the last decade: "Ten years ago [1978], perhaps, none of the women interviewed would have said anything against their husbands or fathers....Whereas now all the women I talked to were able to see themselves as separate and independent of both husbands and fathers" (237). While the laws of Islam, as delineated by Shaaban, are more restrictive for Islamic women than is Western law, it is obvious that the struggles of Western and Islamic women are not that different, and the West has no right to arrogantly cite "backwardness." While Western women may have won some battles already, they are far away from equality and should get off their high horse.

What has slowed down the Middle Eastern world from accepting women as equals has been a matter of religious belief. For generations, women had been taught that the Prophet Muhammad demanded dutiful wives and daughters, and in many Arab countries the law demands it. But that tradition is being questioned. More and more women are encouraged to break out of the role as the (albeit powerful) domestics and take on the right that Muhammad had worked for during his lifetime: the Middle Eastern woman as an equal partner.

At the forefront of this project of reaching woman's equality stands Fatima Mernissi. She argues that since the days of Muhammad, the Prophet, women have had equal rights and have excelled in all aspects of public and private life. But over the course of centuries, patriarchs have rebelled against women's liberation and traditionally used strategic interpretations of the Qur'an to "put women back in their place." Mernissi makes her task "the study of the religious texts that everybody knows but no one really probes, with the exception of the authorities on the subject: the mullahs and imams" (2). She observes that "not only have the sacred texts always been manipulated, but manipulation of them is a structural characteristic of the practice of power in Muslim societies." Since all power, from the seventh century on, was legitimated only by religion, political forces and economic interest groups pushed for the fabrication of (what she calls) false traditions. To believe that the religion of Islam, of Muhammad, wants to see women in the place in which society wants to see them, "to be marginal, and above all subordinate," (24) is to believe incorrectly.

Muhammad, on the contrary, preached and demonstrated that women were equal to men and were to be respected: "In Arabia where power predominated, where the saber was king, this Prophet, who publicly stated that he preferred women to men, was preaching a very unusual message" (63). The Prophet never considered his domestic life as trivial. While he was the military and religious leader of his people, he nevertheless did not consider his home less important. He surrounded himself with strong women and openly discussed his sexuality.

The Prophet's first wife, Khadija, asked him to marry her, a far cry from the arranged marriages which would become the custom centuries later. Umm Salama, another of the Prophet's wives, is considered to be the one who heard the Prophet say that the "two sexes are in total equality as believers, that is, as members of the community" (118), making men and women equal before Allah.

Even among his enemies, Muhammad respected women. Hind Bint 'Utba, who played a central role in the Meccan opposition to Muhammad, was so highly regarded as a capable enemy that her name appeared on the death list after Muhammad had conquered Mecca, an honor (albeit a final honor) previously reserved for men. While the Prophet had tried for equality, opposition was great. Then, "confronted with laws [his opponents] did not like, they tried to distort them through the device of interpretation. They tried to manipulate the texts in such a way as to maintain their privileges" (125).

Mernissi shows that it was a specific orally transmitted tradition, *hadith*, which misogynists used to suppress the rights of women: "Those who entrust their affairs to a woman will never know prosperity" (49). The conveyor of this *hadith*, Abu Bakra, claims to have heard these words from the Prophet directly. But Mernissi questions his integrity. Abu Bakra, she reasons, had much to lose if women came into power. He had been a nobody whom Islam had elevated to status and money, and he could have had reason to keep the faith from changing. It was also a perfectly safe time to pronounce this *hadith*, since 'A'isha, the Prophet's widow, who had tried to revolutionize Islam to bring it back to Muhammad's standards, had just lost a major battle (which is remembered as "the Battle of the Camel," not "the Battle of 'A'isha"). 'A'isha, in particular, and women generally were at the moment in no enviable position. By recalling the *hadith* after the Battle of the Camel, which 'A'isha had lost so miserably and at the cost of so many lives, Abu Bakra was on safe ground. Mernissi accuses him of opportunism (and here is her one major flaw: She is suspicious of men's opportunism but does not expect this same behavior from women). Mernissi states that the misogynistic *hadith* has been passed as a sacred, unassailable truth into our time.

Muhammad also gave women the right to inherit money, which made them financially independent from men and decreased the real or potential wealth of their fathers, husbands, and sons. However, the *hadith* claimed that no one was supposed to favor the foolish (*al-sufaha*), arguing that women were to be considered *al-sufaha*. This adaptation "served them as a springboard for nullifying the new laws" (126). Over time, Mernissi claims, misogynists have developed "Muslim's amnesia" (129). They have forgotten or ignored the laws of Muhammad and consider equality of the sexes as an alien form, a sign of Western intrusion and imperialism. Mernissi reports that very recently a series of books (so-called "woman's books") have been published which ostensibly concern themselves with "the future of Islam" (97), books that aim toward a cleaning of Muslim society of foreign intervention and the resulting change. These books, Mernissi continues, encourage women to return to the values of Islam as these values have been distorted through centuries.

How, asks Mernissi, "did the tradition succeed in transforming the Muslim woman into that submissive, marginal creature who buries herself and only goes out into the world timidly and huddled in her veils?" (194). She believes that Islam took a downward slide under the Abbasid dynasty, the era in the eighth and ninth centuries, remembered as the "Golden Age." This was a time of international aggression by the Muslims, and part of their war loot was women slaves. With the arrival of many women slaves, "the Arab woman was completely marginalized; she had lost all her freedom and pride....Then she began to be treated with contempt" (194). These women slaves became a sort of competition for the Arab women. They educated themselves and tried to improve their conditions by being kept by wealthy men who would take care of them and their children. Their male children could come to power, if things were orchestrated correctly. Ironically, it is exactly this "Golden Age" that the *Arabian Nights* has immortalized forever. So the origin of Disney's *Aladdin* is precisely set in the historically most repressive age for women. How ironic, too, that Disney would make the Middle Eastern woman such a strong and independent person.

Mernissi (at the end of her study) regrets that "it is the image of the woman of the 'Golden Age'—a slave who intrigues in the corridors of power when she loses hope of seducing—who symbolizes the Muslim eternal female, while the memory of...'A'isha, and [other strong and powerful women] awakens no response and seems strangely distant and unreal" (195). If her argument is valid, then this kind of distortion of partial reduction of history was necessary to help the cause of Muslim reactionaries: the concentration of power in male hands.

Were Arab Americans justified in their anger and hurt over *Aladdin*? At least Disney's (accidental) characterization of the woman is not that far from the truth. That is true, but most viewers would not know that. To them, the characterization of the movie's heroine seems to stand in clear opposition to what they thought Middle Eastern women of the mid-1990s were like. And in a sense, this ironic twist makes it even more frustrating for viewers of Middle Eastern heritage.

I further believe that most analyses let Disney off the hook too easily. David Sterritt of the *Christian Science Monitor* writes:

> The movie doesn't deepen our understanding of Eastern mythology, Arabic culture, or anything else of consequence, and it is regrettable that negative ethnic stereotypes are reinforced by some aspects of the picture. But since the point of the show is to revel in sheer fantasy, whimsy, and energy, the most sensible response is to sit back and enjoy the evanescent eye candy it provides.

Well, if that is so, if the movie's goal is sheer entertainment, sheer energy, then why were stereotypes necessary at all? If glitz is all that counts, why could not have Disney presented its tale in a more authentic package, giving everybody Middle Eastern accents or (heaven forbid) having them speak Arabic with subtitles? Why not? Because it is not as simple as Sterritt makes it sound and there is more at stake than "reveling in sheer fantasy." Sterritt's assumption is naive at best. It assumes that we can watch a piece like *Aladdin* without (consciously or not consciously) having the images of stereotyping penetrate us.

Those who did not find *Aladdin* offensive are probably not of Middle Eastern descent. Imagine a high-profile movie set in your ancestral culture: A freedom-fighting GI Joe and Jane, stationed in Germany, fall in love among castles and lederhosen, while the German population, the extras, revel in neo-nazism. Would I be offended? You bet.

Would I have taken my children to see *Aladdin*? Yes, cautiously and uncomfortably, taking care, I would hope, to use the movie as a point of departure for a more broad interest in the Middle East. It was the movie, I am almost embarrassed to admit, that sparked my interest in the Middle East. But I would make sure to tell my kids, as Stewart Klawans of *The Nation* explains, "that the oily fellow with the camel is your typical Norwegian." But the world has changed after last September's events in New York. Westerner's distrust of Middle Eastern culture has turned into fear. It is a moot point now to ponder if *Aladdin*, had it been made ten years later, would have become a success or been released in the first place. My guess would be:

Yes, it would have been released, for all the reasons that Jasmine, if one chooses to see her that way, is very much an American Princess.

Works Cited

Aladdin. Dirs. Ron Clements, John Musker. Animated. Voices: Scott Weinger, Robin Williams, Linda Larkin. The Walt Disney Company, 1992.

Aladdin; Production Information. Unbound package distributed by Buena Vista Studios. Burbank: n.p., n.d.

Britt, Donna. "2 Films Spin Their Own Special Magic." *Washington Post* 13 Nov. 1992:

"Disney Presents *Aladdin*." Unpublished press release by Disney Studios. 1992.

Fernea, Elizabeth Warnock. *Guests of the Sheik.* New York: Doubleday, 1965.

Gorchev, Leila. "When Will It Be Okay to Be an Arab?" *Washington Post* 27 Dec. 1992: C7.

Klawans, Stewart. "*Aladdin.*" *The Nation.* 7 Dec. 1992: 716.

Mardrus, J. C., ed. *The Book of the Thousand Nights and One Night.* Vol. 4. Trans. E. Powys Mathers. 2nd Ed. London: Routledge, 1964.

Mernissi, Fatima.*The Veil and the Male Elite: A Feminist Interpretation of Women's Rights in Islam.* Trans. Mary Jo Lakeland. Reading, MA: Addison-Wesley, 1991.

Nasr, Dr. Vali, Professor of Political Science at the University of San Diego. Personal interview Summer 1993.

Nelson, Charles. Head of Public Relations at Buena Vista Studios in Burbank. Telephone interview. March 1993.

Said, Edward. *Orientalism.* New York: Pantheon, 1978.

Scheinin, Richard. "Angry over *Aladdin*." *Washington Post* 10 Jan. 1993: G5.

Shaaban, Bouthaina. *Both Right and Left Handed.* London: Women's Press, 1988.

Sterritt, David. "Disney Dreams Up a Dazzling *Aladdin*." *Christian Science Monitor* 7 Nov. 1992: 10.

CHAPTER 6

Disney, the Beast, and Woman As Civilizing Force

Kathleen E. B. Manley

In 1991 the Disney Studios released a film version of *Beauty and the Beast*, a tale folklorists classify as one of a large group of tales known as AT 425C, the "Monster Bridegroom" tale type. (Another well-known version of this tale type is "Cupid and Psyche.")[1] Some reviewers saw the Studios' portrayal of Beauty as an improvement over its previous characterizations of Grimms' female protagonists. Janet Maslin, for example, views Belle as a smart, independent young woman, a "better role model than the marriage-minded Disney heroines of the past." Belle does not appear to love only housework and beautiful dresses, and she does not wait to be rescued from a pack of wolves but fights them off herself (1). Other writers find the film open to numerous, sometimes conflicting interpretations (Erb; Downey), and Kathi Maio notes the dangers of perpetuating the fantasy that the love of a good woman can reform a selfish, bad-tempered man (45). Since she is a strong and active woman, Belle indeed appears to be a protagonist who does not reinforce the stereotypes Maslin mentions but does reinforce a stereotype to which Maio alludes: woman as civilizing force. In comparison with two other familiar versions of *Beauty and the Beast*, Disney's characterizations of Belle's father, of her would-be lover, and particularly of the Beast result in increased emphasis on woman as civilizing force.

In two well-known versions of the tale prior to Disney, the Beast does not require character change in order to be acceptable as a suitor for Beauty; only his *appearance* prevents her from accepting his proposals of marriage. The narrative emphasis is on Beauty's lesson about appearances, as Giselle Boras suggests (49). In the Disney version, however, Beauty must change the Beast's character, and she accomplishes this task by resorting to the stereotypical role of woman as civilizing force.

In Western culture, certainly, the stereotype of woman as civilizing force has existed for some time: An early example is the goddess Athena, patron of the Greek city many in the West see as the root of Western culture and a

civilized ideal. In that city Plato theorized about Pure Forms, further sup-
porting the notion of the Beautiful as a path to the Good. The Renaissance
rediscovery of Plato's theories, in fact, encouraged the strong interest in the
arts during that period. Woman as civilizing force also appears in the image
of justice as a woman blindfolded and carrying scales, as well as in the medieval idealization of the Virgin Mary and, in the tenets of courtly love, the
idealization of woman in general. During the Industrial Revolution, too, one
image of woman is that of "Angel in the House," whose duty is to keep the
light of civilization burning in the home and the forces of the jungle outside
at bay. The reference is to Coventry Patmore's book-length poem, *The Angel
in the House*, which provides a good summary of this stereotype about
women. Patmore's narrator has previously had other love interests but is currently held by his beloved's beauty (26); he believes woman is "Marr'd less
than man by mortal fall" (23); and women in general banish his sadness,
providing warmth and life (12). Patmore not only emphasizes woman as
civilizing force but follows the platonic convention of making a beautiful
woman a route to God: "I loved her in the name of God, / And for the ray
she was of Him; / I ought to admire much more, not less; / Her beauty was a
godly grace" (63). Perhaps this role for women is one reason Virginia
Woolf, in 1931, spoke of killing the Angel in the House in order to write
(qtd. in Payne 3). Belle's relationships with men in Disney's *Beauty and the
Beast* reinforce this long-running stereotype of the beautiful woman as civilizing force, a model of acceptable behavior for people in Western culture.

Before the Disney Studios' release of its film and accompanying book,
the versions of this folktale best known to audiences in the United States
were French. According to Jack Zipes, Jeanne-Marie Leprince de Beaumont's eighteenth-century "Beauty and the Beast," based on Mme. Gabrielle
de Villeneuve's longer version of the tale, "is perhaps the most famous in
the world" (231–32). The other version, which is quite similar to Beaumont's, is Jean Cocteau's film *La belle et la bête* (1946). The audience for
these versions differs: Beaumont's was intended for young women (Warner
8), while Cocteau's is definitely for adults (Turner 94–95).[2] A comparison of
the Disney version with these two previous familiar versions is still useful,
however, particularly with regard to the characterizations of the men involved and Belle's resulting relationships with them.

One important change Disney made in comparison with the two previous
well-known versions of *Beauty and the Beast* is the characterization of
Belle's father. In Beaumont and in Cocteau, Beauty's father is a successful
merchant who has experienced a reversal of fortune. In both versions he
bears his losses with dignity and does his best to provide for his family in
spite of his ill luck. In Disney, however, Belle's father, Maurice, is an inven-

tor, but a not-too-successful one. Early in the film, one of his inventions blows up; and Belle rushes home to be sure he is all right. His activities, in fact, evoke the stereotype of the mad scientist, and he is incompetent as well. He gets lost trying to take his invention to an inventors' fair. Belle's role is to provide a civilizing force for her father by taking care of him. She provides the domestic comforts he needs to continue his work.

In Beaumont and in Cocteau the relationship between Beauty and her merchant father is loving and supportive, a contrast to the relationship between the father and Beauty's two sisters. In both pre-Disney versions Beauty's father asks what gift Beauty would like, after her sisters have requested fine clothes and other adornments (Zipes 234; Cocteau 60), and Cocteau's film makes a clear statement that Beauty insists on taking her father's place at the Beast's castle because she believes it was her request for a rose that put his life in jeopardy (104). In Disney, however, Belle has no sisters and makes no request for a rose. When the Beast discovers Maurice at the castle, where the latter has sought refuge after becoming lost, having his horse throw him, and being chased by wolves, the Beast simply becomes inexplicably angry and throws Maurice in the dungeon. Rather than volunteering to take her father's place after he has returned home, Disney's Belle must find Maurice. She offers herself in exchange when she comes upon him, ill, in the dungeon. In taking his place it appears she may be sacrificing the dreams of "something different" she expresses earlier in the film (Henke, Umble, and Smith 238; Gray 160; Downey 195). She rescues him from dangers outside their domestic sphere two other times as well: when Maurice becomes lost during a search for Belle (The Walt Disney Company [WDC] 67), about whom he apparently worries because she is in the Beast's power and outside of the domestic sphere; and when Gaston and his followers come to take Maurice to an insane asylum (72). The relationship is loving and supportive, but rather than one of reciprocity, in which the father attempts to support the family even after he has lost his fortune and Beauty provides support in the form of domestic labor (Zipes 234; Cocteau 30), the relationship between Disney's Belle and Maurice has the added burden for Belle of being similar to that of mother and child. Belle encourages Maurice to continue work on his inventions and rescues him when he makes mistakes. Indeed, he seems almost helpless without her. In addition, Maurice's appearance, which is similar to that of one of Disney's seven dwarfs, encourages the audience to view him as a child who needs a caretaker. By putting Belle in the role of that caretaker, the Disney *Beauty and the Beast* reinforces the Angel-in-the-House stereotype of woman as responsible for making sure that domestic life goes smoothly. The film sets Belle's civilizing role of mother and person responsible for the domestic sphere against the fearsome Outside, making these roles particularly evident in her third rescue of Maurice: When he languishes in the forest on his way to rescue *her*, Belle literally takes him from the forest to the home.

Another difference in characterization between previous versions of *Beauty and the Beast* and the Disney Studios' version is that of Beauty's other suitor. Beaumont's eighteenth-century version has no second suitor, but Cocteau added Avenant, and Disney added Gaston. These two additional suitors differ considerably. Cocteau's Avenant is a nice but rather bumbling ne'er-do-well; he knows that Beauty's sisters do nothing to alleviate her hard work in her father's poor household, and he shows concern for her (30–34). Although Beauty refuses to marry him, she is not shocked or offended by his proposal; indeed, she seems to like him (34–38). At the end of Cocteau's film, Avenant and Beauty's brother attempt to rescue Beauty and steal the Beast's treasure (368); Avenant dies in the attempt, turning into the beast his attempted theft seems to indicate he is (Levitt 52). Cocteau retains Avenant's image, however, by having Jean Marais, who plays both Avenant and the Beast, also play the disenchanted prince (370). John Rieder notes that "[in] Cocteau she loves both the no-good Avenant and the generous, noble Beast, and she ends up getting the best of both worlds only by way of the bizarre exchange enacted in the transformation scene" (238). Avenant has poor judgment and is immature.

Disney's Gaston, in contrast to Avenant, is a boor who needs civilizing (Warner 10). He has no understanding of Belle's interest in books, and worries about the dangers that might occur if women read. His inflated ego causes him to assume that Belle could not possibly reject his marriage proposal (WDC 23–24). Gaston is the epitome of an uncivilized person, believing in the use of force rather than rational discussion, having no interest in the arts, and lacking respect for those he believes to be physically weaker than he (such as Belle and Maurice). In spite of his interest in Belle's beauty—her beauty makes her the "best," according to him—he does not become civilized as a result of that interest nor as a result of her modeling civilized behavior. He serves as a foil to Belle, highlighting her independence and intelligence, and later as a foil to the changing Beast (Warner 11); but for him, Belle's beauty is an object he wishes to possess rather than a means to better himself. Gaston's lack of interest in Belle as a person contrasts with Avenant's sympathy for Beauty in Cocteau's film; Gaston, "the true beast" (Warner 11), responds vengefully to Belle's rejection of his marriage proposal, attempting to have her father committed to an insane asylum (WDC 72) and later leading the villagers in an effort to storm the castle and kill the Beast (74–75). Near the end of the film, Gaston, incapable even of glimpsing the characteristics of civilized life, dies in a fight with the Beast.

Beauty's relationship to the second suitor in Cocteau's version of the tale, then, differs from that in the Disney Studios' version. She likes Avenant, though she also pities him for his immaturity. Gaston, however, she loathes. Unlike the Beast, whose library shows evidence of some interest in civilization, Gaston appears an unlikely candidate for civilized behavior.

The most significant alteration in characterization between the two earlier versions and the Disney *Beauty* is in the that of the Beast. Both Beaumont's and Cocteau's Beasts are adults, whereas the Disney Beast acts like a child. In addition to his bestial appearance, the Disney Beast is immature and has an uncontrollable temper.[3]

Beaumont's Beast appears to lack intelligence, but he is kind, and Beauty comes to look forward to his conversation: "Every evening at supper the Beast paid her a visit and entertained her in conversation with plain good sense, but not what the world calls wit" (Zipes 239–40). The Beast prefers that people speak their minds, and he refuses to allow Beauty's father to call him "lord." He insists on being called "Beast" (236). Beaumont emphasizes the message of her Beast's character—that neither beauty nor intelligence is sufficient in itself—through her description of Beauty's sisters' husbands: One occupies himself with his handsome appearance from morning to night, and the other uses his wit and intelligence to anger everyone around him (242).

Cocteau's Beast, like Beaumont's, dislikes compliments and wishes to be called "Beast" rather than "my lord" (94–96); also, in a conversation with Beauty, he claims to have no wit (150). He differs from Beaumont's Beast, however, in being passionate; according to Betsy Hearne, Cocteau "clarifies the Beast's passionate nature through recurring graphic images of plucked roses, torch flames, hunting impulses, bloodstains, and physical magnetism" (137). Since he is an adult, though, Cocteau's Beast has control over this nature, obeying without comment Beauty's command to leave her room (160). This Beast is a complicated creature, tortured by his bestiality. When Beauty sees him outside her door, covered with blood, he murmurs, "Excuse me...For being an animal...Forgive me..." (178–80). He knows the reason for his enchantment and tells Beauty at the end of the film that his father did not believe in fairies, so the fairies punished the father through the son (374). The reason for Beaumont's Beast's enchantment, in contrast, is unclear; at the end of Beaumont's version the prince simply states, "A wicked fairy condemned me to remain in this form until a beautiful girl consented to marry me, and she prohibited me from revealing my intelligence" (Zipes 244).

Both Beaumont and Cocteau, then, characterize the Beast as an adult who has a strong sense of self and whose problem is one of enchantment rather than character. Beauty learns, through her relationship with the Beast, that appearances are deceiving. The narrative's focus is on her (Boras 50; Erb 53). The Disney Studios, however, created a Beast who, in both the film and the book, behaves like a spoiled child; his bestiality is that of a "little monster" with quite a different sense of self from that of the other two. Though the narrator at the beginning of the film mentions the theme of deceptive appearances, Belle must not only overcome the fear and repulsion she feels at the Beast's ugliness but must also civilize and nurture him. Though a woman in Belle's situation might see that situation as one where she can wield power, a more adult response is annoyance; the mothering, civilizing role does not provide an adult-to-adult relationship. In addition, as Angela Caputi says, the film reinforces the belief that women can turn an ill-tempered monster into a prince if they love him enough (qtd. in Ingrassia and Beck 30).

The Disney Beast's uncontrolled temper and childlike behavior are the primary character differences between this Beast and the Beasts in Beaumont and Cocteau. For example, though the Disney Beast's servants are hospitable to Belle's father, the Beast himself growls at Maurice and throws him in a dungeon (WDC 20). He orders Belle to appear at dinner, and before dinner the servants give him advice; among other suggestions they say he must control his temper. According to the Disney book, the Beast is gruff and awkward when he shows Belle to her room (36); angry as he waits for her to appear at dinner (40); and he roars at her for going into the forbidden west wing (50). The Disney film indicates that his immaturity also appears in his behavior as a hurt child: When he sees Belle in the magic mirror saying she does not want to get to know him, his response is that he is fooling himself and she will never see him as anything but a monster. Similarly, he has doubts before the ballroom scene, saying that he cannot declare his love; Lumiere has to encourage him. He behaves like a spoiled child when she bandages his injured arm: The words used in the book are *roared* and *sulked* (61). Disney's Beast lacks the adult qualities of the other two Beasts and is certainly less introspective than they. His actions are responses to his feelings of the moment rather than thoughtful or considerate. In addition, the reason for his enchantment reinforces his immature character; in the series of introductory scenes in the film, the narrator states that the prince's enchantment is a punishment for his having turned a beggar woman away from the castle door. He is "spoiled, selfish, and unkind" despite having everything he could wish for.

Because of the Disney characterization of the Beast as a spoiled child, Belle's relationship to him is much more that of civilizing force than Beauty's relationship to the Beast in the two previous well-known versions.

In the Beaumont and Cocteau versions, Beauty's relationship to the Beast is that of one adult to another, but in the Disney version she must respond to the Beast as if she were a mother. This motherly response is particularly evident in the scene in which she bandages his injured arm; but throughout the film Disney puts Belle in the position of dealing with a spoiled child. Beyond simply providing a model of civilization, Belle must change the Beast, encouraging him to become an adult who might be a reasonable suitor. The task is not easy; at first she sees him as such a disagreeable companion that on her first night in the castle she refuses to join him for dinner (38–40). Since he mostly roars and growls, he is hardly promising as a pleasing conversationalist. Belle's situation is quite different from that of Beauty in Beaumont and Cocteau; their Beasts state that Beauty is master in the castle (Zipes 239; Cocteau 148), and she looks forward to the Beast's conversation. Even at the end of the Disney film, after the Beast realizes he loves Belle and frees her from her promise so that she can rescue her father, he has not become adult enough to help his servants defend the castle. Instead, he stays in the forbidden west wing and mopes until Gaston finds him. His behavior indicates his dependence on Belle as civilizing force and mother figure; in her absence, his spoiled-child qualities reappear. When he is finally disenchanted, the image of his childlike nature remains. Disney's prince looks more like a teenager than a man. The lack of an adult-to-adult relationship between the two romantically involved characters is an unfortunate model for young women who want a relationship with a man.

Cocteau's film certainly *suggests* a Beast tamed and therefore the possibility of Beauty as civilizing force, but Cocteau's prince is decidedly a man, not a teenager; and the character of the Beast is that of an adult, not a child. Beauty can relate to the Beast as an adult by enjoying his conversation and responding to his passion. Though he is distracted by deer and docs hunt, it is not merely Beauty's influence that changes him; he is a complicated enough creature to feel tortured by these bestial instincts. In most respects, Cocteau's Beast is already civilized. Only once, when she finds him outside her room, does Beauty act in any way which might be interpreted as maternal: She tells him to go and clean himself up (180).

Beaumont's version is very similar to Cocteau's in this regard. Though Beaumont's Beast, like Cocteau's, acts very bestial when he catches Beauty's father stealing the rose, with Beauty he is cordial and polite, someone with whom Beauty looks forward to conversing. He is certainly an adult, and Beauty can relate to him as one. Both Beaumont's and Cocteau's Beasts demonstrate civilized behavior from the beginning and are therefore much less in need of a civilizing force than Disney's Beast.

Three essays on Disney's version of the *Beauty and the Beast* tale explore in particular the question of whether Belle is more of a feminist than other Disney heroines. (None of the three, however, examines the relationships between Belle and her father in their exploration of this question.) Jill Birnie Henke et al. see Belle as having choices and taking action—and therefore a good role model for young women; but reservations about Belle as a feminist protagonist appear in their comment that one way to read the conclusion is that Belle becomes "yet another 'perfect girl' who marries the prince and lives happily ever after" (239). Cynthia Erb explores the homosexual threads in the Disney film, showing how these began, in fragmentary form, in Cocteau's version; she bases her analysis on the assumption of "at least partial gay authorship" (59). Erb disagrees with those who find the Beast violent and brutal but admits that the nature of the film makes possible a number of different interpretations (60). In addition to examining gay subtexts, Erb argues that feminist subtexts exist in the film as well, and she shows how "feminist and gay discourses overlap and converge" (63) at some points. She also states, however, that the feminist discourses "exist in a rather weak, fragmented state" (60–61). Sharon Downey's essay explores the nondiscursive elements in Disney's film as undercutting the narrative some critics (Erb, Warner, Gray, and Boras, for example) see as the Beast's story—a story from a male perspective—and argue that these elements allow an interpretation suggesting empowerment for women.[4] Downey is largely convincing both in showing the importance of nondiscursive elements such as animation and music in opening a space for women's empowerment and in her examination of the dialectic that takes place, as Belle and the Beast become better acquainted, between the different types of power frequently associated with feminine and masculine gender orientation. She does not mention, however, that at least part of Belle's power comes from her choosing the stereotypical Angel-in-the-House role; that Belle is familiar with the role because of her relationship with her father; and that her action (as opposed to passivity) is partly a result of the influence of that role. Some writers, also, do not agree that the nondiscursive elements provide a space for female empowerment; Wilfried Ver Eecke says the "friendliness and gaiety" of the castle's servants cause Belle to be romantically inclined toward the Beast in spite of his character (77n), and Elizabeth Bell comments that in spite of the spectacular displays, the narrative moves toward marriage as a reward and "overwhelms the animated *jouissance* of the musical numbers" (114).

Downey cites the ballroom scene and the "Beauty and the Beast" ballad as indicators that a reciprocal power relationship has developed between Belle and the Beast; the song and scene confirm "his transformation, her legitimacy, and their powerful unity" (202). This same scene, however, is a forceful reminder of Belle's role as the stereotypical Angel in the House, a civilizing force in relation to a Beast characterized as spoiled and immature. The scene, which does not occur in the Cocteau or Beaumont versions of *Beauty and the Beast*, exhibits an aspect of ballroom dancing implied in Julie Malnig's *Dancing Till Dawn: A Century of Exhibition Ballroom Dance*. Malnig says that dance teachers of the early twentieth century "helped...to foster the persona of grace and cultivation" and that these dance teachers inherited nineteenth-century notions equating this kind of dance with proper behavior and good breeding (12). In the Disney book, Belle and the Beast eat together before the ballroom scene, and the Beast "awkwardly" tries to eat with a spoon (62). In the film, the Beast has mastered the spoon just before the ballroom scene, a contrast to his earlier messy eating habits. When they are nearly finished with dinner, Belle rises from the table to lead the Beast into the ballroom. Though the song in the background insists that they are *both* scared, unsure, and unprepared, and Downey sees their dance as "synchronous" (202), it is Belle who shows the Beast how to put his arm around her waist as they begin to dance. He gulps; she has the confidence he gradually gains. She appears to be teaching him to dance, and in this scene the elegant costumes of both characters, the ballroom, and the dancing serve as powerful images of the height of Western civilization. It is significant that after this scene the now more-civilized Beast allows Belle to leave to help her father, and it is also after the ballroom scene that the Beast has "become too human to kill" (WDC 85). Disney's Beast not only changes outwardly as a result of his disenchantment, but thanks to Belle's colonizing influence he changes inwardly as well.[5] Instead of a spoiled, selfish "little monster" who has trouble controlling his temper, he has rather suddenly reached toward adulthood. The importance of the ballroom scene is reinforced at the end of the film: Belle and her disenchanted prince are immortalized, dancing, in stained glass. The contrast between Belle's role as mother figure and civilizer in Disney's film and Beauty's role as discoverer of the reality beneath appearance in Cocteau's film and Beaumont's tale is striking.

The Disney Studios' version of *Beauty and the Beast*, then, in comparison with two other familiar versions of the tale, sends a strong message reinforcing the stereotypical belief that a beautiful woman is a civilizing force capable of taming the beast in a man. Much of this message is a result of the Disney Studios' changes in the characterization of Belle's father, her other suitor, and the Beast; because of these changes, Belle's relationship to these characters differs from that of Beauty's relationship to the men in the Beaumont and Cocteau versions. For her father, Belle is the nurturer, the domestic Angel in the House who keeps the barbaric outside forces at bay. For Gaston, she is desirable as a beautiful possession, but since he has no true respect for beauty, he is incapable of being civilized. For the Beast, Belle is a civilizing force, the woman who changes not only his appearance but also his character. Because of her, he learns to dance and eat with a spoon, becomes capable of love and learns to control his temper. The Disney version helps perpetuate the stereotypical view that the efforts of a beautiful woman can cause a beastly male to become acceptable.

For both men and women, the stereotype of woman as civilizing force can be problematic. Men can use it as an excuse to act like beasts, since they can then depend on a woman to rescue them from themselves and need not take responsibility for their behavior; women may believe their role in a relationship with a man is to mother him, or be a model of civilized behavior, or both. It may also cause women to have an unrealistic belief in their ability to reform a man who treats them badly (Maio 45). Though the woman might feel like a powerful agent who changes the world of beasts through her beauty and her influence for good, in fact she is constrained by a role which requires certain behaviors from her. In spite of her intelligence, independence, strength of character, and ability to take action, as opposed to being passive, Disney's Belle presents an unfortunate stereotype of women in relation to men.

Notes

My thanks to the Faculty Research and Publications Board at the University of Northern Colorado for providing me with a grant which enabled me to complete this work.
1. See Warner for a brief history and discussion of some modern versions of this tale type.
2. Greene discusses Cocteau's eroticism and voyeurism in *La belle et la bête*.
3. See Warner 10, Gray 159, Ver Eecke 77n for comments on the Beast's temper. Gray suggests his psychological profile is that of a wife batterer, while Ver Eecke writes of the Beast in the Disney Broadway musical, "he remains a spoiled brat."
4. Hawkins remarks that the film has leading male and female characters who are fairly well matched in strength and intelligence (263).
5. Jeffords questions the responsibility others, especially women, have to turn beasts into loving men through teaching and modeling (168–69).

Works Cited

Beaumont, Jeanne-Marie Leprince de. "Beauty and the Beast." *Beauties, Beasts and Enchantment: Classic French Fairy Tales.* Trans. Jack Zipes. New York: Meridian, 1989.

Beauty and the Beast. Dirs. Gary Trousdale, Kirk Wise. Animated. Voices: Robby Benson, Paige O'Hara. Walt Disney Pictures Production, 1991.

Bell, Elizabeth. "Somatexts at the Disney Shop: Constructing the Pentimentos of Women's Animated Bodies." Bell, Haas, and Sells 107–24.

Bell, Elizabeth, Lynda Haas, and Laura Sells, eds. *From Mouse to Mermaid: The Politics of Film, Gender, and Culture*. Bloomington: Indiana UP, 1995.

Boras, Giselle. *The Psychological Beast of Disney's* Beauty and the Beast. *Animatrix* 7 (1993): 45–50.

Cocteau, Jean. *Beauty and the Beast: Scenario and Dialogs by Jean Cocteau*. Ed. and annotator Robert Hammond. New York UP, 1970.

Downey, Sharon D. "Feminine Empowerment in Disney's *Beauty and the Beast*." *Women's Studies in Communication* 19:2 (1996): 185–212.

Erb, Cynthia. "Another World or the World of an Other? The Space of Romance in Recent Versions of 'Beauty and the Beast.'" *Cinema Journal* 34:4 (1995): 50–70.

Gray, Elizabeth Dodson. "Beauty and the Beast: A Parable for Our Time." *Women Respond to the Men's Movement: A Feminist Collection*. Ed. Kay Leigh Hagan. New York: Harper-Collins, 1992. 159–68.

Greene, Naomi. "Jean Cocteau: A Cinema of Baroque Unease." *The Bucknell Review* 41:1 (1997): 130–47.

Hawkins, Harriett. "Maidens and Monsters in Popular Culture: *The Silence of the Lambs* and *Beauty and the Beast*." *Textual Practice* 7:2 (1993): 258–66.

Hearne, Betsy. *Beauty and the Beast: Visions and Revisions of an Old Tale*. U of Chicago P, 1989.

Henke, Jill Birnie, Diane Zimmerman Umble, and Nancy J. Smith. "Construction of the Female Self: Feminist Reading of the Disney Heroine." *Women's Studies in Communication* 19:2 (1996): 229–49.

Ingrassia, Michele, and Melinda Beck. "Patterns of Abuse: Special Report." *Newsweek* 4 Jul. 1994: 26–33.

Jeffords, Susan. "The Curse of Masculinity: Disney's *Beauty and the Beast*." Bell, Haas, and Sells 161–72.

La belle et la bête. Dir. Jean Cocteau. Perf. Jean Marais, Josette Day. 1946.

Levitt, Annette Shandler. "The Cinematic Magic of Jean Cocteau." *The Bucknell Review* 41:1 (1997): 42–56.

Maio, Kathi. "Mr. Right Is a Beast: Disney's Dangerous Fantasy." *Visions Magazine* 7 (1992): 44–45.

Malnig, Julie. *Dancing Till Dawn: A Century of Exhibition Ballroom Dance. Contributions to the Study of Music and Dance* 25. Westport, CT: Greenwood, 1992.

Maslin, Janet. "Target: Boomers and Their Babies." *New York Times* 24 Nov. 1991, sec. 2: 1+.

Patmore, Coventry. *The Angel in the House*. London: George Bell and Sons, 1908.

Payne, Karen, ed. *Between Ourselves*. Boston: Houghton Mifflin, 1983.

Rieder, John. "Two Film Adaptations of 'Beauty and the Beast.'" *Literature and Hawaii's Children: Stories as Bridges to Many Realms*. 1992 Proceedings. Ed. Judith Kellogg and Jesse Crisler. Manoa: U of Hawaii, 1994.

Turner, George. "Once Upon a Time There Was *Beauty and the Beast*."*American Cinematographer* 78 (1997): 94–99.

Ver Eecke, Wilfried. "Jean Cocteau: Word and Image." *The Bucknell Review* 41:1 (1997): 57–77.

The Walt Disney Company. *Disney's Beauty and the Beast*. New York: Gallery Books, 1991.

Warner, Marina. "Beauty and the Beasts." *Sight and Sound* 2:6 (1992): 7–11.

Zipes, Jack. *Beauties, Beasts and Enchantment: Classic French Fairy Tales*. New York: Meridian, 1989.

Part IV
Disney Culture

CHAPTER 7

"All That Is Solid Melts into the Air": "The Winds of Change" and Other Analogues of Colonialism in Disney's *Mary Poppins*

Brian E. Szumsky

In an article titled "Walt Disney: Art and Politics in the American Century," Steven Watts writes of Walt Disney's early reputation as an "avant-garde artist" and "modernist" who opposed Victorian constructions of reality both by "blurring the line between animation and reality" and by supplanting Victorian "reason and judgment with impulse" (134). Today, some of these same arguments are used to vilify the megacorporation Disney and its various enterprises. Consider Disney versus Virginia in the "third battle of Manassas," in which Disney scrapped plans to build an American history theme park near the site of the Civil War battlefield. Its decision was forced by the determined opposition of a coalition of historians and wealthy landowners who worried about "traffic jams, pollution" and the subsequent ruin of the "quiet countryside" (Solomon 46). Further, critics like Scott Schaffer argue that Disney distorts real history for the sake of commercial gain. On Disney's use of "localized stories" (from international folktales to histories), Schaffer states that rather than faithful retellings, what occurs is merely a reinscribing of these stories with a typically American value system for use as a "discourse on America's place in the world." Robert Gooding-Williams' article on *The Lion King* begins with a discussion on the difference between entertainment value and ideological content as a way to deconstruct the film's ostensible multicultural message and reveal rather stereotypical assumptions about class and racial demarcations. The representation of history and its cultures, then, or, for our purposes, "disrepresentation," has become a battleground both intellectually and "in the trenches," so to speak, between Disney and its critics.

A discussion about analogues of colonialism in Disney's *Mary Poppins* must take note of the film's historical site, i.e., late Victorian England and of its quasi-historical materials. The film does not purport to show England as it really was at the turn of the century but rather as a stylized, Broadway stage version. The fact that the film is a musical, combining "live action" with animation, exemplifies this "blurring" of history and fantasy discussed earlier. By using its patented mix of live action and animation, Disney created a fantasy as overlay of historical realities (much as the critics charged in the Disney-Virginia episode). Entertainment value does seem to have triumphed over serious ideological or historical content. However, ideological content bubbles to the surface. The dialectic is not, to be sure, Disney's; nonetheless, the materials which the Disney screenwriters appropriated from the novels of P. L. Travers mimic the characteristic spirit of late Victorian and Edwardian critiques or reassessments of various preconceptions of status quo Victorian society. Travers, born in 1906, would have imbibed some of these attitudes in her childhood, in particular through her love of fairy tales. Briefly, the Victorian fairy tale, to which her generation was heir, is noted for its social conscience and its "strong women characters" (Zipes xix)—both of which figure into the materials of *Mary Poppins*.

Though Travers is generally considered a "traditionalist" writer and a social conservative, Patricia Demers points out that "part of her [Travers'] subversive activity is to question accepted ideas" (11). However, this questioning is usually not a search for explicit answers. Travers herself is not a storyteller in the traditional sense, meaning that she does not incorporate explicit moral lessons into her works. She lauds the notion of indirect teaching, saying, "everything I do is by hint and suggestion" (qtd. in Demers 136). Likewise, her creation, Mary Poppins, is equally indirect. She refuses to answer questions and teaches "by the way" (125). In the film, her response to George Banks' demand that she explain herself is, "I never explain." She does not sermonize but rather suggests her meaning through illustration and example, as in the Fidelity Fudiciary Bank–Bird Woman episode. Further, Travers claims that as a writer, she works from "the hodgepodge of life" (qtd. in Demers 1), and that the Mary Poppins books were "entirely spontaneous and not invented, not thought out" (qtd. in Burness and Griswold 122–23). This working model of the writer implies the incorporation of observable elements into her fiction that in many ways tell their own stories—revealing as Travers says, "the truth of things and the one reality that underlies everything" (qtd. in Burness and Griswold 125). Thus, the story's critique, while not consciously undertaken by Travers, writes itself through the chosen materials—a representation, however fabulous, of a social order undergoing change. Her refusal to admit full authorial responsibility enables her to maintain creative and, thereby, intentional distance and is summed up in her claim that "I never said, 'Well I'll write a story...and call it Mary Poppins.' I cannot summon up inspiration; I myself am summoned" (Burness and Griswold 123). This tack also frees her from having to answer questions regarding the "meaning" of Mary Poppins. However, Travers (who worked as a consultant on the film) and her "subversive" ideas are everywhere apparent in the late-Victorian-based materials of Disney's screenplay. The film articulates that the Disney screenwriters, who chose to dramatize and create a storyline from particular events culled from several different Poppins books, can be observed playing cautiously with this colonial critique. Embedded, then, within Disney's popularized retelling of this so-called children's story is a neat, deliberately (to partially) occluded satire of England's (and unavoidably America's) colonial mentality.

Specifically, the film's historical site is the last year of Edward VII's reign and the onset of the "Georgian afternoon," typically described as a temporary extension of the Victorian era. Victorianism as "era" and as ideological battleground becomes a backdrop through which the film's dialectic develops, a dialectic which turns on two pat generalizations: the empowered few and the disenfranchised masses, or more pointedly, Disraeli's "the rich and the poor." This dialectic is played out in the film as a quasi-historical social battle between Victorianism as the classic example of the culture of retention, or more charitably, the culturally stoic (neatly characterized by the father, George Banks), and Victorianism as the culture of social consciousness (embodied by the two female leads and their male counterpart, Bert). The "era" is depicted at its historic denouement when the patriarchal powers are feeling the growing pressure of social change. Consequently, the film is suffused with general instability: the suffragettes, the missing children, even the traditional tea party have become unsettling events, a floating circus of sorts. The very air itself becomes the harbinger of change. Note Admiral Boom's forecasts, Mary Poppins' arrival on the same wind which blew away the conventional line of nannies, the floating tea party at Uncle Albert's. Thus, Marx-Engels' *Communist Manifesto*, itself an indictment of the capitalist bourgeois, suggesting "all that is solid melts into the air," nicely sums up this feeling of instability amid widespread cultural hegemony.

While this paper will not take a strictly Marxist view of *Mary Poppins*, a study of the metaphors of colonization cannot ignore some of the film's more potently class-conscious analogues. Take for example the penultimate dance number in which the chimney sweeps, acting as the proletariat "union of workers" invade the house of the bourgeois Banks. Their entry into the Banks home suggests an uprising (admittedly benign) of the laboring class against its upper class capitalist exploiters. Further, much is made of the contrast between the blackness (by soot) of the sweeps and the whiteness of the Banks home with its attendant racial stereotyping. This contrast exemplifies the Disney screenwriters' images aimed at white American audiences. Note as well that when the children flee the bank, they are confronted by a dark image which initially frightens them. The black image itself (which turns out to be Bert in sooted blackface) insinuates a cultural stereotype equating blackness with fear or danger—a typically Western notion of blackness and certainly potent in America in the mid-1960s. The image of the sooty-faced children themselves is reminiscent of the late-nineteenth-century movement against child labor and the graphic representations of factory and mine working conditions found in Engels' own blue books. The Bird Woman becomes that manifest victim of bourgeois oppression and exemplifies a social mismanagement which degrades its subjects to "such a state that it [the bourgeois state] has to feed [her]" (Marx and Engels 93), as she herself feeds the birds. The preponderance of black smoke pouring into the London skies during the rooftop walk signifies an anti-industrialist image, a sentiment which runs through much Victorian writing, including the works of John Ruskin, Charles Dickens, and Charles Kingsley, and is even contained within the British revival of the fairy tale. Viewed in such a light, these analogues contribute to the ostensibly anti-industrial and antimaterialist tone of Travers' original materials and lead to ideas more central to this discussion.

The dialectic within the film neatly assumes the two "brands" of Victorianism as mutually exclusive: those preservationists of the status quo and the various reformatory and counter groups (also known as the "enemies of the Enlightenment"). These counter groups become popular forces that question the preconceptions of the earlier age; suffragettes looking for the vote and voicing opinions regarding the place of women, the anti-imperialist opposition to the Boer War, the rise of Germany and America as world powers and its effect on Britain as a Western leader. The legacy of the status quo English Victorians, then, with its ordering impulse and secure sense of national identity as a world power, is coming under attack. Through thematics and characterization, the film in its episodic development presents a set of colonial images and analogues which ultimately work as chiding, Horatian (gentle) satire of imperialist Britain.

Though admittedly simplified, Altick's generalization identifies Victorianism as comprised of two strains: the coldly rational (as exemplified by the Utilitarian movement) and the socially conscious (as represented by the emotionalism of the Evangelical movement) (165). Typically, the former denotes a popular representation of "Englishness" which continued into the late twentieth century. Note the uptight Basil Fawlty (John Cleese) in *Fawlty Towers*, and the butler, Stevens (Anthony Hopkins), in Kazuo Ishiguro's *Remains of the Day*. Both play with popular notions equating English identity and Victorian society, character, and values. This depiction of the English upper class as stodgy, myopic, and dysfunctional is an easy target for

U.S. filmmakers always searching for ideal "villains" or foils for U.S. values and norms. These stereotypes confirm U.S. notions of itself as progressive, independent, and compassionate by playing with comfortable generalizations and by presenting England (or any other country, group, society, etc.) as Others with nonconventional or outright wrong perceptions and value systems. The Other is typically depicted as at war with itself (an interesting parallel to the American Civil Rights era) and is used to distance the audience through the use of standard cultural or racial demarcations while, at the same time, confirming that all societies endure these kinds of social crises. In *Mary Poppins* the extended analogue of England and its society is the Banks family itself. As an emblem of status quo Victorianism, much of the film's atmosphere of change and transition is played off George Banks (David Tomlinson). The characterization of Banks is a typical representation of the Victorian father: austere, authoritarian, and conservative. His song "The Life I Lead" elucidates an England built on order, monarchical stability, and mercantile expansionism. "I feel a surge of deep satisfaction / Much as a king astride his noble steed," he sings. The life George Banks thinks he leads is "pleasant," "consistent," and "lordly." He runs his "home precisely on schedule": "It's grand to be an Englishman in 1910 / King Edward's on the throne / it's the age of men." Throughout the song, Mrs. Banks (Glynis Johns) attempts to tell her husband that the children have disappeared. The song, then, becomes particularly ironic, as "the order" which he perceives to be a product of his own value system (and by association analogous to the patriarchal order in general) has already been undercut. Add to this Mrs. Banks' commitment (or better, militant devotion) to the suffragette movement. Her words, "though we adore men individually / we agree that as a group they're rather stupid," act as an indictment of the patriarchal order in general. Those elements, then, which George Banks believes still remain under the patriarchal umbrella have already begun to move out from under it. The onset of social upheaval (as manifested by the women's rights movement and the socially conscious Poppins) becomes localized and mirrored in the Banks family unit. Further, the generalized representation of the patriarchal mentality with its imperialistic and colonizing impulses not only abroad but at home is particularized in the authoritarian structure of the Banks family. The family itself is transformed through George's song into a metaphor for England's monarchical rulers: "I'm the lord of my castle / the sovereign, the liege / I treat my subjects: servants, children, wife with a gentle but firm hand." The father as king rules over his "subjects"—wife, children, domestics—ticked-off in the feudal spirit with "noblesse oblige" thrown in. The ultimate analogue for George's notion of "Englishness" identifies with biology: the "heirs of my dominion." His "molding the breed" suggests a cultural eugenics, with his children as ideological inheritors of the father's Victorian-based legacy. Tradition and the illusion of a "well-ordered" home and thereby society lie at the heart of George Banks' vision of England. When the children tell him about their fantastic outings with Mary Poppins, he objects to all except the fox hunt. "It's tradition," he says. "I don't mind that."

The Fidelity Fiduciary Bank (with Bank as the family's namesake) is, in many ways depicted as the engine of imperialistic and colonial impulses. The elder Dawes' song, "Fidelity Fiduciary Bank," in its attempts to seduce Michael into investing his tuppence, calls upon a "sense of conquest" and a "sense of stature." Dawes, Sr., goads George Banks into singing that investments can make you "part of railroads through Africa," "dams across the Nile...plantations of ripening tea." These colonizing images are underscored by the profit motive (credit, purchase, foreclosure, chattels) through which stature and influence expand, i.e., imperialist and, by association, capitalist objectives. His appeal for investment is an appeal for continuum (of colonial ideologies of the forefathers) and parallels George's "cultural eugenics." The Victorian age was, as Arnold wrote, a time when "not a creed...is not shaken, an accredited dogma...is not shown to be questionable, and a received tradition...does not threaten to dissolve" (qtd. in Culler 306). With cultural and ideological threats of this kind, from Darwin to the suffragettes to the decadents, the Victorian forebears, like the bank and George Banks (apropos), saw the best interests of England in a clear-cut hierarchical value system (race, gender, class), a preservation of tradition, and a scrupulous materialism. Both banks (George and institution) become Victorian utilitarian solicitors for a cashiered society incapable of emotional attachment. Note Marx's critique of the bourgeois family which has "reduced the family relation to a mere money relation" (Marx and Engels 82), and "the pound is up" (Sherman and Sherman) as a deification of money and the monumentalizing of a capitalist value system. The physical proximity to the bank (across the street) of the homeless Bird Woman (Jane Darwell) juxtaposes the presence of extremes in a capitalist, caste-structured state, i.e., the widening gaps between wealth and poverty. Disraeli, writing in 1845, identified "[two] nations (rich and poor); between whom there is no intercourse and no sympathy" (23). Michael's deposit into the bank would represent an investment into a materialist, compassionless England, one which does not recognize the Others of society—women, children, the disenfranchised such as the Bird Woman. All of these groups are marginalized in a patriarchal, mercantile society. The major parodic representation of the bank is its infirm director, who, while preaching about the importance of the strength of the English banks, is physically unstable, teetering throughout his number. "While stand the banks of England, England stands," and vice versa. Dawes' grab for Michael's tuppence and the resulting "run on the bank" suggest a middling capitalistic greed and a certain inherent societal mistrust of the entrenched hierarchy, respectively.

From George Banks to Dawes, Sr., to Admiral Boom, the film's continuous jabs at the colonial mentality come mainly through its male characters. Admiral Boom (veteran British actor Reginald Owen) appears as a representative of the past glory of the British military. His diminished position as nothing more than a senile clock-tower operator suggests impotency and ineffectualness. He is a parodic representation of the state of British naval power in the face of modernization of military technology and the rise of Germany's and America's military powers, a character who is already nearly an anachronism. As an amateur weatherman, he notes the change in the winds, marking its meteorological or nautical significance but not its metaphoric possibility as an analogue for societal unrest. George Banks, as well, shares the Admiral's social myopia. Like his counterpart Admiral Boom, he is removed from the societal boil. Both characters move through the film in a disoriented, out-of-touch fashion. Both insinuate themselves into the "you think I can't see past the end of my nose" mentality, in full denial of what is going on around them. While Dawes, Sr., and the members of the Board of Directors are insulated by the bank as ideology and as physical space, and Boom, sitting atop his house, is also somewhat removed, by contrast Banks is "in the mix," so to speak. His failure to understand what is going on around him is informed by self-preservation and is tied in with the thinking of older Victorians like Dawes, Sr., and Boom. Banks is quick to place the blame for his feelings of instability on Mary Poppins for upsetting the status quo, even though he, as well as the other capitalists, unwittingly has been the cause of not just a familial rupturing but a cultural one. While George succeeds in business, he fails at home. His position in the British bank indicates his own (as well as his society's) supplanting of mercantilism over compassion. His emotional distance from his children, masked by an authoritarianism, contrasts with the compassion that Mary Poppins instills in the children for the Bird Woman.

Bert (Dick Van Dyke, who also plays Dawes, Sr.) stands alone as the major male character who acts outside of bourgeois mentality and proscriptions. As a chimney sweep, he represents not only the Marxist proletariat, but the classic cultural insider-outsider. This profession (he has several in the film besides chimney sweep) sets him outside of the capitalist money machine. Yet as a man of "many hats," he can also be seen as an entrepreneurial opportunist who can read the "winds of change" for monetary survival. He is exploited by the system, yet by cleaning the houses of those bourgeois, he does, ostensibly, enter their world if only temporarily and superficially. Note his dialogue with George Banks, which provides, for the latter, an epiphanic moment. The scene contains a less-than-confident reprise of Banks' earlier song, "The Life I Lead." Where the earlier number exhibited a supremely confident male worldview, the reprise, which contains some rather lofty, quasi-heroic lyrics, sounds dismal by comparison. "A man has dreams of walking with giants," he sings, but "before the mortar of his seal / has a chance to congeal / the cup is dashed from his lips / the flame is snuffed abourne / he is brought to wrack and ruin in his prime." The lyrics, a curious collection of mixed metaphors, combined with Bert's rather obviously leading remarks, help Banks realize his emotional distance from his children and accept the responsibility for bridging that gap. By design, Bert becomes the antithesis to George Banks, an example of the story's dialectic of class and ideology. His lower social status is suggested by his various occupations as street musician, sidewalk artist, and chimney sweep, his street urchin-like dress, and his apparent homelessness—he is always found in the park or on the street. Also note his overdone Cockney accent. His inherent understanding of Mary Poppins and what she represents stands in sharp contrast to Banks' own cultural and ideological provincialism and his distance from personal and social realities. In giving a ride to the Irish-brogued fox in the chalk picture set piece, Bert displays his own subversive tendencies, saving the fox from annihilation (or colonization) at the hands of the (English) hounds. His aesthetic and imaginative propensities demonstrate his own willingness to look beyond those self- and culturally imposed boundaries and restrictions of someone like Banks, whose patriarchal and imperialist inheritance has become hard and fast identity. Bert's aestheticism, "it's all me own work from me own memory," can be compared to Ruskin's "centering of beauty in one's own imagination" (qtd. in Altick 288). Bert's ability to "please the crowd," to affirm and reward their expectations (note the film's opening scene) presents the artist as wish-fulfiller; an aim akin to the Disney enterprises as a whole. However, Bert's aestheticism, when influenced by Mary Poppins, becomes more Ruskinian in intent—the role of art as nothing less than the salvation of society, or, at the very least, the stirring of social consciousness. It was Ruskin, after all, who wrote, "The first schools of beauty must be the streets of your cities, and the chief of our fair designs must be to keep the living creatures round us clean, and in human comfort" (qtd. in Roe 318).

With Bert, the two female leads Mary Poppins and Mrs. Banks represent ideological counters to the Victorian status quo. Mary Poppins (Julie Andrews) becomes that Victorian anathema, the "enemy of the Enlightenment." Significantly, she arrives when the winds change direction. As an agent of change, wearing the guise of her society (the typical Victorian nanny appearance: umbrella, carpetbag, and black attire), she can work for change and subvert cultural biases from the inside (as the Victorian poet). Note her handling of the Bird Woman episode, in which the father's culturally biased construction and prejudice is displaced with compassion. For Mary, the children become either thoughtless ingesters of their cultural inheritance or critical thinkers. Her commute on the eastern "wind of change," as forecasted by Boom and her own independent, self-sufficient personality, present her as both a supernatural and a human female figure. Her magical powers signify her as a fairy figure, a "good witch" of sorts. As a strong woman character, Mary mirrors the suffragette devotions of Mrs. Banks and can be seen as her quasi-supernatural counterpart. Both women express attitudes which counter the institutionalized societal constructions of the patriarchal mind-set. A certain mirroring effect is apparent between Mary and Mrs. Banks. Mary Poppins becomes a projection, a cultural fantasy, of the liberated, self-sufficient woman. The ordinarily demure Mrs. Banks, who subserviently defers to her husband in all matters at home (somewhat tongue-in-cheek), metamorphoses into the prototypical fighter for women's rights. Her song "Sister Suffragette" argues for a matriarchal movement to counter patriarchal control. The song's lines "we're clearly soldiers in petticoats," "shoulder to shoulder into the fray," and "we're fighting for our militantly" state the belligerent analogue in no uncertain terms. Her words "casting off the shackles" and "clapped in irons" connote images of slavery and repression. These analogues work to supplant social protest marches with more threatening images of open rebellion and hyperbolize suffragette rallies into military campaigns. What they point to is the restlessness and desperation of a society engaged in ideological conflict.

Unquestionably, the *Mary Poppins* project must have been terribly appealing to Disney. Regardless of the inherent ideological content (the materials are fairly saturated with anticolonial sentiment), Disney recognized the appeal of the materials for a popular audience. Since the quality of the materials are such that they cannot be disengaged from the ideological presence of their creator, the studio unavoidably preserved some of the (unconscious?) implications of Travers' original critique. Indeed, Travers herself said "I don't know why *Mary Poppins* is thought of as a children's book" (qtd. in *Contemporary Authors* 448). What Disney's *Mary Poppins* project did was move the story out of the realm of sociopolitical discourse and into the realm of family entertainment. In short, the studio developed a film and an ending to soften Travers' apparent critique. Note the fact that the status quo, though given a run for its money, is restored. George Banks is reinstated to his job at the bank as a member of the Board of Directors. Though led to believe that there has been a cultural change of heart, the viewers see only the status quo at the end. Attendant to this, Mary Poppins' departure is silent and unobtrusive, a jarring contrast to her earlier presence. Believing her job is complete, i.e., the reuniting of the Banks family under a more compassionate (or feminized) male figure, she chooses a quiet leave, one which even the children do not seem to notice. As a prelude to the last scene, Mrs. Banks' suffragette banner becomes the tail of a kite and the final scene shows the Banks family as well as the other board members flying kites. This sequence connotes the taming of these "winds of change." The ploy, then, diverts attention from the ramifications of the earlier dialectic and asks viewers to focus on Disney's happy ending. The film's conclusion becomes problematic because the corrective, satiric quality of the earlier material is apparently undercut by the Disney closure. The "happy ending" is meant to deflect the audience's concerns for the sociopolitical dialectic and to replace this social compassion with a "take care of one's own" ethic. Socialism is simply not an American (and therefore not a Disney) value. The absence of most "counter" characters, such as the Bird Woman, the suffragettes, and Mary Poppins, suggests that it will be business as usual; however, the entrenched patriarchy will appear less tense about it. The audience, like the children, is not supposed to notice this absence. This omission stands as Disney's resolution to the struggles for cultural hegemony apparent in the earlier episodes. The only subversive figure to appear in the final scene is Bert, who, as a hawker of kites, is seen demonstrating his entrepreneurial ability to use the system for his own benefit. While the "meaning" of these events is intentionally blurred to produce a happy ending, society is preserved because certain threatening ideologies of the fringe element have been absorbed into the process. The kite flying, though suggestive of a certain frivolity (the stodgy behavior of the patriarchal power structure becomes suggestively "laid back" in the kite-flying sequence), comes with "strings attached," with the old guard still holding those strings.

How then does one reconcile the film's rather neutral ending with the preponderance of sociopolitical implications of the earlier material? Disney's resolution of tension does little but reaffirm its own "aim to please" and sociopolitical leanings. Certainly at the heart of the film's ending is an affirmation of the "nuclear family." Because the storyline of the ruptured family unit runs throughout the film as an analogue for larger issues of British monarchy, the class system, and colonialism, the film's conclusion asks the viewer to accept the unified Banks family as an analogue for reaching cultural accord. The family unit becomes a bulwark against social upheaval. Further, as Giroux suggests, a unified family unit is an analogue for a culture which is ideologically unified. In emphasizing the preservation or reunification of the nuclear family, the happy ending is assured and the filmmakers have dutifully recast the dangerous sociopolitical discourse into a safe American commonplace. The "aim to please," then, might have justifiably weighed heavily in Disney's decision.

A second possibility is that Disney wanted to sidestep issues and criticism of America's own imperialistic endeavors which the materials might suggest. Note America's post–WW II position as world power and policeman against communism to expand American democracy and influence as a policy of "cultural imperialism" disguised in anti-leftist rhetoric. Quite possibly, Disney saw the political expedience of staying away from outright damning of British colonialism because of its ideological proximity to then current American foreign policy and affairs. The comparison between England in the nineteenth century and America in the twentieth is striking. American involvement in Asia in the 1950s and 1960s, culminating with the undeclared war in Vietnam, can stand alongside the English presence in Africa and Asia as well as the unpopularity of the Boer War at the turn of the century. Further, Travers, writing in the early 1930s (the first book of the *Mary Poppins* series being published in 1935), may have been influenced by the anti-industrial sentiments of W. H. Auden; and Pylons, Walsh, and Da Gradi (Disney's screenwriters for the project) could possibly have been influenced by these same ideas articulated in the 1960s. The relationship of Victorian England to modern America is nothing new. Richard Altick, writing some eight years after the initial release of the film, alludes to the "modern analogues" of Victorianism, pointing out that the Victorians lived in a world "remarkably [frighteningly?] like our own" (x). Combined with the anti-industrialist images of the sooty-faced children and the factory-like black chimney smoke billowing thickly into the sky, Victorian critiques of industrialization become melded together with a 1960s American radicalism.

On a final note, Disney's relationship to the United States government goes back to World War II, when the studio was called upon to make propaganda films to support American involvement (Schaffer). The following Disney press release from 1955 associates the Disney organization with America itself:

> Disneyland will be based upon and dedicated to the ideals, the dreams, and the hard facts that have created America. And it will be uniquely equipped to dramatize these dreams and facts and send them forth as a source of courage and inspiration to all the world. (qtd. in Schaffer)

The political leanings and involvement of the studio with the government would have proscripted a movement away from any rhetoric which could be construed as anti-American. The "local story" was meant to stay local and distant, and the Disney "spin" was to reinterpret these materials for a conservative American audience and to neutralize the sociopolitical implications of the story.

Works Cited

Altick, Richard D. *Victorian People and Ideas*. New York: Norton, 1973.
Burness, Edwina, and Jerry Griswold. "P. L. Travers." *The Paris Review Interviews: Women Writers at Work*. Ed. George Plimpton. New York: Modern Library, 1998.
Culler, A. Dwight, ed. *Poetry and Criticism of Matthew Arnold*. Boston: Houghton, 1961.
Demers, Patricia. *P. L. Travers*. Boston: Twayne Publishers, 1991.
Disraeli, Benjamin. "The Two Nations." *The Portable Victorian Reader*. Ed. Gordon H. Haight. New York: Viking, 1972. 22–23.
Giroux, Henry. "Beyond the Politics of Innocence: Memory and Pedagogy in the Wonderful World of Disney." *Socialist Review* 23 (1993): 21 Dec. 1996.<http://www. socialistreview.org>.
Gooding-Williams, Robert. "Disney in Africa and the Inner City: On Race and Space in *The Lion King*." *Social Identities* 1.2 Aug. 1995. 23 Sept. 1996. <http://209.21.154.1/titles/13504630.htm>.
Marx, Karl, and Friedrich Engels. *The Communist Manifesto*. Trans. Samuel Moore. New York: Penguin, 1979.
Mary Poppins. Dir. Robert Stevenson. Perf. Julie Andrews, Dick Van Dyke, David Tomlinson, Glynis Johns. The Walt Disney Company, 1964.
Roe, Frederick William, ed. *Victorian Prose*. New York: The Ronald Press Company, 1947.
Schaffer, Scott. "Disney and the Imagineering of Histories." *Postmodern Culture* 6.3 May 1996. 23 Sept. 1996. <http://muse.jhu.edu/journals/postmodern_culture/toc/pmc6.3.html>.
Sherman, Richard M., and Robert B. Sherman. "Fidelity Fiduciary Bank." *Mary Poppins*, 1964.
——. "The Life I Lead." *Mary Poppins*, 1964.
——. "Sister Suffragette." *Mary Poppins*, 1964.
Solomon, Julie, et al. "Disney: A Sudden Surrender in Virginia." *Newsweek* 10 Oct. 1994: 46.
"Travers, Pamela Lyndon." *Contemporary Authors: New Revision Series*. Ed. James G. Lesniak. Vol. 30. Detroit: Gale Research Co., 1981.
Watts, Steven. "The Avant-Garde Walt Disney." *Wilson Quarterly* 19.4. Autumn 1995. 21 Dec. 1996. <http://wwics.si.edu/>.
Zipes, Jack David, ed. *Victorian Fairy Tales: The Revolt of the Fairies and Elves*. New York: Methuen, 1987.

CHAPTER 8

Notes from the *Aladdin* Industry: Or, Middle Eastern Folklore in the Era of Multinational Capitalism

Christopher Wise

Following the 1992 release of the animated Disney extravaganza *Aladdin*, the film's opening song "Arabian Nights" created somewhat of a stir in the popular media because of its breathtakingly anti-Semitic lyrics, so obviously loaded with bigotry toward the Arab world. After pressure was exerted by members the American-Arab Anti-Discrimination Committee in July of 1993, The Walt Disney Company finally removed some of the more offensive lyrics from the home video version of *Aladdin*, specifically deleting references to the threat of bodily mutilation by Arabs.[1] Oddly, references to the Middle East as a "barbaric" place were unaltered, much to the chagrin of Albert Mokhiber, president of the antidiscrimination group.[2] Over fifteen years since the publication of Edward Said's *Orientalism* (1978), it is both striking and saddening that contemporary stereotypes of Arabs have changed so little in American popular culture, in fact verifying Said's once startling thesis that the U.S. media compulsively seeks to prove that "Semites [i.e., Arabs] are at the bottom of all 'our' troubles" (286). However, the offensive lyrics of Disney's song, while notable in their lack of subtlety, do not in themselves convey the extent of anti-Arab and anti-Islamic sentiment that the film *Aladdin* promotes.

In the following essay, I will briefly sketch a few of the more disturbing implications of the film's narrative, setting aside the indisputable fact that *Aladdin* is thoroughly and dangerously racist in its depictions of Arabs. To say that *Aladdin* is racist is merely to state the obvious. Instead, I will seek to demonstrate how the film functions as a symbolic resolution of the contradiction (for Westerners mainly, especially Americans) of the persistence of

Islamic theocratic government in the era of former president George Bush's "[whole] new world order." In other words, I will attempt to show how the film vilifies Islamic Law, or *sharia* (law that is based upon the Qur'an), promoting instead a largely Western notion of "freedom"—which means essentially the freedom to exchange goods, or, in the language of *Aladdin*'s narrator (the voice of Robin Williams), the freedom to buy, sell, and trade "the finest merchandise in Agrabah [an approximate anagram for Baghdad]." In more specific, theoretical terms, my argument will draw upon Fredric Jameson's *The Political Unconscious* to suggest that Disney's *Aladdin* represents a "First World" attempt to creatively resolve the "problem" (or ongoing crisis) of an "archaic" Middle Eastern economy or "mode of production" that refuses easy penetration by multinational capitalism, largely because of Islamic religion, custom, and tradition.[3]

Aladdin, Jasmine, and the Genie are all victims who seek their freedom from social oppression, or from being "trapped" by law and outmoded custom: This is the unifying link and common thread of the film. Aladdin, like the title character in Douglas Fairbanks, *The Thief of Baghdad* (1920)—the precursor and actual model for Disney's *Aladdin*—must steal bread from local vendors in the Agrabah marketplace in order to live. Aladdin is morally upright, however, in that he steals only enough to survive. Furthermore, he gives away what he steals to less fortunate children, who are also starving victims of an unjust and suffocating social order. Additionally, Aladdin risks a great deal by his life of crime in that the punishment for stealing in Agrabah, as is well known, is having one's hand cut off by the authorities. Aladdin is also victimized by his social class status in that he is born a "street rat," though he vows not to die one. His quest to marry the princess Jasmine is in some sense a quest in the vein of American Horatio Alger tales: the well-worn story of the upwardly mobile rise of an ambitious young man (the "diamond in the rough"); only Aladdin seems to be confronted with a social system that is much more obsolete and oppressive than anything young Horatio Alger ever dreamed of. Not surprisingly, lead Disney animator Glen Keane deliberately modeled the image of Aladdin on the American actor Tom Cruise, especially of *Top Gun*, "who carried himself with a kind of confidence and an air of invincibility" that Disney sought to convey.[4]

Not only in the film's opening-song lyrics, but all throughout *Aladdin*, Disney exploits Western superstitions regarding corporal punishment in the Middle East, specifically the penalty of having one's hand cut off for theft, a punishment that is actually mandated in the Qur'an and in *hadith* literature.[5] For example, when Princess Jasmine first visits the Agrabah marketplace, she too is brutally grabbed by the wrist and asked, "Do you know what the penalty is for stealing?" Indeed, it is surprising that there are any hands left intact in the city of Agrabah, given the frequency and ease with which this punishment is administered.[6] In a more important sense, however, Jasmine is a victim of the Law, or tradition, which callously dictates that she must marry a wealthy, foreign prince, regardless of her personal desires. When Jasmine's father reminds her that "the law says [she] must be married to a prince," Jasmine simply replies "The law is wrong!" Nothing more need be said because, by this point, it is quite clear to everyone that the Law is the real problem or issue. In fact, the Law even interferes with the plans and desires of Jafar, the evil, hook-nosed vizier to the King.

At the beginning of *Aladdin*, Princess Jasmine has never even been outside in the city streets, though she dreams of freedom constantly: "I can't stay here and have my life lived for me," she tells her tiger Raja. When she flees the palace and takes refuge with Aladdin in his secret hideaway, Jasmine contradicts Aladdin's longing for the ease of royal life by telling him that, in the palace, "you're not free to make your own choices." Their romantic epiphany, however, or the moment when they awaken to their true feelings for one another, occurs when they both realize that they are equally "trapped" in their own separate ways: Indeed, they utter this word simultaneously, as they gaze longingly into one another's eyes.

Of course, the Genie is also trapped. He wants to be his own master: He longs for freedom because no master has yet wished him out of the imprisoning lamp. The three main characters, Aladdin, Jasmine, and the Genie, are all thwarted and degraded by senseless traditions, customs, and laws. They must all *submit* to demeaning enslavement by the Law. Another way to say this is that they are imprisoned by a society that demands that they *submit* to the hopelessly outmoded dictates of the Qur'anic Word. *Islam*, of course, is the Arabic word for submission—submission to the will of God. *Muslim* or *Moslem*, which is the participle form of *Islam*, also means "one who submits." As *Aladdin* makes clear, Islamic or Qur'anic law is archaic, stultifying, terroristic, evil, and corporeal: It may cut off your head just as easily as your hand.

If Disney's *Aladdin* seeks to vilify *sharia* (Islamic law), a rapid survey of recent events in the Middle East would seem to demonstrate both the urgency and the seriousness of the threat that Islamic "fundamentalist" and theocratic revolution now poses to Western economic policies. While the Islamic Shi'ite revolution in Iran has consistently frustrated U.S. policy since the late 1970s, the rise of pan-Islamic "fundamentalism" in the Sunni world (i.e., in places like Egypt, northern Sudan, and Algeria) has caused considerable alarm in the West. In North Africa, for example, nongovernmental Sunni groups are the best organized and loudest voices that call for free elections—elections that would no doubt mean the end of democracy in a world where Western-style democracy itself is often regarded as both "idolatrous" and "inappropriate" for Muslims.[7] In fact, even many Muslims who are not particularly hostile to the West do not believe that democracy will serve as a valid solution to their problems, especially Euro-American styles of democracy promoting free speech, separation between church and state, and *riba* (interest on loans).[8]

The thematic obsession in Disney's *Aladdin* with Islamic *hu-dud* laws, or laws prescribing stoning, whipping, and amputation for breaches of *sharia*, strikingly replicates the concerns of recent Western journalism on the Middle East, especially whenever the subject of *sharia* is broached.[9] Besides keeping inventory on the minor "absurdities" of Islamic law, news accounts have consistently ridiculed efforts, for instance, the state of Kelantan in Malaysia and nations like Iran and the Sudan to impose *sharia* in their economic, banking, and insurance systems. Of particular concern to Western journalists is the ban on *riba*, a banking practice that is viewed by most Muslims as un-Islamic. In Pakistan, for example, the reimposed ban on *riba* caused foreign lenders to withdraw from a multimillion-dollar hydroelectric project near Karachi, an event characterized by *The Economist* as yet another example of Islamic theocratic fanaticism.[10]

The fact that many Muslims cannot accept Western concepts of international or multinational law—in a word, any legal system that would grant sovereignty to *nations* (i.e., human beings) rather than *God*—has also been a source of considerable frustration in recent accounts of Middle Eastern news. Commentators bemoan the legal headaches and complexities that *sharia* creates in the development of international trade, the privatization of national economies, the expansion of media technology, and the shape of educational reform. In the case of Iran, *sharia* is dismissed as a disappointment at best, though most often it is described as clear failure. A reporter for *The Economist* recently stated that "like the shah, the Islamic regime rules through repression.... Corruption and *parti-bazi* (exploiting personal connections) are as widespread as ever; the difference is that nowadays the clerics are the ones handing out the favors."[11]

In nearly every recent American news account regarding the expansion and implementation of *sharia* in places like the Sudan, Pakistan, and Iran, the message seems clear: The Islamic world is a dangerous (and backward), faraway place—"where they cut off your ear if they don't like your face." In all of these accounts, the elasticity, rigor, and sophistication of traditional Qur'anic interpretative practices are elided and repressed to promote a largely jingoistic and childish understanding of *sharia* as a legal or judicial system.[12] For example, the Western media nearly always conflates Christian fundamentalist religion with so-called Islamic "fundamentalism," a term that evokes born-again Protestants who insist on the literal truth of the Bible.[13] However, as opposed to the anti-intellectual bias of fundamentalist Protestants in the United States, Islamic interpretation may actually be more analogous to Rabbinic and Catholic interpretative traditions that encourage "multilevel" and polysemous readings of the biblical text.[14] In fact, Catholic, Jewish, and Muslim hermeneutics (or approaches to sacred scripture) have all deeply influenced or "cross-pollinated" one another throughout their respective histories.

As in the case of Protestant fundamentalism, however, we are led to believe that Islamic "fundamentalism" encourages only a literal reading of the Qur'anic text, hence the ease with which the *hu-dud* laws are administered in *Aladdin* and in other Western representations of the Islamic world. In the Sudan, Pakistan, Iran, and Kelantan, the "traditional" Islamic punishments seldom have been carried out, a fact that even the most hostile accounts of recent events in the Middle East have freely admitted. While the *hu-dud* laws are seldom imposed anywhere in the Islamic world, their infrequent administration is generally attributed to the shoddiness and incompetence of Muslim bureaucracy, or to petty conflicts and differences in leadership styles among judges.[15] In the case of Iran, for example, in one account we are given the fantastic explanation that *sharia* is so rarely imposed "because so many Iranians lost limbs in the war with Iraq that limblessness is no longer a sign of shame."[16] Though *sharia* systems are far from flawless, they are obviously a great deal more complex and sophisticated than the heavy-handed caricatures U.S. media accounts would have us believe.

In Disney's *Aladdin*, what prevents the "whole new world" from coming into being is, quite simply, "that stupid old law," in the words of Princess Jasmine. Like any good feminist, Jasmine is appropriately outraged when she comes across Jafar, Aladdin, and her father discussing her arranged marriage: "I'm not a prize to be won!" she shouts indignantly at them. "How dare all of you sit around deciding my future!" Later in the film, the evil Jafar places Jasmine in a time amulet, the sand literally pouring over her, drowning and killing her—like *all* Muslim women who are hopelessly crushed under centuries of Islamic oppression.[17] Not surprisingly, Jasmine succumbs to Aladdin's suit only when he reluctantly agrees that she is *not* a prize to be won, that she should be free to make her own choices. When the law, tradition, and custom are circumvented, the consequences are truly dazzling: Immediately, Aladdin and Jasmine climb onto the magic carpet from the Cave of Wonders and fly away into the stars. Disney's hit song "A Whole New World" unfolds in appropriate MTV fashion as the "whole new world" below reveals something of its magnificence and splendor. Among other wonders, we see the pyramids and the Sphinx of Egypt, the Acropolis in Athens, and finally the palace of the last emperor of China. The binary opposition pitting the prison house of Islamic tradition over and against the free marketplace of open exchange, or the freedom of individual *choice*, operates all throughout *Aladdin*'s narrative. In the end, when Aladdin wishes for the Genie's freedom, even Jasmine's bumbling father must finally agree that "[i]t's the law that's the problem." The King therefore decrees: "From this day forth the princess shall marry whom she chooses." Everyone is happy now: Aladdin has successfully risen above his station, Jasmine has gotten around "that stupid old law," and the Genie is free. To the amusement of all, the Genie zooms wildly over the palace, shouting, "I'm free, I'm free, free at last. I'm hitting the road, I'm off to see the world." Not surprisingly, once his long-desired freedom is obtained, the ecstatic Genie sports a Florida-style vacation shirt, suitcase, and Goofy hat, and is off to visit—where else?—Disneyworld.

Postscript

Following September 11, 2001, the political relationship between the United States and the Middle East has dramatically altered in many obvious and far-reaching ways. At the time the above article was written in the mid-1990s, I responded primarily to *Aladdin*'s thematic emphasis on the Islamic tradition as a retarding force, especially as a belief system that inhibited the expansion of multinational capitalism from the West. In retrospect, my article lacks a sufficient acknowledgment of the fact that consumer products like Disney films have indeed found a ready market in the Arab world, which continues to purchase and enjoy Disney's *Aladdin* films and similar claptrap from the United States. Despite a significant boycott of American products following Israeli military operations in the spring of 2002, the Arab world has more generally resigned itself to the feeling that globalization is an irreversible process, and that boycotts of U.S. goods and services will inevitably harm Arabs far more than they will Americans or Israelis. As a resident of Amman, Jordan, I have asked numerous locals their feelings about Disney's *Aladdin*, and the vast majority have expressed to me far more reservations about the fact that U.S. tax dollars continue to fund Zionist imperialism and apartheid—a reality that directly affects the majority of the people of Amman of whom approximately 75% are Palestinians—whereas *Aladdin*'s obvious stereotyping of Arabs is so commonplace and laughable that it hardly merits lengthy discussion. Ignorant Western fantasies about the Arab world (i.e., that Arabs are "barbaric," that Islamic women are victimized by their religion, etc.) may be shrugged off, but the fact that U.S. tax dollars continue to underwrite the illegal occupation of Palestine, as well as racist laws aimed at Arab Christians and Muslims living under Israeli rule, cannot be so easily dismissed. The tragicomedy in all this lies in the United States' ongoing obliviousness to the overwhelming receptivity of Arab peoples to American culture and its products, including consumer goods like sleek Disney films. To speak then of the "Disneyfication of *our* children," as alluded to in the articles by Ayres and Buhler, must be qualified with the acknowledgment that the "our" in this title unavoidably includes Arab and Arab American children who are also brought up on a steady diet of Disney products.

Arab parents cannot be unaffected when watching their children play with the latest Disney toy imported into the Middle East from the United States. Those who might normally be indifferent to global politics find themselves placed on the defensive with friends and relatives. They must ask themselves questions like "Should I allow my child to play with Mickey Mouse?" If so, will I betray my brother who was killed in Ramallah? My uncle who lost his home in Bethlehem? My niece who dreams of becoming a suicide bomber? What if all I really want is to be left alone? When will the Israeli occupation end so my children can play with their Disney products in peace? Since the Gulf War, the United States has repeatedly failed to grasp that Arabs are ready trading partners— that "they" do not hate "us" in the slightest—but want merely for the Palestinian-Israeli crisis to be resolved. Once America wakes up from its fifty-year slumber, this process of "getting on" with things in the Arab world will inevitably involve *more* Disneyfication, the proliferation of *more* U.S. imports in the Arab world, especially film products like *Aladdin*. More importantly, it will involve greater democratization of Arab government and other civil institutions (of which the single largest impediment remains U.S. foreign policy in the Middle East). It is no accident that the largest anti-Zionist protest in Washington's history, following massacres in Jenin and the Israeli siege of PNA (Palestinian National Authority) headquarters in the spring of 2002, united the efforts of U.S.-based Palestinian supporters and countless anti-World Trade Organization (WTO) protesters. In this instance, the struggle to bring an end to the illegal occupation of Jerusalem/Al-Quds, the West Bank, Gaza, and Golan Heights was rightly perceived by protesters as analogous to the fight to open the WTO to fair democratic representation on behalf of those most directly affected by its decisions. Ten years following the American-Iraqi war for Kuwait, it is far more difficult to entertain leftist or Islamist fantasies that American-style globalization can simply be arrested in the Middle East, or even that fast-food joints like McDonald's, Taco Bell, or KFC may forever be kept out of "unspoiled" places like Aqaba, Marrakech, and Damascus, but no one may doubt that multinational corporations like McDonald's and Disney may be transformed into more responsible, humane, and democratic organizations. If the critique of cartoons like *Aladdin* seems like so much "political correctness" to the jaded U.S. consumer, it bears remembering that the fact of globalization means that Disney products are no longer the exclusive concern of Americans. This too is a consequence of multinational capitalism. American indifference to Arab realities—in fact, to the Arab world's *appreciation* of U.S. culture—is at least partly to blame for the terrible events of September 11, 2001, not to mention Afghanistan's and Palestine's sufferings in the months that followed. The cavalier insensitivity of films like *Aladdin* has directly contributed to the culture of misunderstanding that now prevails in the United States, and has prevailed in the years that led "us" to the controversies in which "we" and "our" children are now embroiled.

Notes

1. The exact words of the song "Arabian Nights," written by Howard Ashman and Alan Menken, are as follows: "Oh, I come from a land / From a faraway place / Where the caravan camels roam. / Where they cut off your ear / If they don't like your face / It's barbaric, but hey, it's home!" References to mutilation were replaced by Disney with descriptions of the desert climate and geography.
2. *New York Times* 11 July 1993.
3. Though this is obviously not the place to engage the largely scholastic question of which "mode of production" (in classical Marxist terminology) may appropriately designate or signify the economic systems of theocratic Islamic nations like Iran, Pakistan, the Sudan, and so on, Marx's much-embattled concept of the Asiatic mode of production, traditionally signifying those economic systems organized around the "sacred" or "religious," may serve my purpose here in a heuristic or provisional sense.
4. *New York Times* 8 Nov. 1992.
5. Like the Torah, or Mosaic law, Islamic law often can seem harsh and "primitive" by contemporary Western as well as Middle Eastern standards. Thomas W. Lippman, in his book *Understanding Islam*, comments: "In [prehistoric Arab] society where incest, infanticide, polygamy, banditry, slavery, and vendetta were common, the criminal code of Islam can be seen as one of moderation and progressive reform, not the dark regimen of cruelty and reaction often depicted in the West" (92).
6. Despite the fact that, in recent history, this traditional penalty has seldom been carried out in *any* part of the Islamic world, there is another more obvious problem with Disney's narrative of corporal terror in the Middle East, namely the fact that the Islamic value placed on almsgiving, which is one of the pillars of the faith, makes stealing for bread (i.e., the plight of Jean Valjean in Hugo's *Les Misérables*) virtually unthinkable within an Islamic context; that is, within a context where bread, shelter, and money are freely given to those in need.
7. For example, during elections last year in Algeria (1992), a leader of the FIS (Islamic Salvation Front) stated his view to a Western reporter that "democracy is sheer idolatry" (*The New Republic* 27 Jan. 1992: 7).

8. "There are a sizable number of middle class people in the Arab world," stated Mustapha Kamel Said, a political science professor at Cairo University, "who feel that democracy doesn't promise them anything" (*U.S. News & World Report* 21 Jan. 1991: 25). It is important to note, in this regard, that the word "democracy" itself is a Western word of Greek origin. Generally preferable in the Middle East is the Arabic word *shura,* which means "consultation" and better serves values of Muslims, especially insofar as it historically arises from an Islamic context and worldview.

9. In a recent article in *The Economist,* for example, a correspondent in Lahore, Pakistan, opened his brief "exposé" by stating that "the law is a peculiarly cruel ass in the Islamic Republic of Pakistan" (5 Oct. 1991: 36).

10. 5 Sept. 1992: 38–39.

11. Islamic revolution, so *The Economist* concludes, is much like Iran's "horrible 'Islamic beer'": "Served in brown bottles straight from the fridge, this amber alcohol-free drank looks almost like the real thing. Then it goes flat and warm and tastes like prunes. Most Iranians prefer Pepsi" (11 May 1991: 38).

12. Ironically, in *Debating Muslims: Cultural Dialogues in Postmodernity and Tradition* (1990), authors Michael M. J. Fischer and Mehdi Abedi point out that contemporary literary theorists like Jacques Derrida, Edmond Jabès, and Emmanuel Levinas (perhaps the most influential cluster of late-twentieth-century philosophers) are all steeped in traditional Judeo-Muslim hermeneutics. In fact, Fischer and Abedi argue that in the disorienting world of postmodernity, it may well be the West today that has the most to learn from the interpretative sophistication of Islamic hermeneutics, especially as an "intellectual interlocutor in the modern world scene, as in the days when [Islamic culture] gave form to the nascent 'Western civilization'" (xxi).

13. No equivalent of the word "fundamentalism," or even the concept, exists in Arabic or in Islam. For example, Benazir Bhutto, the prime minister of Pakistan, once ironically said of the former prime minister of Pakistan Nawaz Sharif that "he was no 'Islamic fundamentalist'"—to which Sharif quickly replied, "But there are no fundamentalists in Islam" (*The Economist* 20 Apr. 1991: 33).

14. In Augustinian and Thomist hermeneutics, the biblical text may be read on at least four different levels: the literal, the allegorical, the moral, and the anagogical. In Rabbinic or Jewish hermeneutics, the text may be read "forty-nine ways positively and forty-nine ways negatively": which is to say, there is an infinite number of ways to read the Torah (i.e., seven, which is the number of perfection, times seven equals forty-nine, or infinity).

15. *The Economist* 4 Apr. 1992: 47–48.

16. *The Economist* 4 Apr. 1992: 48.

17. Of course, all of this is not to say that women *are not* oppressed in the Middle East but rather to demonstrate the audacity of the West for, once again, positioning itself in the role of liberating savior. For example, in Akbar S. Ahmed's recent *Postmodernism and Islam: Predicaments and Promise* (1992), the Western depiction of Muslim women as "disempowered victims" is turned on its head quite effectively. Ahmed states, rather, that "rape, mutilation, and abuse" seem to be the destiny of *Western* women in the eyes of most Muslims (247). "There is an inherent tendency in Western society," Ahmed suggests, "to view women as hate objects, one which is glibly projected onto Western media images of women in Islam" (247). Also, see Gayatri Chakravorty Spivak's "Can the Subaltern Speak?" where she explores the problem of "white men saving brown women from brown men" (297).

Works Cited

Ahmed, Akbar S. *Postmodernism and Islam: Predicaments and Promise.* New York: Routledge, 1992.

Fischer, Michael M. J., and Mehdi Abedi. *Debating Muslims:Cultural Dialogues in Postmodernity and Tradition.* Madison: U of Wisconsin P, 1990.

Jameson, Fredric. *The Political Unconscious: Narrative As a Socially Symbolic Act.* Ithaca: Cornell UP, 1981.

Lippman, Thomas W. *Understanding Islam: An Introduction to the Muslim World.* Revised Ed. New York: Mentor, 1990.

Said, Edward. *Orientalism.* New York: Vintage Books, 1978.

Spivak, Gayatri Chakravorty. "Can the Subaltern Speak?" *Marxism and the Interpretation of Culture.* Eds. Cary Nelson and Lawrence Grossberg. Urbana: U of Illinois P, 1988.

Part V
Disney Literature

CHAPTER 9

Shakespeare and Company: *The Lion King* and the Disneyfication of *Hamlet*

Stephen M. Buhler

The works of William Shakespeare come not as single spies but in battalions: One is introduced and reintroduced to them by all manner of interpreters. The plays especially are packaged in highly mediated form. The mediation ranges from pedagogical structures to schools of criticism, from edited text to hypermedia, from stage to screen, with all their conventions, expectations, and formulas. The work of adapting one of Shakespeare's plays often involves much more than the playtext itself. In the case of Disney's *The Lion King* (released in 1994), not only does *Hamlet* undergo re-presentation and transformation, but so do several well-established modes of interpreting the Shakespearean corpus.

As the film repackages *Hamlet* and draws upon Shakespeare as a cultural authority enshrined by other cultural authorities, *The Lion King* also participates in an appropriative project of resistance—one that both claims and discredits certain kinds of cultural capital. Disney productions have long specialized in rewriting canonical or traditional texts in "popular" form; the practice, seen in Walt Disney's early silent cartoons, is meant to be seen as populist, even egalitarian. The refigured stories, however, tend to suppress cultural complexities found in the original texts that might sustain genuinely democratic readings. A potentially unsettling text such as *Hamlet* loses much of its destabilizing force in the kind of reverential and canonical treatment that is both echoed and challenged in the revision.

Shakespeare's plays have been claimed, reformulated, and adapted by the various technologies of the information age. Examples include two treatments of *Romeo and Juliet*, as filtered through late-twentieth-century media. Baz Luhrmann's *William Shakespeare's Romeo + Juliet* retains the language of the playwright (albeit in a drastically cut text) while enlisting the aid of visual-overload techniques refined in music videos and television commercials. Troma Pictures' *Tromeo & Juliet* gleefully grafts all manner of trash-culture trappings—from golden-age Hollywood camp and drive-in movie sex 'n' gore to post-punk fashion—onto the classic drama. Less daring, but still formidable, projects include making Shakespearean plays in digitalized performance and in textual variants immediately accessible to the imagination of any reader/hacker through interactive video and hypertext.[1] Even the Bard's name has undergone an e-mail seachange: SHAKSPER is an electronic discussion group available over the Internet for scholars, directors, actors, readers, and others, all linked by an interest in Shakespeare. The group is, of course, a font of information about the personalities of those involved in the Shakespeare industry and about the character of Shakespeare studies generally.

One SHAKSPER debate centered not on Shakespeare's travels along the information superhighway but on his presence in *The Lion King*. The animated film sparked lively and sometimes intemperate responses from Shakespeareans. An opening salvo argued that this sort of appropriation—which included using the *Hamlet* parallels as a selling point in some promotional materials—was little short of sacrilege. The corporate entities that come under the Disney aegis were said to be in utter and irreconcilable opposition to the values represented by the enterprise of reading, staging, and studying Shakespeare's plays. Return firings noted that Shakespeare himself shared in the entrepreneurial spirit to no small degree. Most contributors admitted that the Bard could be every bit as opportunistic as Uncle Walt and (literally) company, at least when it came to reworking old material. Many of the exchanges, then, dealt with the basic question of whether Will and Walt are mighty opposites or kindred spirits.

One possible reply to that question is "as you like it"—though the intensity and pervasiveness of Disney marketing (as in the promotional materials for *Hercules*) make it difficult to sustain such tolerance. Both sides of the above debate agreed that Shakespearean texts are of value, even while they disagreed as to what values are most effectively communicated in appropriated form. I have invoked a Shakespearean tag here to suggest that there is indeed common ground and to acknowledge the tendency of people on both sides to quote their favorite author (or author-function) in order to make their separate cases. Sometimes even Disney's severest critics unknowingly approve of the alliance with Shakespeare: One professor praised the film *Renaissance Man* as preferable to the handling of Shakespearean materials in *The Lion King* without realizing that the former is also a Disney production, released through its Touchstone Pictures subsidiary. One of my favorite echoes of Shakespeare in any oeuvre can be heard in Disney's *Beauty and the Beast*, as the villain, Gaston, sings out one of Lady Macbeth's lines:

"Screw your courage to the sticking place!" The borrowing works well not only because of its subtlety, a hallmark of Howard Ashman's skill as a lyricist. The quote contributes to the film's impact because the parallel is as apt and rich as it is clever. In Shakespeare's play, Lady Macbeth exploits notions of manhood in order to goad her husband into murder. In the animated feature, the aggressively masculine Gaston invokes the very notions of manhood in which he is trapped so that he can goad his fellow villagers into storming the Beast's castle. Ideas of manliness and what it means to be human come into conflict with ideals of humanity and humane conduct.

Much has been made of the lack of such revisionist thinking in *The Lion King*. Commentators have criticized the film for a variety of, at best, insensitivities and, at worst, outrages. Few critics, though, have treated the film's indebtedness to Shakespeare as yet another strike against it. Some disdain for Disney's appropriations from Shakespeare is partially motivated by a desire to protect the Bard from association with such aspects of the Disney heritage as the misogyny and racism that play recurring roles in the company's entertainments. But despite Shakespeare's own trafficking in such issues and his sometimes vulnerable position as a canonical figure, no one has worked up an argument establishing Shakespeare's own responsibility for the film's often striking lack of cultural awareness. I would suggest that there is something to this polemical approach, because an undue reverence for a specific and very limited model of "Shakespearean culture" keeps the makers of *The Lion King* from generating more of the same kind of productive parallels occurring so happily in *Beauty and the Beast*.

The closing credits to *The Lion King* could accurately include the phrase "Additional dialogue—and story ideas—by William Shakespeare." Juliet's impassioned query, "What's in a name?" appears and is subjected to a vaudevillian, even burlesque, treatment: Timon, a wisecracking meerkat, shouts out the line with gospel fervor during a musical interlude devoted to the subject of flatulence, a condition suffered by Puumba, a warthog. The viewer is, of course, asked to supply a continuation of the quote and to realize that a warthog "by any other name would smell as," well, as warthogs do. Timon's own name, somewhat perversely pronounced, suggests a connection with Shakespeare's disillusioned anti-hero—although improvised lines by Nathan Lane, who provides Timon's voice, may be more responsible for the parallels than the efforts of the lyricist of record, Tim Rice, or the screenwriters.[2] Together, Timon and Puumba provide parallels less to, say, Rosencrantz and Guildenstern, and more to Falstaff, the anti-heroic sidekick to Shakespeare's Prince Hal: Timon shares Sir John's cynicism and self-regard, while Puumba shares his appetite and girth.

Additional credits should include Jessie L. Weston's *From Ritual to Ro-*

mance and E. M. W. Tillyard's studies of the mythology of monarchy in Shakespeare's time, especially his *The Elizabethan World Picture*. An apt alternative title for the film would be *Disney's The African World Picture*. The approach to Shakespearean materials in *The Lion King* is deeply indebted to the state of undergraduate-level college teaching of literature from the early 1960s through the early 1980s. The myths of the Fisher King and of the correspondential relation between the microcosm of the body politic and the macrocosm of nature are vividly invoked as the Pride Lands, the true lion king's domain, degenerate into a barren desert during the usurper's rule; certainly part of Weston's appeal to scholars and teachers shaped by the New Criticism was T. S. Eliot's acknowledged borrowing from her work in *The Waste Land*. The patterns of nature—what the film calls, compulsively, the Circle of Life—have been violated by a political act, since it is the usurpation (more than the fratricide that made it possible) that keeps the landscape so desolate. Having completely naturalized the institution of monarchy, the film can then show how a political act can magically revivify the natural world. If the time is out of joint, then Simba, the Hamlet figure of *The Lion King*, must set it right by occupying the throne. He, however, finds it not a "cursed spite"—as Hamlet does after his first encounter with his father's spirit (1.5.188)[3] but an absolute joy to learn of this weighty responsibility. The apparent deviation from the Shakespearean source, though, may not be a simple case of revision. It may also reflect the triumphalist approach sometimes taken in interpreting Shakespearean tragedy; one notable example is J. Dover Wilson's *What Happens in "Hamlet,"* which presents the slaughter concluding the play as auspicious in itself (287) and Hamlet's "bearing" throughout the scene as even more so.[4]

Once the true prince has purged the kingdom, the Pride Lands restore themselves to the lush and fecund state in which they appeared at the film's opening. *The Lion King* constructs and enacts the natural "Circle of Life" by framing its story with nearly identical scenes that present a newborn heir to the throne not only to the movie audience but also to the animal subjects eagerly attending these royal audiences. The film also constructs its realism by, in effect, impersonating technical limitations. The African savanna is shown to be teeming with "real life," from the plants to the insects to the largest mammals. In sharp detail, ants walk along a tree limb, each carrying a leaf. The effect of clarity in the foreground is enhanced by an out-of-focus background in which indistinct shapes move. Suddenly, those figures come into focus, revealing themselves to be more animals en route to the presentation of the lion prince, while the still active ants are blurred. The inability of conventional camera lenses to maintain a single field of focused vision across great distances in depth has been strategically re-created to enhance the illusion of remaining within—even entering more fully—the natural world. Akira Lippit has noted how in film, which is "in many respects the exemplary technological medium, the figure of the animal resumes the task of his namesake *animus*, generating life in the form of animation" (822). *The Lion King* here uses technology to mask its technological control over appearances; it also uses the "animal kingdom" to breathe life into a correspondential view of things strikingly at odds with any kind of egalitarianism. Rather like Hal, another—if more complex—true prince, Disney strategically adopts what is "base, common, and popular" (*Henry V* 4.1.38), in the phrase of Hal's former companion, Pistol, to strengthen its position.

When the infant Simba is presented to the other animals at Pride Rock, the sun breaks through the clouds, further validating his status as the true prince. A correspondential order, which Tillyard asserts was unquestioned in Shakespeare's time, is vividly rendered here: The sun, the king of planets, demonstrates his kinship with the lion, the king of beasts. In response, the assembled animals pay homage by cheering and bowing. Some even genuflect, in response to Simba's being held aloft by Rafiki, a baboon who serves as the realm's spiritual leader.[5] In his most influential study, Tillyard quotes from *The Learned Prince*, Thomas Blundeville's 1580 verse adaptation of one of Plutarch's *Moralia*, to show how, in the "Elizabethan view," the natural world is in sympathy with both the divine will and the political order. In this passage, Tillyard observes, the "correspondences are between God, the sun, the prince, reason, and justice":

And like as God in heaven above
The shining sun and moon doth place
In goodliest wise as best behove
To show His shape and lively grace,
Such is that Prince within his land
Which, fearing God, maintaineth right
And reason's rule doth understand,
Wherein consists his port and might.

But Plato said God dwells above
And there fast fixt in holy saws
From truth He never doth remove
Ne swarves from nature's stedfast laws;

And as in heaven like to a glass
The sun His shape doth represent,
In earth the light of justice was
By Him ordain'd for like intent. (20)

Mas'ud Zavarzadeh, in his analysis of "the ideological work of the contemporary mainstream film," notes that film's success in "naturalizing the ruling social order" is often achieved not only by asserting the ideology's "obviousness" but also by "testifying to the existence of a real world whose reality is documented in the film" (20).

The process of naturalization is obvious in a text like *The Learned Prince* and in a film like *The Lion King*, but the specific ideological import is not so obvious in the latter. The mainstream film intersects with a naturalized social order that no longer holds; further, the film intersects not only with Elizabethan modes of naturalization but with a Shakespearean text that can serve both to reinforce and to critique such processes in relation to any social order. The film also intersects with a technology that both foregrounds and effaces its independence from the "real" even as it artfully represents the natural.

While *The Learned Prince* initially includes the moon as an exemplar of divine grace, Tillyard overlooks it. A similar exclusion is at work in *The Lion King*, as the Pride Lands are defined exclusively by the more obviously royal—and male—sunlight. Mufasa, Simba's father, shows his son the extent of their realm early one morning. They rule "everything the light touches," as all darkness is circumscribed, even othered. Mufasa sustains the solar correspondence, informing Simba that a king's reign "rises and falls with the sun." The Food Chain is linked with the Great Chain of Being. While there may be differences in degree and diet, all animals—whether carnivore or herbivore, predator or prey—are mortal. Death, the great leveler, serves to excuse the exercise of power in life, though later, death does not absolutely end a king's reign, after all. Later, having just rescued his errant son from attack, Mufasa feels apprehensive about his and his son's mortality. Appropriately enough, his confrontation with the penitent Simba occurs at dusk and early evening. So Mufasa is able to reveal to his son the true nature of the stars: They are, he avers, where "the great kings of the past" continue their benevolent reign beyond death and keep watch over their successors. Even though this speech traces the Chain of Being into transcendence, extending temporal and patriarchal rule into eternity, the invocation of ghostly fathers is not primarily meant to inspire awe either in Simba or in the audience. Instead, Simba is told this as a defense against future loneliness when he inherits the throne. Simba is assured that he and his royal dad will continue to be "pals," as the lion cub says, despite time and death.

For now, though, the rightful monarch is as secure in his course as the sun in the sky. There is, however, a usurper waiting in the wings. The film's villain is named Scar, brother to Mufasa. Not only does he serve as the Claudius figure for this revision of *Hamlet*, he shares to some degree—as do many Disney villains—in the charm and charisma of Richard III. He, also, like Richard Crookback, is marked by his disfigurement. The scar for which he is named is crescent shaped; his planet is the moon. In place of Richard's hired assassins, *The Lion King* offers a comic trio of hyenas, who are gleefully immoral. Hyenas are nocturnal creatures and thus outcasts from the sunny Pride Lands: Their association with the dark apparently allows their usefulness to the great Circle of Life as scavengers to be forgotten. They are instead dismissed as poachers upon the royal hunting grounds. The very recognizable voices for these "dark" and shadowy clowns have provoked considerable comment: Whoopi Goldberg and Cheech Marin provide decidedly urban versions of African American and Hispanic American speech for Shenzai and Banzai respectively, while Disney stalwart Jim Cummings jabbers maniacally as the dim Ed. Many listeners have taken offense at the stereotypical nature of these voices, especially given Disney's sometimes appalling depiction of nonwhites and long-standing ideas of Africa as a "dark" continent.

But *The Lion King* complicates matters by having African American actors James Earl Jones and Robert Guillaume provide the voices for Mufasa and Rafiki—though casting Matthew Broderick as the adult Simba is dreadfully consistent with commissioning British popmeisters Elton John and Tim Rice to provide the songs. Even this has unexpected resonances, however: European imperialism is glanced at both lyrically and in the casting of other roles. The voice of British comedian Rowan Atkinson is given to Zazu, a devotedly officious and toadying hornbill in Mufasa's service. Zazu remonstrates with his "young master," Simba, for his headstrong ways: "If this is where the monarchy is headed, Count me out: / Out of service, out of Africa—I wouldn't hang about." Rice's lyrics touch on latter-day scandals involving attenuated royalty, on traditions of class, and even on Isak Dinesen's recollections of colonized Africa—or at least on Meryl Streep's performance as Dinesen/Karen Blixen. The most obvious interloper is Scar himself, whose voice is supplied by the unmistakably English Jeremy Irons (who is making the portrayal of villains from the Old World a major component of his career). While Susan Miller and Greg Rode, in a study entitled "The Movie You See, the Movie You Don't," are alert to how a range of British and other accents establish racial and class stereotypes in *The Jungle Book* (92–93),[6] the categories are less well established in *The Lion King*. Unlike George Sanders' suavely imperial Shere Khan in the earlier film, Irons' Scar has no real or lasting power.

After his first plot against Simba fails, Scar resolves to eliminate his brother, Mufasa, and the heir, together. He is angered into revealing his plans when Shenzai casually disparages his potency in comparison fasa's. Scar may be "so proper" even though he is not king, but his very name can inspire an ecstasy of fear and, it is implied, desire: After shuddering deliciously in response to Banzai's saying "Mufasa," Shenzai cannot resist urging him, "Do it again." No wonder that Scar will later prohibit the mere mention of his late brother's name. His setpiece, the song "Be Prepared," starts with visual and auditory echoes of totalitarianism (ranks of hyenas march as if in the Nuremberg rally in Riefenstahl's *Triumph of the Will*) and ends with Scar presiding over a kind of witches' sabbath. Scar perches upon a narrow peak, parodying the presentation ceremony upon Pride Rock. The etymological connections linking *pride* and sexuality are likely pertinent here, but the clearest significance is expressed correspondentially. No sun shines during the night of Scar's political revelry or on the shadowy lands that are the hyenas' proper home; instead, a crescent moon shines in crooked sympathy with the usurper's schemes.

Scar's lack of potency is part of yet another revision, this time of Freudian readings of *Hamlet*: Because this Claudius is asexual, there can be no provocation of Oedipal guilt. Instead, Scar stages the murder of Mufasa so as to instill guilt in Simba. There is no primal envy—beyond Scar's own— that might subsequently lead to guilt, as commentators have perceived is Hamlet's case. Simba does experience shame regarding his father's wife, as Scar quietly asks of him: "What will your mother think?" But since Scar does not take Mufasa's place with Sarabi, Simba's mother, nothing of the Oedipal rivalry can be brought to a crisis. No new heir will be produced; in fact, the decline of the Pride Lands into the Waste Land strongly suggests that Scar's is indeed a "barren sceptre."[7] This parallel to *Macbeth* (3.1.61) is reinforced by Simba's flight, which bears a resemblance to Fleance's escape after his father's assassination. Scar is not informed that his henchmen have indeed only "scorch'd the snake, not kill'd it" (3.2.13), so he calmly announces the deaths of Mufasa and Simba, reluctantly assuming the throne in the manner of Richard III. The heir to the throne, he believes, has died in an African gorge—if not the tower—and the moon rises over Pride Rock in sinister approval. The Disney version appropriates psychoanalytic readings of *Hamlet* and makes them far less unsettling; it accordingly makes the relationship between fathers and sons unquestionably benign, no matter how troubling it may be in the Shakespearean source.

While in self-imposed exile, Simba finds refuge in an Edenic landscape and in the carelessness enjoyed by Timon and Puumba. Their motto is *Hakuna Matata*—"It means 'No Worries' for the rest of your days," as the song goes. While the Swahili phrase conjures up notions of suitably Falstaffian irresponsibility, it also echoes colonialist stereotypes of native "laziness." Simba is being derelict in his duties, and a sign of his degradation is his new diet: No longer a noble predator, he feasts on insects with his newfound allies. Timon's charming ignominy is underscored by his mocking rejection of any transcendent, correspondential order. When Simba recalls his father's identification of the stars with "the great kings of the past," the meerkat cannot contain his hilarious contempt. "You mean a bunch of royal dead guys are watchin' us? (Laughter.) Who told you something like that? What mook made that up?" he asks, marveling that anyone could believe in what is so obviously a fiction. The construct is, to his mind, a politically expedient one at that: We must be expected to behave ourselves, if all these "royal dead guys" keep watch over their descendants and their descendants' subjects. Here, writ small, is the disquisition of honor delivered by Falstaff, another ally and misleader of a royal youth. But if Timon revives Sir John's cynicism and Puumba embodies the old knight's girth and devotion to the Prince as individual and as monarch, Simba is no Hal. His irresponsibility is genuine, rather than calculated. His inaction, on the other hand, does bear some resemblance to that of Hamlet: "Conscience" truly puzzles Simba's will, if only because of the false guilt deliberately instilled by Scar.

Simba needs first the prompting of Nala, his cubhood companion, and Rafiki, the Pride Lands' shaman, to overcome his reluctance to return home and take action against a sea of troubles. What decides matters, of course, is the counsel of Mufasa's spirit. As Simba is a revised Hamlet, Nala is Ophelia reconfigured as the Prince's ally and consort. This Disney feature is fairly open about its sexual politics: The encounter between the erstwhile playmates may begin with the horseplay they enjoyed as youngsters, but it moves swiftly to something like foreplay. Nala draws Simba out of an exclusively homosocial adolescent state into a more "mature" sexuality as part of his preparation for assuming his rightful place as king. It is intriguing to consider, then, how Nathan Lane, who provides Timon's voice, insisted in interviews that Timon and Puumba were not just homosocial but gay; the first gay couple in a Disney cartoon, Lane argued.[8] This aspect of *The Lion King* likely reflects yet another engagement with a school of Shakespearean criticism: The comedies, especially, have often been presented as studies in the development of male (hetero)sexuality and sociality.[9] While Nala's and Simba's mutual attraction is a necessary stage, however, it is insufficient to draw him back to face his responsibilities. Nala's early exclamation at discovering that Simba is alive—"Your mother! What will she think?"—is probably unhelpful on a number of levels. It will take the ghostly will of the father, as mediated by Rafiki, to prompt Simba's return.

Rafiki's own potency is figured by his staff and dual gourds, but it is his verbal aggressiveness that most goads the Prince. Robert Guillaume plays the role as a Griot, while Rafiki himself plays the holy fool, maneuvering Simba into a desire to pursue his identity as "Mufasa's boy." Here the connections with *Hamlet* and a famous film version of the play are notable both for their frequency and for their alterity. Hamlet avers that the question is "To be or not to be?"; according to Rafiki, the question instead is "Who are you?" He then, Horatio-like, promises to show the leonine Hamlet his father. Simba follows him, going through a maze of vines reminiscent of the passageways traversed by Laurence Olivier in his film (released in 1948) of the play. Olivier's Hamlet confronts his father's spirit on a high tower overlooking the Danish coastline; he returns to the same spot to meditate, famously, on "the question."[10] Instead of a long, slow climb, Simba makes a brief descent to another threshold where earth and water meet. Where Olivier had Hamlet gaze down into a turbulent sea and at that point meditate on life, death, and action in the play's most famous soliloquy, Disney and company have their young Prince gaze into a placid stream. With Rafiki's encouragement, Simba looks "harder" and his reflection turns into that of his late father.

Turning his gaze upward, Simba sees his father in the stars and in the clouds. As eagerly as Hamlet, but with none of the dread implicit in the Shakespearean exchange (and stressed by Olivier), he drinks in the words from the apparition—

> Mufasa: Simba, you have forgotten me.
> Simba: No, how could I?
> Mufasa: You have forgotten who you are and so forgotten me. Look inside yourself, Simba. You are more than what you have become. You must take your place in the circle of life....Remember who you are. You are my son and the one true king. Remember who you are.

The repetitions of "Remember" continue, clearly indebted to the Ghost's farewell—"remember me" (1.5.91)—at the end of his first appearance to Hamlet.

All the differences from the Shakespearean playtext lead to very different conclusions. The appearance of his father's ghost sends Hamlet into utter turmoil and toward his tragic end, but the spirit that appears to young Simba initiates the resolution of his problems and hastens him toward the obligatory happy ending. Mufasa even repeats the word "remember" as stars shine through the breaking clouds after fire and rain purge the Pride Lands. Instead of the fatal scene that "cries on havoc" even to martial Fortinbras, comes a renewal of the benevolent "Circle of Life" under the reign of the natural, supernaturally sanctioned monarch. Scar, the Claudius figure in the film, is indeed hoist with his own petard, as his attempt to betray his allies backfires; but Simba is as guiltless of his uncle's death as he is of his father's. The figure who displays Falstaffian irreverence, Timon, and the one who displays

Falstaffian dimensions, Puumba, both earn their places at court and banishment at the new king's hands. Even they, like Hal, come to feel that "[i]f all the year were playing holidays, / To sport would be as tedious as to work" (*1 Henry IV* 1.2.204–05). Timon and Puumba are redeemable Falstaffs; their participation in the battle to regain the throne for Simba—unlike that of Sir John at Shrewsbury—is eager, daring, and effective, if still comedic.

Disney productions tend to authorize fatherly counsels completely, while Shakespeare—far more honestly and compellingly—reveals them as deeply problematic. Shakespeare himself, along with many figures from English literature and culture, is presented by Disney as a kindly patriarch from the past. Over the decades, Disney has followed the strategy, initiated in the early twentieth century, of promoting English literature as a preserve for "Anglo-Saxon" culture in the United States (Brown 230–31 and Buhler 219, 235–36). The strategy is strongly in evidence in the pairing of *Wind in the Willows* and *The Legend of Sleepy Hollow*, complete with an opening shot of a stained-glass library window depicting the lamp of knowledge. The former tale is introduced by Basil Rathbone, whose appearances as Sherlock Holmes helped to assert an Anglo-American alliance throughout the Second World War. That alliance has been reflected in film after film: The list includes *Alice in Wonderland, Peter Pan, Treasure Island, 101 Dalmatians* (in both animated and live-action formats), *Mary Poppins, The Jungle Book, The Sword in the Stone*, even *Robin Hood*. The process may have come full circle in *The Great Mouse Detective*, drawn from the Basil of Baker Street series of Holmes pastiches for children. Even as the patrimony of English letters is invoked, however, the fatherly counsels of Shakespeare, Stevenson, and Kipling get insistently, radically rewritten. It is true, on the one hand, that some of the English writers are women and that much of their sly and subversive messages get domesticated in the Disney approach to adaptation. What can one say happens, though, when the texts of men writers—the will of literary fathers, in effect—are resisted in ways both reverent and irreverent?

Such resistance is rarely revolutionary, much less rebellious. Most of the time, it merely bows to the designs of corporate growth and the dictates of market research. But implicated in the search for new markets is Disney and company's own struggle with the burdens of family (Lewis 96–99): studio heads faced with changing tastes that Uncle Walt might loathe to acknowledge, much less cater to; creative personnel struggling to acknowledge—however obliquely at times—the shadowy regions that were and still are so often a part of the Disney domain. Further dramas involve occasional attempts directly to redress the sins (artistic and ideological) of the father, but these are often overwhelmed by more regular efforts to maintain inequities in matters of credit and compensation for work. One version of Shakespeare's own counsel on such matters is that great art and wide audiences can coexist; social fabrics and constructs can be faithfully replicated and severely scrutinized at the same time as profits can be made. As Shakespeare once wrote, in *Hamlet*,

> This above all: to thine own self be true,
> And it must follow, as the night the day,
> Thou canst not then be false to any man. (1.3.78–80)

Wait a minute. That is advice given by Polonius, another father and father figure, a character by turns doddering and cunning, untrusting and untrustworthy, severe and sentimental. Perhaps he is the one—not Hamlet junior or senior, not even Claudius—who truly holds the mirror up to Disney and company.

Notes

1. The MIT Shakespeare Electronic Archive is increasingly operational, after years of work by Peter S. Donaldson and Janet Murray of MIT, Larry Friedlander of Stanford University, and numerous others. The first public version of the archive was beta-tested at the Folger Shakespeare Library in 1997. "Hamlet on the Ramparts," a public Web site culled from the archive, is accessible at <http://shea.mit.edu/ramparts>.
2. The screenplay is credited to Irene Mecchi, Jonathan Roberts, and Linda Woolverton; seventeen individuals are listed as having contributed to the film's "story."
3. References to Shakespeare's plays are taken from *The Riverside Shakespeare*.
4. The persistence of triumphalism can be seen in Jorgensen (124–35).
5. Annalee R. Ward sees the film's evocations of spirituality—and of a natural link between virtue and predatory power—as unproblematic. This kind of transcendence is one of several "values" presented that she considers "noncontroversial, prosocial" (175–76). Another approvingly "mythic" approach—this time of both film and sourceplay—is offered by Rosemarie Gavin as the basis for a teaching strategy.
6. Miller and Rode suggest interesting parallels between Disney's Mowgli and Shakespeare's Prince Hal (92–93).
7. In the sequel, *The Lion King II: Simba's Pride*, Scar is posthumously awarded a mate, Zira, who bears two sons, Kovu and Nuka. Despite the obvious enmity between this would-be dynasty and Simba's clan, Kovu falls in love with Kiara, Simba's daughter, thus providing the film with a parallel to *Romeo and Juliet*. The sexual politics of the original not only allows Scar no real potency but also withholds any chance of active resistance from Sarabi, Mufasa's bereaved mate.
8. As in an interview with Charlie Rose, for public television, which aired in summer 1994.
9. Norman Holland summarizes a number of psychoanalytic approaches to maturation in Shakespeare; see his discussions of *All's Well That Ends Well* (152–54) and *Twelfth*

Night (278–79). Marjorie Garber has reexamined the issue, specifically considering depictions of women's adulthood in the plays (123–43).
10.   On both the general and the very personal psychology of these scenes in Olivier's *Hamlet*, see Peter S. Donaldson (40–42).

Works Cited

Beauty and the Beast. Dirs. Gary Trousdale, Kirk Wise. Screenplay by Roger Allers and Linda Woolverton. Walt Disney Pictures Production, 1991.

Bell, Elizabeth, Lynda Haas, and Laura Sells, eds. *From Mouse to Mermaid: The Politics of Film, Gender, and Culture*. Bloomington: Indiana UP, 1995.

Brown, Stephen J. "The Uses of Shakespeare in America: A Study in Class Domination." In *Shakespeare: Pattern of Excelling Nature*. Eds. David Bevington and Jay Halio. Newark: U of Delaware P, 1978.

Buhler, Stephen M. "Antic Dispositions: Shakespeare and Steve Martin's *L.A. Story*." *Shakespeare Yearbook* 8 (1997): 212–29.

Donaldson, Peter S. *Shakespearean Films/Shakespearean Directors*. Boston: Unwin Hyman, 1990.

Garber, Marjorie. *Coming of Age in Shakespeare*. London: Methuen, 1981.

Gavin, Rosemarie. "*The Lion King* and *Hamlet*: A Homecoming for the Exiled Child." *English Journal* 85.3. Mar. 1996: 55–57.

Hamlet. Dir. Laurence Olivier. Two Cities Films, 1948.

Holland, Norman. *Psychoanalysis and Shakespeare*. New York: McGraw-Hill, 1964.

Jorgensen, Paul. *Lear's Self-Discovery*. Berkeley and Los Angeles: U of California P, 1967.

Lewis, Jon. "Disney After Disney: Family Business and the Business of Family." *Disney Discourse: Producing the Magic Kingdom*. Ed. Eric Smoodin. New York: Routledge, 1994.

The Lion King. Dirs. Robert Allers, Rob Minkoff. Screenplay by Irene Mecchi, Jonathan Roberts, and Linda Woolverton. The Walt Disney Company, 1994.

The Lion King II: Simba's Pride. Dirs. Darrell Rooney, Rob LaDuca. Screenplay by Flip Kobler and Cindy Marcus. Walt Disney Home Video, 1998.

Lippit, Akira Mizuta. "Afterthoughts on the Animal World." *Modern Language Notes* 109 (1994): 786–830.

Miller, Susan, and Greg Rode. "The Movie You See, the Movie You Don't." Bell, Haas, and Sells 92–93.

The Riverside Shakespeare. Ed. G. Blakemore Evans. 2nd Ed. Boston: Houghton, 1997.

Rose, Charlie. Interview with Nathan Lane. Public Television. Summer 1994.

Tillyard, E. M. W. *The Elizabethan World Picture*. London: Chato and Windus, 1943.

Ward, Annalee R. "*The Lion King's* Mythic Narrative." *Journal of Popular Film and Television* 23.4. Winter 1996: 171–78.

Weston, Jessie L. *From Ritual to Romance*. Cambridge UP, 1920.

Wilson, J. Dover. *What Happens in* Hamlet. 3rd ed. Cambridge UP, 1951.

Zavarzadeh, Mas'ud. *Seeing Films Politically*. Albany: State University of New York P, 1991.

CHAPTER 10

Disney's *Tempest:* Colonizing Desire in *The Little Mermaid*

Richard Finkelstein

Because of its huge and successful penetration in several converging media markets, the Walt Disney corporation can exemplify theories about the increasing power of commercial culture and the subsequent impoverishment of citizens. More than any other media conglomerate, Disney has succeeded at creating an illusionary community by promising kinship and communication, the kind of participation that Ewen and Ewen tie to individuals isolated in a corporate industrial world (42). Its heavy marketing of "family values," its group of well-known characters present in stores and at home in Disney "parks," its giveaway toys for fast-food mealtimes, its films and spin-off clothing, diapers and toys, its TV stations and TV news, all let it permeate every aspect of daily life, private and public. If the individual means of mass communication have been submerged into an interlocking system (Bogart 3), Disney represents both commercial culture and the larger community because isolated citizens participate in a kind of virtual community by engaging with its products. In Adorno's scheme, consumer culture becomes an extension of production itself (26). People who buy Disney things (including communications products) themselves become standardized according to its product model.

Although cultural criticism about Disney films has circulated through academic, journalistic, and popular media, the critic consuming these entertainment products confronts special problems. If critics use their learning to demystify the mechanisms through which Disney films manage public values and the American marketplace, they risk reifying the product they distrust. In seeking to expand its empire, Disney presents a particular kind of American culture as having values which transcend national boundaries. But to step back from a product is to lend it and the critic the air of autonomy (Benjamin 221). It exists in an independent field of artistic production capable, as Pierre Bourdieu suggests, of imposing its own norms on both product and consumption (3). Adorno warns critics that unless they recognize their own cultural values, they implicitly assume that culture transcends the flux of markets (32). When addressing Disney, it is especially hard for an academic critic to "both participate in culture and not participate" (33); in this case, to avoid becoming either standardized or too irregular to be understood.

One means for escaping from this circuit is paradoxically by joining in temporarily while traversing the cultural landscapes it transmutes. *The Little Mermaid* presents an ideal opportunity for evaluating the means through which Disney manages and distributes cultural knowledge and energy. It breaches the permeable boundaries between three very different cultural systems, gaining its cultural capital by drawing on each. Based on the Hans Christian Andersen tale, Disney adapts its progenitor for the American marketplace by imbuing it with familiar elements from Shakespearean comedy and romance (much as *The Lion King* draws on *Hamlet*, and the Fates in *Hercules* resemble the witches in *Macbeth*). Walter Benjamin's suggestion that, in principle, a work of art has always been reproducible (218) especially resonates with folktales. Developed from varied oral traditions, folk stories can contain little if any "essence." (Andersen himself also knew the renderings of Goethe's *Melusine* and Fouqué's *Undine*.) As Jack Zipes has shown, Andersen's version is not a text of rarefied purity. It reflects the anxious participation of its own author in a particular class and psychological configuration which stresses a Protestant ethic, essentialist ideas of natural order, and the value of suffering, humiliation, and self-torture (71–94). The Disney film thus is not desecrating a purer, more appealing version, but is part of a system which creates "ideals" by substituting signs for experience using an earlier fictional system which did the same.[1]

The film's use of Shakespeare tacitly acknowledges its creators' awareness that because every folktale version emerges from the cultural configurations of its time, it competes with others to effectively impress a message on audiences. The most successful story, then, finds a way to legitimize itself. When it creates distinctions, in Bourdieu's terms, that version wants the audience to accord it "a privileged position in a social space whose distinctive value is objectively established in its relationship to expressions generated from different conditions" (56). In other words, using Shakespeare makes *Mermaid*'s design for living seem legitimate and all others arbitrary.

Any writer's choice for anchoring the value of his or her fable is overdetermined. However, because "Shakespeare" occupies some readily identifiable positions within Anglo-American and even international culture, this institution's presence in Disney's *The Little Mermaid* has some targeted effects on the film's arguments and the cultural relationships in which it participates. As many Shakespearean critics have recently demonstrated, Shakespeare plays a central role in the creation of national character and thus patriarchy, even as the understanding of "Shakespeare" itself reflects this ethos (Bristol, McEachern, Sinfield). Because his lines are regularly taken out of context, his works are easily moralized and thus have come to be seen as stating moral truths.[2] His image is always central to struggles between high and low culture—indeed, to the identity of high culture itself (Levine, Stephen Brown). That the public regularly thinks of Shakespeare as teaching "transcendent truths" seems a statement needing no confirmation with citations.

By legitimizing *The Little Mermaid* with issues raised by Shakespeare's *Tempest*, Disney shapes its audience's perception of itself as a community laid out along a grid of relationships between gendered and ungendered authority, sexual license and discipline, patriarchy and national identity, culture and nature.[3] The changes which the writers use Shakespeare to impose on Andersen's story reveal a surprising alliance between Puritanism and the marketplace. They also show an alliance between a patriarchal nationalism and a feminism, two ideologies which often contest one another over the female body. Indeed, although criticized by many for eroticizing its heroine,[4] *Mermaid* actually works hard to discipline the body as a means of standardizing consumption.

* * *

Far from being a gentle writer of unsophisticated tales, Hans Christian Andersen was an extraordinarily well connected, well traveled, and voraciously well read man who overcame terrible deprivation to become the first widely read Scandinavian writer from the working classes (Zipes xiii). His diaries reveal an extensive knowledge of Shakespeare, whose works he "devoured" in 1825 and with whom he identified at least for a time (ix, 21; Kofoed 212). His diaries also reveal that he saw several of Shakespeare's works staged. When visiting England he was repeatedly conscious of being at locations which were settings for specific plays, including *Henry VI*. He viewed sculptures of Shakespeare's characters, including Ariel, Titania, and Puck, which inspired a fantasy about writing a poem on the last figure (187). But by far his longest diary entry (over 20 lines of printed text) with regard to Shakespeare came after seeing a London performance of *The Tempest* in 1857. Interestingly, he particularly noted the performances of Ariel, Miranda, and Caliban but did not even mention Prospero. He returned home exhausted and declared to his diary, "My blood [sic] hot!" (Andersen 257).

It is hard to connect Andersen's "The Little Mermaid" to Shakespeare and even harder to apply to it the diary's remarks on *The Tempest*, made twenty years after he claimed to have invented the tale. It is nonetheless striking that the words he used to describe Ariel (a "lovely figure") and Miranda ("sentimental, bloodless and yet captivating") could apply also to his mermaid; so too, could his typically nineteenth-century reading of Puck and his kin as creatures of fantasy. His rapture over the play could imply a long-term affection for it but certainly confirms his intense involvement with Shakespeare.

Although "The Little Mermaid" wears a Shakespearean aura, the structure of Andersen's tale is very different from Shakespeare's comedies and romances. His characters inhabit a female-dominated world—the mermaid king is barely mentioned (almost like Prospero who is absent from the narrative). The mermaids are both tremendous sources of support for the heroine and founts of inspiration and independence; the enticing stories of the human world come from a grandmother. Merwomen, however, are also the source of destructive powers. The witch, who offers the mermaid a Faustian bargain to gain feet, perhaps doubles the grandmother or the absent mother for her ambivalent yoking of separation to danger (Soracco 409).

The filmmakers preserve and intensify many of the cultural configurations and Shakespearean hints in Andersen, while splicing in their Shakespearean structure. In the nineteenth-century version, swimming up to gaze at humans is presented as a female rite of passage when each mermaid sister turns fifteen. In Disney, this ritualized journey becomes a more generalized romance quest in which an adolescent heroine must overcome blocks (primarily, her father and the Sea Witch) to gain her desire. Perhaps the most significant change, with regard to the narrative, is that the father is given both vastly increased presence and a name: the large, imposing King Triton, whom even Prince Eric's sailors know in advance (as if he were Poseidon). Disney explicitly represents Ursula the Sea Witch as Triton's enemy, an opposition absent from Andersen. Indeed, her presence has also grown. Exploiting an impulse latent in Andersen's text, a human romantic interest. Of course, the film finally ends festively, with the mermaid in a gorgeous dress and having a big wedding, attended by merpeople and humans, while Andersen's mermaid gains the hope of salvation through three hundred years of work after sacrificing herself.

The addition of parental blocking figures,[5] the festive ending, the movement in and out of the often dangerous human world—all suggest that Disney's writers were familiar with the tremendously influential analyses, rooted in Shakespearean comedy, by Northrop Frye.[6] Written in the late 1940s, Frye's analysis of comedy dominated English departments for at least a generation following his own, and it would be unlikely that college-educated writers would be unfamiliar with interpretations of Shakespeare influenced by it. A brief synopsis of Frye might use *A Midsummer Night's Dream* as an example: A parental blocking figure, supported by law (Duke Theseus), prohibits his daughter from marrying the object of her desires. She runs from him and his domain to a place of greater freedom but also danger—to a forest rife with chaotic magic. However, the special nature of this domain sorts out the relationships between the mixed-up lovers so that they can return to their old place, but they find it and its authorities reformed. The lovers' values—and their determination to act on their impulses—remove the blocks to their happiness, which dominate the first part of the play.

Ariel's quest in Disney's movie follows this pattern closely, particularly with regard to her relationship with her father. The film's opening minutes show Sebastian, like Shakespeare's Philostrate, orchestrating performances for his lord. Although many journalists noted her desire for human things, for material possessions, Ariel says she has many things already but that she wants *more*. Her father's desires as blocks are summed up by Sebastian's deceptively charming calypso song, which concludes, "Someone needs to nail that girl's fins to the floor." Ariel's defining desires represent themselves in her song, which (reprised at her wedding) identifies dancing, feet, walking, running, seeing the sun, exploring, "knowing what people know," and "becoming part of that world" as her goals—in short, being different from her father and becoming integrated into a new society. Not just things, but knowledge of behaviors, customs, and rules would show her kinship with that world. The assault on her companion Sebastian, the crab, in Eric's palace is a displacement of the dangers for her in a world of which she is ignorant, like the dangers which Shakespeare's Hermia dreams of in the forest.[7]

However, much more in the film (such as the heroine's name itself) shows the writers introducing *The Tempest* vividly into Andersen's tale. In the late romance, although the father figure plans to give away his daughter, he still recalls other Shakespearean blocking parents by erecting temporary obstacles. (Ferdinand is made to do pointless, arbitrarily set tasks to slow the growth of his relationship with Miranda.) The film begins with a scene not found in Andersen but much like the first scene of *The Tempest*: Before the credits, a dark boat makes its way through the sea while its occupants engage in a class-inflected discussion (in Shakespeare, an argument about who should decide proper nautical conduct, since the tempest is already sinking the ship). While the sailors speculate about King Triton, Prince Eric and his counselor Grimsby declare they have never heard of either him or merpeople. They perhaps know what Shakespeare suggests but which did not occur to Andersen: that the storm which will engulf them originates with an anthropomorphic figure; in Shakespeare, the more human Prospero.

Absent from *The Little Mermaid* is Prospero's central antagonist, Caliban, whose behavior focuses the rebelliousness and assaultiveness of others in the play, including Stephano, Trinculo, Antonio, and Sebastian. However, to create Ursula, the film inflates (quite literally) the role of Caliban's mother, the witch Sycorax (who, according to her son, had taken the island for herself and him). Though dying before Prospero's arrival in *The Tempest,* Sycorax in some ways represents his principal antagonist, since both she and he colonized and ruled the island with supposedly opposing kinds of authority. Disney's film transforms this opposition into the central dramatic struggle between good and evil.

Reading Shakespeare within postcolonial theory, famously first done by Francis Barker and Peter Hulme and by Paul Brown, late-1980s academic criticism frequently took Caliban's part to implicate *The Tempest* within imperialist or colonial projects.[8] Within this perspective, the colonized are often seen as feminized. Iconographically female as the Other, Caliban's role actually merges with his mother's and together they become Ursula in *The Little Mermaid.* Shakespeare's presence thus lets the writers use Ursula, like Sycorax and Caliban, to create a colonial subtext. And she is unambiguously, essentially evil, unlike her "son," whose evil is by the same critics seen as culturally constructed, as Shylock claims for himself in *The Merchant of Venice.* Exchanging gender, while traversing the issues of colonialism, identity, and evil is Disney's main strategy for producing cultural reconfigurations.

What's in the name Ariel? Shakespeare's Ariel is a sprite, not unlike the ethereal mermaid of Andersen's version. However, Disney has worked an exchange: As the central character struggling for her independence, the corporate Ariel conflates Miranda and Shakespeare's spirit in her innocence, her announced desire for knowledge, and of course, her position with regard to her father.[9] Implied parallels which Shakespeare makes between Miranda and Caliban multiply in *The Little Mermaid*: Although in some ways an agent of Ariel's father's restrictions, Ursula also becomes a far less innocent version of Ariel's maturing desires and, of course, provides some means to gaining those desires. The first image of Ursula in the movie is of her putting on lipstick, and she wears an enormous amount of eye shadow. When Ariel is frightened about being left voiceless, with thrusting hips the sea witch tells her, "Use your body language."

* * *

Borrowing Miranda, Prospero, and Sycorax from Shakespeare reconfigures

Andersen's story into a romance quest crossed with a war between opposing forces of domination. The triadic configuration of the three central characters, with the help of Shakespearean elements, conflates a colonialist project with a parable illustrating Foucauldian sexual discipline, involving not just Ariel but her absent mother. It also allows the authors to present Ariel's separation and individuation project, like the definitions of good and evil, as essential, rather than the product of culturally shaped patterns.

As Ingwersen and Ingwersen note, Disney substitutes a patriarchal merkingdom for Andersen's matriarchal one, in which the grandmother seems both principal parent and figure of authority. Because it omits the grandmother, the film shows only the negative side of female rule (415). As in many of Shakespeare's comedies and *The Tempest*, a girl comes of age without any woman present to whose cultural or psychological place she can aspire. In fact, as Peter Erickson, Lynda Boose, and many others have shown for Shakespeare's comic heroines, Ariel's rebelliousness gives way to accommodation with a different patriarchal system: In the end, she integrates herself within a society where her husband's role supplants her father's.

However, by dropping the self-sacrifice of Andersen's mermaid and changing the presentation of her beautiful voice, Disney intensifies other tensions within this cultural formula. From Hermia to Viola and Rosalind, perhaps most obviously for Isabella in *Measure for Measure*, entrance into marriage means taming transgressive behaviors or speech—effecting Isabella's silence. However, the key to Disney's ending is that Ariel regains her voice—Eric had been looking for a singing woman all along, and her voice becomes his evidence that she was the one who saved him. Ariel's singing closes the film, joining with the chorus as the credits scroll. Ariel's marriage to Eric may mark her success at removing the parental blocks to her happiness, but the reemergence of her voice marks her triumph over Ursula, who had stolen it.

Joining the new patriarchal order of the human world thus also means subduing all that Ursula represents—winning a sexualized competition in which Ursula/Vanessa's marriage to Eric was only a small part of a larger goal: to emasculate the king and, by taking him, dominate his realm. Disney reads Shakespeare's patriarchal text in effect to focus more on discipline of Ursula than on Ariel's exchange of one system for another. Indeed, the film's imagery suggests that Ariel's successful incorporation into Eric's class-inflected patriarchy can only happen through exploding Ursula's overblown body.

Her body is not only large but connects with a wide range of issues toward which the film takes a strong attitude. Disney's animators invest Ursula's fleshy body with a range of signifiers which have historically been used both to construct women and to identify essential biological facts about them. At her first appearance she wears that heavy makeup. When singing "Poor Unfortunate Souls," she jiggles her breasts and swings her wide hips to underscore her points. She is not just flesh but also a Puritan nightmare of a female sexual body. It is Ursula who tells Ariel in song that men do not like girls who talk—"Men don't like a lot of blabber / They think a girl who gossips is a bore / ...It's she who holds her tongue who gets her man." It seems strange that a powerful woman who talks so much would make such arguments.

And yet not. Ursula is constructed by the quintessential American patriarchal corporation (guarding family values) for an American audience, positioned within a Shakespearean scheme which presents Sycorax/Caliban as a threat to a patriarchal ruler who uses art to manage nature. As Patricia Parker has shown, women have, since biblical times and certainly in Shakespeare, been identified by male writers with "fatness"—with lacking sexual discipline and with inflation, multiplication (cf. her octopus "legs"), and proliferation, including especially the proliferation of texts and words. Ursula's transgressive, sexualized body encompasses all these disorderly traits. As if to underscore that she signifies this cultural set of disruptive images, the film marks her temporary triumph near the end by having her blow herself up to gigantic proportions, with lightning, storm, and fireworks issuing from her. The triumph of Eric and Ariel, created by the same patriarchal corporation, over Ursula, becomes the disciplining of the female "fatness" she represents, very much including the sexual license and expression of female sexual desire toward which she encourages Ariel.[10] Ursula's fatness is thus an enemy not just to Ariel, but to the discipline required for creating standardized patterns of consumption which benefit large corporate bodies.

But even in the final struggle, Ursula shows herself a mother. When two of her eel servants are killed by Eric, she whimpers, "Babies...my poor little poopsies." Indeed, the stylization of her breasts and hips in particular presents her not just as an object of female sexual desire, but of maternity. She imprisons captives in her lair after reducing them to small but large-headed creatures with tiny, thin tails. Their appearance recalls tadpoles, even sperm. Either way, they signify that she is a mother (much more vividly than in Andersen's tale) who wants her "children" regressed.[11] In a pattern Janet Adelman has found repeatedly in Shakespeare's plays, the film thus links a mother's expression of her sexual desire with destructiveness toward her children. The comedy encourages the audience to believe with Hamlet that a mother's blood should be tame, and to expect destructiveness if maternity and sexual desire coexist. The film makes Ariel's triumph over a competitive, sexualized maternal figure the prerequisite to maturity.

Demanding this discipline of adult, female desire also shapes the film's colonial subtext. As in Andersen, the merworld, in general, is presented as a natural paradise, in opposition to the human world of culture. In the film, Eric's ship, by contrast, has a carved, very formal looking *clothed* wooden mermaid on its bow. Sebastian's song "Under the Sea" might remind a Shakespearean of *Henry V* on the greatness of England: The sea world is a place of harmony among many varieties of fish. They can all join together in song: "Each little snail here / Know how to wail here." But as in *Henry V*, or in *The Tempest* for that matter, maintaining a strict hierarchy contributes importantly to this harmony—implied by Sebastian's assertion that "everyone has a nice place," and "can sing his part in the song." Order and hierarchy are celebrated as part of nature.

However, perhaps because of the difference between the commercial cultures of Andersen and Disney, or even just the need for a happy ending, the film is ambivalent about going natural. Triton's opponent, Ursula, with whom he wars for control over this natural paradise, creates both the world of "culture" to which she helps Ariel escape and the darker side of the natural paradise. No one in the natural merworld wears makeup; despite her bloated body, Ursula's affectations recall those of her skinny society sister, Cruella De Vil from *101 Dalmatians*. Yet at the same time, in encouraging Ariel to pursue "love at first sight," despite Triton's Father Capulet-style punishments, Ursula facilitates what postromantic youth culture imagines to be the kind of natural love which opposes parental matchmaking. Even this natural goal is layered with parental culture: Although helping Ariel to leave her father and competing with him like Caliban with Prospero, Ursula presents devastating blocks that actually ally her goals with Triton's. Ursula is thus more an equivocal dark side of both nature and culture than a representation of either one.[12]

The film conquers and eradicates all that she represents: competitions for control of a physical place and or control of human individuals. Particularly through her connection to Caliban and Sycorax, it casts her as the Other against which successful societies position themselves as a means to distracting both individual citizens and competing groups from seeing that their culture contains the demonized elements. The "natural" King Triton with his harmonious state may also be an authoritarian ruler (willing to explode the treasures of an individual opposing him) with a hierarchical force maintaining concord. (Indeed, his master of the revels originally planned to "nail" Ariel and serves as a courtier/spy before reluctantly joining love's cause.) Physical desire is obviously part of Ariel's nature and useful to her in her quest. However, Disney films are notoriously skittish about showing such longings in their heroines; this film pretends Ariel's physical desire is not central to her mission by deconstructing Ursula's designs. (She even becomes Vanessa to usurp Ariel's place.) Prospero finally does admit to having physical necessities: "This thing of darkness I acknowledge mine." The film cannot make a similar admission because it is too committed to disciplining human energies which could disrupt a kind of national identity: a belief in being a harmonious system where everyone—different species of fish in the film, of class, race, and ethnic groups in America—has a voice. At the same time, the film markets a world in which unsettling psychological and behavioral impulses can be disciplined out of existence.

Ariel's family does come to her wedding in the festive ending, which celebrates the union of nature and culture in her marriage to Eric; but they swim away before the credits, as if to suggest an unbridgeable difference between these two realms. (Triton's sadness at losing Ariel suggests he does not expect to see much of her after her wedding.) And nature has in many ways lost: Ariel regains and keeps human legs; she will live in a world where artists carve mermaids in statuary and cooks carve crabs for luncheon parties. Ariel originally sought this world of culture for the freedom and the pleasure she imagined it to have from her very earliest knowledge of it. Was the promise of her learning fulfilled? Ariel's ancestor, Shakespeare's Miranda, is famously innocent of all knowledge and experience other than that given to her by her father—so much so that when she sees Ferdinand for the first time, she does not know what kind of creature he is, since she has not seen males of any species other than her parent and Caliban. With Ariel's innocence, the film courts laughter, much as Shakespeare does with Miranda's. Although Ariel seems much more independent than her progenitor, and has been collecting objects from the human realm, she knows almost nothing of it. Given the number of her treasures, she seems to have been frequenting sea wrecks for some years. Yet she knows as little about them as Miranda does about men: On Scuttle's advice she combs her hair with a fork, thinking it a "dingelhopper" for this purpose, and misuses other things as amusingly. She is not just misusing the items; she is also getting them wrong as signs, wrenching them from their natural functions.

Miranda thinks that Ferdinand might be a spirit when she first sees him; in her "crush," she mistakes the male body for a sign of something transcendent. Ariel's experience with signs is more complicated, partly because her lover is associated with many things when Miranda's is not. Ariel's collected human objects, at the center of which (as in Andersen) stands the Prince's statue, communicate her several longings and the film's many ambivalences. Because the movie is more a coming-of-age romance quest than *The Tempest*, Ariel's things ironically signify her ideal love. Because they represent the object of her desires and his milieu, they also signify the adult heterosexuality and separation which her Shakespearean father briefly crushes. Human made, this garden of things also represents being "part of that world" which she so much desires: They are a sign of culture. Ariel understands little of either love or human communities, sharing the innocence and inexperience of Miranda.

Within this romance, then, art and culture are goals toward which one aspires as long as the artifacts can be separated from the real bodies, with real desires, that created them. Were Ariel to have membership in a mermaid aesthetic movement preaching art for art's sake, her desire for objects might signify a desire for transcendent good in the freedom she wants. However, she isn't looking with what Bourdieu sarcastically calls a "pure gaze" (3). Benjamin's "aura" for her includes the heterosexual longings and "culture" which she wants to live out. Ariel and the film confuse the physical signifiers of transcendent, ideal love with physical things. Themselves possessed and understood, such things would actually help her. They would let her participate in a real community, which the film measures by her success in forming an adult heterosexual attachment.

Marketed to an increasingly multicultural, late-twentieth-century consumer culture, this kind of construction gains socioeconomic resonance. Ariel resembles the people in stories related by Ewen and Ewen, in which images of consumer products have a mystical power for people planning to immigrate to America in the first half of this century (45–47). These images gain their power from the fact that the would-be consumer is innocent of both the real product and its social signification within its original culture. Because of Ariel's innocence, for a long time signs of the human world substitute for experience, leading to the film's suggestion that gaining a sign itself gives one access to a real experience of community. Eric's experience of Ariel mirrors hers of his things: Because she cannot talk, he can only rely on the gestures she makes and his attraction to her physical self. Yet the film suggests that signifying gestures, absent of real communication, can be the basis for transcendent love.

Ariel's desire to leave her natural world for the world of men is thus also a desire to leave a world of communal song for a realm where signifying replaces other forms of communication. Of course, Eric's superhuman heroism and Ariel's own in the face of Ursula's apocalyptic assault provide actions which show that their gestures represent real presence. However, the process which Baudrillard describes—in which everything, including affect and emotions is channeled into signs—explains the film's contradictory ending (*Sign*). Amidst the festivity of Ariel's marriage there is that departure of her merfamily and friends. The film reifies culture over nature. But, as if wanting to have it both ways, the final images feature the francophone cook chasing Sebastian around the barge with a cleaver. This time, the crab and his friends quickly shatter his adversary, suggesting that "natural" talents can always make a comeback. The human, adult culture lacks some of the energy of nature, a theme indicated primarily through Ariel's commitment to its signs. In fact, the wedding's promise is that Ariel and Eric will supplant the vacant dialogue of their courtship with real exchanges they couldn't have when Ursula owned Ariel's voice.

* * *

The voice itself is the circulating sign most central to the plot, and it focuses the film's politics of identity. Its return to Ariel cements the alliance between her and Eric which finally defeats evil. Gaining Ariel's voice was Ursula's first step in enacting her plan to gain control over nature by subduing King Triton. However, in the latter part of the plot, the viewer's focus is on Ursula's use of it for trapping Eric by making him believe that she— "Vanessa"—was the rescuer with the beautiful voice. This floating voice is presented as the principal evidence for Ariel's identity in the realm of culture. It must be a natural part of her: Early in the film she is so distractible that she forgets to participate in an important performance before the king. Because it is hard to imagine her coming regularly to rehearsals, her voice— described by Andersen as the most beautiful in the world—must be an expression of a miraculous natural talent.

All want to manage Ariel's voice in much the same way that they want to control her use of her body. Her father is very proud of her singing, but part of his pride is the thrill of control: When she does not perform for him, he flies into anger. Ursula, of course, uses it for her ends and, save Triton's bargain with her, would keep Ariel in a tadpolelike, dehumanized state, after winning the competition. It thus does not just express, but *is* the essence of Ariel's identity—transcending her "body language," her appearance, or her good actions.

Ursula loses precisely because her disciplined use of this magical treasure briefly lapses; Ariel wins because she submits completely to her cause. Just before Vanessa's stolen wedding to Eric, Ursula declares her triumphant expectations to a mirror and is overheard by Scuttle. Ariel's patience with Eric and their adventures, though, show that she has learned the kind of discipline she lacked when earlier wandering from appointments. (This change seems especially clear to members of the audience who can recall Andersen's tale, in which the mermaid chooses sacrifice by refusing the witch's offer to gain a human soul by killing the prince.) Disney's argument seems to be that people who make disciplined use of an essential self will triumph.

Body language, appearance, and good actions—as in Ariel—express this self but cannot be the cause of success.

The film thus enacts its commitment to Puritanical ideologies of the body by presenting the physical self as a dispensable sign and by its emphasis on discipline both material and intellectual. This Puritanical feel is not contradicted by the film's much noted indulgence in material rewards, epitomized by Ariel's grand wedding and the products she spawns. Indeed, within Protestant ideology, election brings reward. The film offers an experience of things to its audience, and thus to the buyers of "spin-offs," within its forceful portrayal of good and evil as recognizable entities knowable in any experience or set of ideas. For example, Disney has hardened the story of Ariel's maturation, of her self-preparation for heterosexual marriage, into a process more strict than in Shakespeare. Instead of the many choices permitting the playful experiments of Shakespeare's comic heroines, one representative of Ariel's options is presented as entirely evil and the other as entirely good. Using the formula of heroic romance, in which a hero overcomes obstacles preventing maturation, hardens the fluid representations of sexuality in Shakespeare's plays, and particularly the culturally constructed feel of good and evil in *The Tempest*, into fixed, mythic natures: This "essentiality" makes the competing positions seem immutably opposed, and thus makes the story of female maturation appear universal. As Baudrillard suggests, ideology can reduce symbolic material into a form which, more than most, provides the appearance of transcendence (*Sign* 144–45).

When plots focus on women, they tend to investigate "personal life," in part because women have been seen as guardians of issues related to the private sphere (Williamson 106). In encouraging the repression of maternal bodies, *The Little Mermaid* struggles to order some of the most private elements of experience into a form conducive to standardization. *The Little Mermaid* circulates sexuality to manage it by borrowing two plot structures from Shakespeare—one concerned with controlling female bodies, the other with geopolitical competition and dominance. As a result, its Puritan instincts merge with its participation in a capitalist standardization of products and consumers. Instead of referring to biological multiplication, seen as disruptive, disorderly in its unpurified form, Disney's female body refers to multiplying things.

Turning to Shakespeare to effect such functions is inevitable. The high mimetic dynamics of this film, *The Lion King*, and perhaps *Beauty and the Beast* result in Disney movies expressing cultural ideologies in a manner analogous to that of Renaissance drama within its own milieu. Yet more historically specific mechanisms are also at work. It is not surprising that in the same years—the Reagan/Bush eighties—during which Shakespeareans found good figures in *The Tempest* increasingly suspect, Disney produced a film celebrating their sunniness. Using Shakespeare to reify its narrative, a Shakespearean *Little Mermaid* participates in a larger cultural project to reclaim Shakespearean themes—even Shakespeare himself—for the conservative structure of the marketplace.

Indeed, *The Little Mermaid* appeared within a marketplace also presenting many Shakespeare films which carefully manage the sliding line between high and low culture to gain a heterogeneous audience. If, as Raymond Williams suggests, the film industry mediates between sectors of culture and the economy (408–9), *The Little Mermaid* is a prime example of economic shifts shaping the definition and reception of "culture." Lawrence Levine points out that what is elite and what is popular are always being redefined (230). During periods of socioeconomic shift, renegotiations of distinctions between haut-bourgeois and elite culture occur as different groups try to claim their own distinction. One effect of this process is to further reify the signs of what have always constituted cultural, educational, and academic capital. Demand for the products bearing these signs increases. This process is apparent, for example, in the explosive growth of American opera audiences during the last two decades, or the popularity of Shakespeare and Austen on film. However, as new groups gain wealth, influence, and thus an increasing share of the consumer dollar, another effect of America's two-decade-long redistribution of wealth is to raise what used to be ignored and reduce the prestige of once iconographic figures. Disney's use of Shakespeare testifies both to the current perception of Shakespeare as an icon for value and to the Shakespeare industry's increasing need to compete with other media producers. Disney, like Branagh and others, does not so much contain and colonize its audience as help it to authorize itself with systems of value. *The Little Mermaid* interprets Shakespeare, and *The Tempest* authorizes Disney. Each authorial institution shapes the other's place in defining the intertwined psychological, cultural, and political identities of its consumers.

Notes

1. Here I am employing Baudrillard's notion that an object/advertising system substitutes an idea of relationships for experience so that even effect and emotions become signs. Andersen's tale wonderfully illustrates this theory. The Christian aspirations of Andersen's

mermaid for immortality, through alliance with a world which does not admit her, reflects Andersen's own participation in nineteenth-century Danish society. Andersen har-
nesses both his experience and effect within spiritual symbols of his own invention, such
as sea foam. See Baudrillard, "The System of Objects," 24; Zipes 7, 71–94. Disney uses
many of Andersen's constructions to create its own signs to gain market penetration.

2. Dunn; see also McManaway; for an example see Quincy Adams.

3. These are the issues critics now find central to the play. For a thorough review and critique, see Skura.

4. See, for example, Bendix, and debates in the popular press. Bendix provides a useful if
partial review of press attitudes toward the film.

5. As in Shakespeare's comedies, such as *A Midsummer Night's Dream*, the blocking figure
is the father. However, as Soracco notes for Andersen's version, the Sea Witch may double the absent mother and allow the story to explore issues related to maternal desire to
keep a daughter close. Hence, though antagonists, Ursula and Triton are related blocks to
Ariel's desires, and in some ways Ursula enacts Triton's desire to limit Ariel's development (408–9).

6. Although I regularly refer to "Disney" as a corporate writer throughout this essay, the
actual script credits go to John Musker and Ron Clements. I prefer reference to a corporate author, though, because of the dozens of people involved in all areas of production
and the processes of revision and marketing which greatly diminish the role of the "author" in films generally, particularly in one such as this.

7. Given Grimsby's interest in having Eric marry well, it is surprising that he is so polite to
Ariel at her first dinner (even after she blows pipe ash in his face) until the film juxtaposes this interaction with Sebastian being chased by the cook with the meat cleaver.

8. See also Halpern, Wilkes.

9. In fact, the film is exploiting the many parallels Shakespeare's play presents between
members of Prospero's "family": Miranda, Ariel, even the arguably naive Caliban are all
to some extent unlearned, "natural," and struggling for their freedom.

10. Interestingly, as she rises from the sea, her fluid body has become rigidified, and one
cylinder arises—which turns out to be a prong from Triton's stolen crown. If one reads
this phallic rendering of Ursula's stolen power as a sign that she has transgressed the
iconographic boundaries of her gender, one sees Disney suggesting that when "female"
qualities triumph, they transmute themselves into a tyrannous version of positive patriarchy.

11. Laura Sells understands the embedding of Ursula within gynophobic imagery of a smothering mother more related to the sanitization of Ariel's loss of power than to regression;
she argues that Ariel must trade her connection to female symbols in order to join the patriarchy (181).

12. Sells suggests that Ursula is relegated to the position of the repressed, which keeps a system functioning. The film actually pretends she can be eradicated (181).

Works Cited

Adelman, Janet. *Smothering Mothers in Shakespeare's Plays*. New York: Routledge, 1992.
Adorno, Theodor. *Prisms*. Cambridge: MIT P, 1981.
Andersen, Hans Christian. *The Diaries of Hans Christian Andersen*. Ed. Patricia L. Conroy
and Sven H. Rossel. Seattle: U Washington, 1990.

Barker, Francis, and Peter Hulme. "Nymphs and Reapers Heavily Vanish: The Discursive Contexts of *The Tempest.*" *Alternative Shakespeares.* Ed. John Drakakis. London: Methuen, 1985. 191–205.

Baudrillard, Jean. "The System of Objects." *Selected Writings.* Ed. Mark Poster. Stanford: Stanford UP, 1988. 10–28.

———. *For a Critique of the Political Economy of the Sign.* Trans. Charles Levin. St. Louis: Telos P, 1981.

Bendix, Regina. "Seashell Bra and Happy End: Disney's Transformations of 'The Little Mermaid.'" *Fabula* 34 (1993): 280–90.

Benjamin, Walter. "The Work of Art in the Age of Mechanical Reproduction." *lluminations.* New York: Schocken Books, 1969.

Bogart, Leo. *Commercial Culture: The Media System and the Public Interest.* New York: Oxford UP, 1995.

Boose, Lynda. "The Father and the Bride in Shakespeare." *PMLA* 97 (1982): 325–47.

Bourdieu, Pierre. *Distinction: A Social Critique of the Judgement of Taste.* Cambridge: Harvard UP, 1984.

Bristol, Michael. *Shakespeare's America, America's Shakespeare.* London: Routledge, 1990.

Brown, Paul. "This Thing of Darkness I Acknowledge Mine: *The Tempest* and the Discourse of Colonialism." *Political Shakespeare: New Essays in Cultural Materialism.* Eds. Jonathan Dollimore and Alan Sinfield. Manchester: Manchester UP, 1985, 48–71.

Brown, Stephen. "The Uses of Shakespeare in America: A Study in Class Domination." 1939. *Shakespeare, Pattern of Excelling Nature.* Eds. David Bevington and Jay Halio. Newark: U of Delaware P, 1978.

Dunn, Esther Cloudman. *Shakespeare in America.* 1939. New York: Benjamin Bloom, 1968.

Erickson, Peter. *Patriarchal Structures in Shakespeare's Drama.* Berkeley and Los Angeles: U of California P, 1985.

Ewen, Stuart, and Elizabeth Ewen. *Channels of Desire: Mass Images and the Shaping of American Consciousness.* Minneapolis: U of Minnesota P, 1992.

Frye, Northrop. "The Argument of Comedy." *English Institute Essays, 1948, 1949.* New York: Columbia UP, 1949. 58–73.

Halpern, Richard. "'The Picture of Nobody': White Cannibalism in *The Tempest.*" *The Production of English Renaissance Culture.* Eds. David Lee Miller, Sharon O'Dair, and Harold Weber. Ithaca: Cornell UP, 1994. 262–92.

Ingwersen, Niels, and Faith Ingwersen. "Splash! Six Views of 'The Little Mermaid'—A Folktale Approach." *Scandinavian Studies* 62 (1990): 412–15.

Kofoed, Niels. "Hans Christian Andersen and the European Literary Tradition." *Hans Christian Andersen: Danish Writer and Citizen of the World.* Ed. Sven Hakon Rossel. Amsterdam: Rodopi, 1996. 209–56.

Levine, Lawrence. "William Shakespeare and the American People: A Study in Cultural Transformation." *Rethinking Popular Culture: Contemporary Perspectives in Cultural Studies.* Eds. Chandra Mukerji and Michael Schudson. Berkeley and Los Angeles: U of California P, 1991.

The Little Mermaid. Dirs. Ron Clements, John Musker. Animated. Voices: Jodi Benson, Christopher Daniel Barnes, Pat Carroll. The Walt Disney Company, 1989.

McEachern, Claire. *The Poetics of English Nationhood, 1590–1612.* Cambridge UP, 1996.

McManaway, James. "Shakespeare in the United States." *PMLA* 79 (1964): 511–18.

Mukerji, Chandra, and Michael Schudson, eds. *Rethinking Popular Culture: Contemporary Perspectives in Cultural Studies.* Berkeley and Los Angeles: U of California P, 1991.

Parker, Patricia. *Literary Fat Ladies: Rhetoric, Gender, Property.* New York: Methuen, 1987.

Quincy Adams, Joseph. "The Folger Shakespeare Memorial Dedicated: April 21, 1932: Shakespeare and American Culture." *Spinning Wheel* 12 (1932): 212–31.

Sells, Laura. "Where Do the Mermaids Stand? Voice and Body in *The Little Mermaid.*" *From Mouse to Mermaid: The Politics of Film, Gender, and Culture.* Eds. Elizabeth Bell, Lynda Haas, and Laura Sells. Bloomington: Indiana UP, 1995. 175–92.

Sinfield, Alan. *Cultural Materialism and the Politics of Dissident Reading.* Berkeley and Los Angeles: U of California P, 1992.

Skura, Meredith. "The Case of Colonialism in *The Tempest.*" *Shakespeare Quarterly* 40 (1989): 42–69.

Soracco, Sabrina L. "Splash! Six Views of 'The Little Mermaid'—A Psychoanalytic Approach." *Scandinavian Studies* 62 (1990): 408–12.

Wilkes, G. A. "*The Tempest* and the Discourse of Colonialism." *Sidney Studies in English* 21 (1996): 42–55.

Williams, Raymond. "Base and Superstructure in Marxist Cultural Theory." Mukerji and Schudson 407–23.

Williamson, Judith. "Woman Is an Island: Feminism and Colonization." *Studies in Entertainment.* Ed. Tania Modleski. Bloomington: Indiana UP, 1986. 99–118.

Zipes, Jack. *Fairy Tales and the Art of Subversion: The Classical Genre for Children and the Process of Civilization.* New York: Methuen, 1988.

CHAPTER 11

Mulan Disney, It's Like, Re-Orients: Consuming China and Animating Teen Dreams

Sheng-mei Ma

As Chinese legends have it, Mu Lan's family name is Hua, or, in Maxine Hong Kingston's Cantonese version, Fa. Inspired most likely by Kingston's *The Woman Warrior* (1976), the 1998 Disney animation *Mulan* calls the protagonist Fa as well. But in the film, she largely goes by her first name, while called Ping during her cross-dressing disguise. The rendering of her given name, Mulan, in the pinyin system, thus ridding it of the more defamiliarizing space and capitalization, makes possible easy identification between the young audience and the protagonist with an English-sounding name. Lest I be found a carping critic on the point of Mulan's spelling, one must realize that Mulan, along with the dragon-lizard Mushu, are in fact exceptions to the rule of Chinese-sounding names. They are outnumbered, based on Disney's accompanying children's book, by Fa Zhou, her father; Fa Li, her mother; Shan-Yu, the Hun chieftain; Chien-Po, the bald giant; Cri-Kee, her familiar; and others. The splitting of the word "cricket" to create the monosyllabic "Cri-Kee" demonstrates the Orientalist context, within which Mulan's more English-sounding name appears. Indeed, the overwhelming majority of characters have names which are at once exotic and familiar—the precise Orientalist formula of projecting the self's deepest longings onto the Other, a magic mirror dwarfing and caricaturing none other than the self taken to be someone else. The yoking of strangeness and banality in Orientalist representations succeeds in accommodating and domesticating the unknown. Hence, Mulan's steed is Khan, after Genghis Khan. Her companion, the dragon-lizard, is Mushu, after Mooshu Pork. Her masculine disguise is called Ping, after an imperial court mandarin in Puccini's *Turandot* (1926).

Mulan's hidden last name, however, is Disney. Mulan Disney now joins the lineage of animated female characters, all of them with suppressed surnames—Snow White, Cinderella, Sleeping Beauty, Jasmine in *Aladdin*, Pocahontas, Belle the Beauty, and others. Although endowed with various cultural and national identities, they are all, by blood, children of Disney. Reflecting the desires of the multicultural, Gen-X (-Z?) audience in the United States these characters are composites based on images, stereotypes, and fantasies of the Other. With respect to images of Asians in the 1990s productions, they are no longer blatantly racist, like the sly, bucktoothed, cross- and slit-eyed, and pidgin-speaking Siamese cats in *Lady and the Tramp* (1955) and in *The Aristocats* (1970).[1] Having said that, one hastens to add that Mulan and her nineties siblings, born out of multiculturalism, serve to manage, within the United States and elsewhere, the drastically changing demographics and the concomitant conflicts of cultures; the Disney bunch not only entertains but brings into conformity with the adolescent American sensibility an alienating and occasionally hostile world. Just as the global village is becoming increasingly complex daily, Disney offers simplistic visions of the exotic Other—China—to allay the audience's fear. Bent upon "re-orienting," pun intended, rather than "dis-orienting," Mulan draws from Orientalist fantasies of yore, notwithstanding the inflections of contemporary youth culture. The waves of laughter during a screening of Mulan are perhaps expressions of children's innocence, cheering them up before the long journey into William Blake's experience.

The dish Mooshu Pork brings into being the character Mushu, with unmistakable association with Chinese cuisine. Mushu's concluding line of the film is "Call out for eggrolls!" for the dancing party of Fa Mulan's ancestors in celebration of her triumphant return. Whether Chinese take-out, appetizer, or entree, the fetish of Chinese food has so interpellated the Western consciousness that Disney never bothers to capitalize on Mushu's origin, as it were, until the last line of the film. However, Mooshu Pork is a corruption from the standard yet nearly unpronounceable spelling of, in Wade-Giles, *mu hsu*, or, in pinyin, *muxu*. Moreover, the second vowel in Mooshu should be "ü." Clearly a long-standing compromise with English-speaking customers, the entree has always been listed on the menu as Mooshu Pork. After all, one is not likely to order a dish he or she cannot vocalize. The seeming chaos of an Orientalist culinary universe to many Westerners must be commanded linguistically ("Let there be—Mooshu!") before it can be consumed.

Consuming China

In *Mulan*, the sensory consumption of China is predicated on the abundance of iconography of the Orient, which can be divided into three categories: animate icons, inanimate icons, and human relationships. Animate icons in Mulan consist of animals and insects, of which the Magic Kingdom boasts a long tradition. The protagonists of *Mulan* are almost always accompanied by nonhuman familiars, such as Mulan's puppy, the black horse Khan, the dragon-lizard Mushu, and the cricket. Although playing second fiddle to Mulan, these familiars are instrumental in moving the plot, in generating fun, and in Orientalizing this Disney product for consumption.

The Voice of the demoted and diminutive dragon-lizard Mushu is dubbed by the actor Eddie Murphy, whose jokes stem largely from streetwise black lingo. Mushu's lines gush out with dizzying speed, one which befits the MTV pace of the film and the short attention span of a young audience. When subjected to prolonged contemplation, however, Murphy's performance reveals its schizophrenic nature. Murphy has always been a chameleon of a comic, changing himself into a host of black characters with entirely different physical and speech traits. Makeup artists worked wonders on Murphy in *Coming to America* (1988), where he triples as a barber, a singer, and an elderly Jewish man (the only role transgressing racial lines, with a stereotypical Jewish nose and a strong East European accent), in addition to an African prince. Murphy once again doubles as an obese scientist and a playboy in *The Nutty Professor* (1996). Responding to blackface performances from Al Jolson's to Gene Wilder's in *Silver Streak* (1976), the talented Murphy pays back in kind. Whereas previously having strived to impersonate another race (the Jewish man), Murphy-Mushu is unadulteratedly "black." Whereas the Jewish Murphy impresses through how thoroughly he sheds his blackness, the Chinese Murphy wears race like the emperor's new clothes, unabashedly exposing an ebony self. Perhaps Murphy has no choice: The Jewish man speaks with a heavy accent, but not one which crosses into racist caricature; however, it would be inexcusable had he adopted the singsong Chinese pidgin for Mushu's dialogues.

It is tempting to attribute the difference of Murphy's Jewish and Chinese personae to the diverging demands of live-action films and animations. Realism has come to dictate Hollywood dramas. Hence, to perform a particular race, one has to be like that race, or at least take on the outer trappings and stereotypical images of that race. Any mismatch between physical traits and dialogues defeats the realistic facade. Animations are make-believe, supposedly free from the bondage of the real and the factual. Dubbing for animations, furthermore, entails the paradox of a voice *divorced from* the body and yet *belonging to* the body. Although filmically the audience do not see Murphy, they know it is him, particularly when Disney's advertising campaigns never fail to include the Hollywood stars lending their voices to its animations.

The difference between live-action dramas and animations aside, the alarming fact remains, however, that Murphy expends no effort to acquire any semblance of Chinese-ness, whatever that means linguistically. Supposedly performing in yellowface, there is simply no pretense as to his blackness. One of the multicultural plo(a)ys of the 1990s Disney productions, Mushu juxtaposes irreconcilable ethnic elements of Orientalist appearance and black English, as if racial differences could be resolved accordingly. The other extreme of Disney's dubbing practices is the racial essentialism in having prominent Asian American performers do Chinese characters: Ming-na Wen for Mulan, B. D. Wong for Shang, and Pat Morita for the Chinese emperor. Disney's facile approach to multiculturalism is a wish-fulfillment, deriving from and hence validating racial stereotypes. The transparency of race inherent in Murphy's inner-city black dialect bespeaks the relative powerlessness of the Asian American constituency; Disney takes this calculated risk of offending a particular minority for the potential profit it may garner from the majority and other minority groups.

In terms of Orientalist appearance, Mushu is the caricature of a dragon, the trite trope for China, equipped with long strands of goatees. Almost all the major characters, it goes without saying, sport "proper" Orientalist markers—slant eyes, round moon faces, long straight hair, and goatees for males. In addition to her steed Khan and her dragon guardian Mushu, a cricket accompanies Mulan as well. Notwithstanding the precursor of Jiminy Cricket in *Pinocchio* (1940), the choice to adopt a cricket in the cast accentuates the limited repertoire of Orientalism, resorted to by Westerners whenever the need to represent China arises. Bertolucci in *The Last Emperor* (1988), the first film ever made by a Westerner inside China after the Cultural Revolution, features a grandiose scene at the Forbidden City where Pu Yi—the last emperor of the Ching dynasty—is inaugurated. Amidst hundreds of kowtowing officials, the young emperor is hooked by the sound of a cricket and eventually discovers its whereabouts. After a lifetime of impotence, corruption, and suffering, the gardener Pu Yi in the People's Republic of China returns at the end of the film to visit the Forbidden City, where he retrieves, miraculously, the cricket cage hidden behind the throne. While allegedly making a historical film of epic proportion, Bertolucci sees fit to integrate magical touches via a cricket to highlight Pu Yi's childlike innocence. The Chinese American novelist Amy Tan, likewise, introduces a grasshopper alongside Kwan in *The Hundred Secret Senses* (1995). The cricket in Mulan is made to symbolize good luck, and much amusement stems from how Cri-Kee fails its task.

The iconography of China includes as well props or inanimate icons. The film opens with the Great Wall and ends with the Forbidden City.[2] In between the well-known historic sites, tired Orientalist objects are repeatedly deployed: the dragon flag which Shan-Yu burns on the Great Wall, the dragon statue in Mulan's family garden, the dragon wallcovering in the emperor's palace, the dragon cannons which annihilate Shan-Yu's army, the dragon dance concealing Shan-Yu's henchmen, the dragon pendant bestowed upon Mulan by the emperor. Besides dragons, plum blossoms decorate a classical Chinese garden where a traditional scene of filial piety between Mulan and her disabled father unfolds. No films on ancient China are complete without some kung fu sequence. As such, the commander Shang, later Mulan's intended, trains the new recruits in martial arts. The final showdown between Mulan and Shan-Yu takes place on the grounds of the Forbidden City, embellished with traditional Chinese lanterns and fireworks. Other seemingly authentic details of China abound, such as Mulan's hair comb, chopsticks, and ink brush. Mulan eats with chopsticks, but no Chinese would be so ill mannered as to thrust the chopsticks upright on the rice bowl. No rice bowls, for that matter, would pile up like a mound. She writes with a brush, but her calligraphy winds up on her wrist.

Finally, human relationships are constructed in accordance with clichéd notions of the East. Mulan attempts to bring "honor" to her family by attending the bride selection, which proceeds, incidentally, with monotonal music and monosyllabic lyric. Another manifestation of the constricted repertoire of Orientalism, Disney's foregrounding of "honor" harks back to Puccini's *Madame Butterfly*, where the Japanese geisha commits ritual suicide upon discovering her shame and dishonor. Similar to Amy Tan's rehashing of the trope of grasshopper in *The Hundred Secret Senses*, David Henry Hwang in his self-styled "deconstructivist" *M. Butterfly* (1988) borrows as his recurring motif Puccini's line "Death with honor / Is better than life / Life with dishonor" (15). Both of Chinese extraction, Tan and Hwang are so deeply immersed in Western culture that their respective attempts to subvert Western hegemony end up perpetuating that hegemony.[3]

Failing to "honor" her family through marriage, Mulan subsequently embodies "filial piety" in substituting for her ailing father in battle. Disney, however, overdoes the Orientalized social customs in presenting an exposed Mulan on the verge of being beheaded. As the military consul makes clear, tradition decrees capital punishment for the offense of cross-dressing. Neither the folk legend of Hua Mu Lan nor the extant "The Ballad of Mulan," written anonymously during the sixth century A.D., depicts this crisis. If anything, "The Ballad of Mulan" offers an almost uneventful transformation from her male disguise back to femininity. "Just lend me a fleet-footed camel / To send me back to my village," requests Mulan of the emperor. "When my parents heard I was coming, / They helped each other to the edge of town" (Liu and Lo 79). What is missing in the translation is the gender-specific references, namely, "send me back to my village" should be "send boy [son] back," while "When my parents heard I was coming" should be "When my parents heard girl [daughter] was coming." The awkward literal renditions hope to bring out the gender switch as Mulan moves from her public role in the presence of the emperor to her private self in the family. The social context entails a gender switch.

Disney, on the other hand, is more concerned with creating suspense to hold the audience's attention. It is surely a boost to the dramatic tension when Mulan is saved only by Shang's love and hence his countermanding of the so-called tradition, but the sword lifted above Mulan's neck nevertheless sharpens the perception of a misogynist Orient, where, in Maxine Hong Kingston's memorable words, girls are "maggots" and "worse than geese." Other than the sexist mores, another site where taken-for-granted Chinese rituals emerge is the family shrine or temple in the garden. Fa Zhou is seen there performing ancestral worship. In the wake of Mulan's disguise, transparent spirits of ancestors hold council as to how to prevent Mulan from "dishonoring" the family. After Mulan's feat of rescuing the emperor and killing Shan-Yu, the ancestors at the temple, signaled by Mushu's "Call out for eggrolls!", burst into rap music and dance, the background for closing credits. In the same vein of the multicultural violence of handcuffing yellow-face with black English, Disney fills the old bottle of Orientalist images with the not-so-new teen dreams.

Animating Teen Dreams

Billed as family entertainment, Disney's animations appeal to all age groups. Children are, of course, the main consumers of Disney products. In the case of *Mulan*, months prior to its release in movie theaters in the summer of 1998, an entire array of products—toys, stuffed animals, clothes, backpacks, paper cups, paper napkins, and so forth—flooded the market, culminating in the animation itself. While the cartoon may be the centerpiece, it is but one of Disney's marketing strategies capitalizing on the image of an Oriental girl stamped on every product. For children to acquire a piece of this Orientalist fantasy, adults must be persuaded to purchase them, a transaction of money and commodity, of desire and symbol, which implicates both children and adults. Moreover, it is unlikely that children would frequent movie theaters without parental escort. Even when the videocassette of a Disney animation is played, at times to babysit children, adults may steal a glance or two at the TV screen.

Beyond practical considerations of commodity consumption, the magic of the Magic Kingdom lies squarely in fantasies of teenage years, fantasies shared by children and adults alike. Although viewed culturally as a transitional period when much unease and self-doubt are felt, adolescence remains the ideal age, glamorized in the slim, anorexic bodies of fashion models, fetishized in the coolness of a Leonardo DiCaprio on the silver screen. Each generation of moviegoers, of course, hails its own DiCaprio, celluloid teen idols whose great-grandfather is James Dean. Freud's "Creative Writers and Day-Dreaming" helps to illuminate the fascination with teens. As a child grows, Freud maintains, "he stops playing, gives up nothing but the link with real objects; instead of *playing*, he now *phantasises* [sic]." Freud proceeds to dissect the difference between children's play and adults' fancy:

> A child's play is determined by...the wish to be big and grown up.... On the one hand, he [the adult] knows that he is expected not to go on playing or phantasising any longer, but to act in the real world; on the other hand, some of the wishes which give rise to his phantasies are of a kind which it is essential to conceal. Thus he is ashamed of his phantasies as being childish and as being unpermissible. (438)

Part of the "unpermissible" fancies of transgression lie in Disney's (for lack of a better term) "anti-family" undercurrents, despite its self-promotion as family entertainment with family values. Nearly all Disney characters are from broken families: Mulan has a crippled father and has to substitute for him in battle; Pocahontas, Ariel the mermaid, Jasmine, and Belle grow up without mothers; Simba's father is stampeded to death; Snow White and Sleeping Beauty endure cruel stepmothers; Bambi, the gypsy Esmeralda in *The Hunchback of Notre Dame* (1996), and Tarzan (1999) are orphans. Such widespread absence of parents can be interpreted both as children's and as adults' desire for autonomy. In either case, family members sitting next to oneself have to be extinguished, at least temporarily, clandestinely in the dark isolation of a theater. It is tempting to decipher this recurring motif of bereavement as highlighting the importance of family via its absence, but Disney's happy endings never involve the formation of new families by protagonists. Characters are formulaically teenagers engaged in premarital romance—no family, no children, no responsibility. Whenever characters unite after great travail, the animation ends and they never become married couples. A marriage would mean not only family obligation but a cessation of the youthful adventures outside of parental supervision just experienced by audiences of all ages.

As a result, Disney's target audience, children, openly dream of growing up into teenagers; the adults secretly dream of regressing into teenagers. The former group wishes to empower itself by romanticizing teens, such as Wendy and her brothers taking flight with Peter Pan; the latter wishes to shirk responsibility and a lifetime of disenchantment through a nostalgic look backward, as does Wendy's father reminiscing about his winged days at the conclusion of *Peter Pan* (1953). From either point of view adolescence is seen as a time of looking cool, of experiencing adventures away from home, and of finding self-identity. Disney's decision to highlight the trio of teen dreams in Mulan is unequivocally exposed when contextualized with the animation's unacknowleged source of inspiration, Kingston, as well as with Kingston's unacknowledged source of inspiration, "The Ballad of Mulan."

The look is paramount to adolescents. Almost all of the Disney animations feature handsome teenage protagonists, who talk and move like typical American youth. Consider, at the outset, the hair fetish. Belle in *Beauty and the Beast* (1991) constantly runs her finger through the lock of hair curled around her forehead. Even the young lion Simba in *The Lion King* (1994) has bangs fallen over his eyes à la DiCaprio or Brad Pitt. Although John Smith dubbed by Mel Gibson in *Pocahontas* (1995) appears to be more mature, his bangs boast two swirls which could be stabilized only by generous applications of hair gel. Then there is Tarzan, with boyish hair in his eyes and with his flying through the jungle as if he were rollerblading (as indeed the Tarzans do at Disney's Animal Kingdom). The hair fetish in *Mulan* is elevated from a symbol of gorgeous looks to one of gender, the pivotal motif in this story of cross-dressing.

When Mulan decides to substitute for her father, she cuts her hair with the masculine symbol of a sword, leaving in place of the conscription scroll her hair comb, a gift from her mother. During her disguise as the recruit Ping, her hair is tied in a bun like all other Chinese male characters. (By contrast, the "barbarian" invaders of Shan-Yu and his henchmen have long untied hair.)[4] The only moments when her hair is loosened are when her identity is at risk of being revealed. As she disrobes and unties her hair to bathe in the pond, her colleagues suddenly join her. After the battle, an injured Mulan is naked in bed with hair soon to be loosened, at which time her masquerade comes to an abrupt end. In subsequent scenes, Mulan sports loosened hair, for she has been uncovered. In order to bait Shan-Yu and save Shang, who has fainted, Mulan pulls back her hair to reveal her former self.

Mulan's alter ego, the girl doll, likewise has long hair waving in the wind. Upon the snowy grave of Shang's father, against the sword and helmet which serve as the tombstone, Mulan leaves the doll. The proximity of the masculine sword and the feminine long hair foreshadows Mulan's imminent danger in battles against Shan-Yu and against Chinese patriarchy. Also with this ritual to commemorate the dead, both Shang and Mulan are cut loose from their past, growing into "manhood"—a general and a male soldier. While prominently displayed in a number of scenes, the doll is largely forgotten in the bulk of the animation. Structurally, the doll resembles a Freudian slip, a revealing yet somewhat awkward detail. It materializes out of, literally, thin air, as Shan-Yu's falcon returns from a reconnaissance and drops it into the chieftain's hand. Just as it reappears beside the grave, the doll is destined to be buried in the snowstorm.

Always looking cool, Disney protagonists like Mulan experience adventures to satisfy a shared human longing, adventures found outside of parental guidance and outside of home. A G–rated film turns out to smuggle in, subconsciously, a message about the cessation of family. The dearth of reflection on the part of Disney's family-oriented consumers over this and many other blatantly contradictory issues was predicted in 1944 by Horkheimer and Adorno in *Dialectic of Enlightenment*:

> Real life is becoming indistinguishable from the movies. The sound films...[leave] no room for imagination or reflection on the part of the audience, who are unable to respond within the structure of the film, yet deviate from its precise detail without losing the thread of the story; hence the film forces its victims to equate it directly with reality....[The sound films] are so designed that quickness, powers of observation, and experience are undeniably needed to apprehend them at all; yet sustained thought is out of the question if the spectator is not to miss the relentless rush of facts. (126–27)

Given this bleak vision of what Horkheimer and Adorno call "the culture industry" epitomized by movies, one way to escape from the tyranny of filmic images lies in slowing down the "rush," in lengthening each moment by means of a historicist juxtaposition with earlier texts. History or time then derails the breathless presentness of Disney animations. For instance, the contemporariness of Mulan—its appeal to teen dreams of the nineties— becomes readily apparent when one contrasts *Mulan* with Kingston's *The Woman Warrior* and with "The Ballad of Mulan." A key moment of *Mulan* occurs as Mulan transforms herself into a male soldier. Animation at its best, this sequence with no dialogue develops visually through fast-paced action of Mulan cutting her hair and stealing away, punctuated by the exciting soundtrack. This sequence is preceded by a defiant Mulan storming away from the family dinner table and, subsequently, curling up beneath the dragon statue, soaking wet. Upon reaching a decision, Mulan walks barefoot into the family shrine to undergo her conversion. Although set in an exotic locale, each episode closely mirrors the routine behavior of rebellious teenagers—slouching and pouting by oneself, tiptoeing to sneak off. In addition, the sequence is achieved by means of MTV techniques, such as "quick cuts" and "funky camera angles" (Owen 5), the latter most apparent in the tracking shot of nothing but Mulan's bare feet walking into the family temple.

However, this "running away" sequence radically deviates from the Chinese poem "The Ballad of Mulan" as well as from Kingston. "The Ballad" depicts Mulan's substitution as a family decision rather than a solo performance. The poem opens with a distraught Mulan at the spinning wheel, responding to the question of the cause of her sadness thusly:

> "Last night I saw the draft list—
> The Khan's mustering a great army;
> The armies' rosters ran many rolls,
> Roll after roll held my father's name!
> And Father has no grown-up son,
> And I've no elder brother!
> So I offered to buy a saddle and horse
> And campaign from now on for Father."
>
> In the eastern market she bought a steed,
> At the western a saddle and cloth;
> In the southern market she bought a bridle,
> At the northern a long whip;
> At sunrise she bade her parents farewell,
> At sunset she camped by the Yellow River;
> She couldn't hear her parents calling her,
> She heard only the Yellow River's flow surge and splash. (Liu and Lo 78)

Mulan volunteers "to buy a saddle and horse / And campaign from now on for Father" in answer to an unknown interlocutor. Although one is at liberty to interpret the quotation marks surrounding the first stanza above as indications of Mulan's interior monologue, the second stanza intensifies the sense of social interaction due to an exchange of ideas. The purchase of a horse and other equipment befitting a recruit is most likely engaged in by the family as a whole, considering how paltry a young unmarried woman's private funds must have been, if any, in the sixth century A.D. Mulan then bids farewell to her parents, and her thoughts return to them twice in the repetition of "She couldn't hear her parents calling her." The line "At sunrise she bade her parents farewell" is somehow mistranslated by Arthur Waley as "In the morning she stole from her father's and mother's house" (113). The original Chinese reads *tsao tz'u yeh niang chu*, literally translated as "morning—bid farewell—father—mother—leave." The key word is *tz'u*, "bid farewell," which indicates that Mulan does not furtively run away from home. Unless Waley bases his rendition on an entirely different version of "The Ballad," it is inconceivable that such a renowned sinologist would have missed so badly.

Waley furnishes the only support Disney could possibly marshal to justify its presentation of a Mulan leaving surreptitiously in the wee hours of the morning, which presupposes that Disney is even aware of the existence of this ballad. Moreover, Mulan Disney reveals her true pedigree by devoting herself, like most of her animated siblings, to a series of carefree adventures, totally blocking out her worried parents. Mulan Disney has, in a manner of speaking, turned her back on the very meaning of the tale of Mulan in China. The Mu Lan legend has long been regarded as one of the many deeds of filial piety. For instance, the illustrated *Hundred Tales of Filial Piety* by Chang Tse-tung of the Ching dynasty features a Mu Lan surnamed Wei instead of Hua. These acts of *hsiao*, or filial piety, promoted by Chang and others tend to be masochistic sacrifices, such as defrosting a hole on a frozen river with one's bare torso in order to catch a fish for the stepmother, or feeding mosquitoes with one's naked body so that the parents can sleep undisturbed. The former hero eventually becomes a high-ranking government official, the latter a Taoist master. In Confucian thought, these characters embody the basis of the moral code—filial piety, out of which springs an ordered, highly stratified human society. While retaining the theme of self-sacrifice, Disney has assuredly excised the heavy didactic, moralistic tone of the Chinese Mulan.

Even the other American Mulan, Kingston's phantasmic woman warrior in "White Tigers," from *The Woman Warrior*, fails to live up to Disney's amnesic escapade. The apprentice of martial arts in Kingston is so homesick that she is allowed to look into a magic gourd for her parents. Furthermore, on the eve of the woman warrior's setting out on behalf of her father, Kingston deliberately transposes the tale of the Sung dynasty general Yueh Fei onto Fa Mu Lan. In other words, the tattoo on Mu Lan's back with sacred vows of revenge belongs originally to the legend of Yueh Fei. "[My father] began cutting; to make fine lines and points he used thin blades, for the stems, large blades," narrates Kingston. "My mother caught the blood and wiped the cuts with a cold towel soaked in wine. It hurt terribly—the cuts sharp; the air burning; the alcohol cold, then hot" (41). With the meticulous depiction of its gradations, the excruciating pain inflicted upon the woman warrior by her parents signifies the anguish of identity formation of minorities in the 1970s. Deemed too "gross" for a young audience, Disney proceeds to turn the only inscription in the film into Mulan writing calligraphy on her wrist in hope of outwitting the matchmaker's standard questions. In chronological order, an anonymous poet in the sixth century A.D. sings of Fa Mu Lan's filial piety and patriotism; similar traditional morals inform the tale of Yueh Fei; Mulan is collected in didactic stories of filial piety to edify the public throughout various dynasties; a Chinese American novelist grafts the twins of Mulan and Yueh Fei as a trope for ethnic and feminist identity; Disney's animation accentuates the clandestine playfulness of gender reversal and adolescent adventures away from home.

The same transformations across time occur in Disney's battle scene. The charge of the barbarians and the ensuing avalanche are stunningly real, a panoramic spectacle of computer-generated virtual reality. The fighting, however, is absent in "The Ballad," inhabiting literally the space between two stanzas:

> After a hundred battles the generals are dead,
> Ten years now, and the brave soldiers are returning!
> Returning to audience with the Son of Heaven,
> The Son of Heaven, sitting in his Luminous Hall.
> ....
> Then the Khan asked what Mulan desired. (78)

On the other hand, the battles in Kingston unfold in the tradition of martial arts and *wu-hsia* film genre. Concurrent with Mulan's growth as a formidable general, her femininity grows as well in terms of the fetus in her womb inside her enlarged armor.

The woman warrior's clashes with her enemies culminate in the enthroning of the people's emperor at the Forbidden City. An ancient story acquires a modern twist:

> I stood on top of the last hill before Peiping...the land was peopled—the Han people, the People of One Hundred Surnames, marching with one heart, our tatters flying. The depth and width of joy were exactly known to me: the Chinese population....[The people] inaugurated the peasant who would begin the new order. In his rags he sat on the throne facing south and we, a great red crowd, bowed to him three times. (50)

Kingston has, in this scene, overlapped several images of Tiananmen fresh in the collective memory of her 1970s American readership: Mao Tse-tung's announcement of the founding of the People's Republic of China in 1949 and the surging Red Guards' chanting of "Long Live Chairman Mao!" during the height of the Cultural Revolution. Moreover, the novelist ingeniously blends such recent events of proletarian mass movements with the dynastic traditions of "the throne facing south."

The teen dreams Disney perpetuates are part of the youth consumer culture. As a result, *Mulan* simulates some of the cinematic conventions in Hollywood. The arch-villain Shan-Yu is disposed of by Mulan via a firecracker which resembles a rocket, hence the amalgamation of Orientalist icons and contemporary filmic clichés in action thrillers. Stabbed in the stomach by the rocket, a phallic symbol, Shan-Yu lifts off into the air, thus recycling the incredible ending of villains being speared and carried away by rockets, such as the demise of John Travolta in John Woo's *Broken Arrow* (1996). Prior to the rocket attack, Mulan frames the position of Shan-Yu with her fingers like a professional photographer, underlining her coolness in the face of monstrosity. Broadly speaking, the party culture of adolescents is made to infect even ancestors' spirits at the conclusion of *Mulan*; phantoms in classical Chinese costume break out into dance in consonance with rap music. Likewise, the longing for romance dictates that Shang seek out Mulan, at the urging of the emperor.

Teen dreams revolve around, as Freud puts it, "growing up" or fashioning self-identity. For the majority of the white, Gen-X audience to see themselves in Mulan's self-discovering saga, they must find race and, for half of the audience, gender transparent in order to identify with her. Chineseness in *Mulan* is presented as exotic dresses to be tried on by spectators, as role-playing, neither of which poses soul-searching, gut-wrenching deconstruction of one's subjectivity. A perfect analogy is Americans' love affair with Barbie dolls. The series of Barbie collectibles includes Barbie the Chinese Empress, modeled after the Ching dynasty's Empress Dowager, in Manchurian dress, cap, accessories, and the darker skin tone. This Chinese empress' sisters include Barbie the French Lady and a host of other racialized dolls. The fascination with Barbie stems from the ease of transmutations of the self, an entity of consciousness projected by the doll owner onto the doll's naked body. There appear to be as many Barbies as there are her apparels, yet Barbie remains fundamentally unchanged in her smile and her fashion model figure. As a consequence, the doll owner is able to assume multiple roles in imagination, facilely and superficially, just as Barbie is made to change into her sundry outfits. For that matter, Disney's nineties characters, despite their divergent racial backgrounds, exhibit an amazing degree of similarity physically and temperamentally. The French Belle of 1991 resembles the Arab Jasmine of 1992, who resembles the Native American Pocahontas of 1995, who resembles the gypsy Esmeralda of 1996, who resembles the Greek Meg of 1997, who resembles the Chinese Mulan of 1998. Disney's dominant genes dictate the look and the behavior of its brood of idealized adolescents, whereas race and culture become, ironically, recessive genes. To illustrate Disney's subsuming of race and culture into adolescent desires, one turns to the scene of fireworks and the dragon dance at what appears to be the Hall of Supreme Harmony (*Taihedian*) at the heart of Beijing's Forbidden City in—not *Mulan*—but *Aladdin*. This fleeting glimpse—along with those of the Taj Mahal, the Parthenon in the Acropolis, the Thomas Jefferson Memorial, and other famous sites—provides the backdrop for the teen romance unfolding between Aladdin and Jasmine on the magic carpet traveling through time and space.

Indeed, Disney has exploited Orientalist images as racial markers. What follows is an investigation of Disney's strategies of racial dichotomy between us and them, between the Hans and the Huns. American moviegoers instinctively take the side of the "good guys," the Hans defending themselves, a natural human reaction to any alleged struggle of the virtuous against the evil. Race and gender differences of the characters from the audience are elided in an abstract identification with the good. This is not to deny the spellbinding "power of the dark side," as James Earl Jones intones in his black cape and helmet in *Star Wars*. Before one plunges into race, however, it is important to reiterate Mulan's search for a new gender, which constitutes nothing less than a fun-filled game for both boys and girls. To act like a man, Mulan has to learn to walk, talk, spit, and fight like one. The awkwardness of this process is exemplified in her hesitation and stammer before naming herself "Ping," popularized as masculine through *Turandot* but remaining equally feminine to Chinese ears. Masculinity becomes a role Mulan assumes, in the same way that white youngsters would identify with a Chinese-looking yet American-acting Mulan.

To empathize with the Hans, the dominant Chinese race, the audience must be made to reject the Other—the Hun invaders. The polarization of race manifests itself in the Huns' gray skin tone and in the Hans' fairer skin tone. Disney accomplishes this further by rendering Shan-Yu and his followers as animalistic, predatory barbarians. With fingers like hawk's talons, the steep forehead of a gorilla, eyes and eyebrows squashed together, and two pointed snake fangs, Shan-Yu is, arguably, simian. He hangs upside down like an ape; he scales the Great Wall and climbs trees; he sniffs at the doll which his falcon brings back from its scouting. With his superhuman strength, he bursts out of snow that annihilates his entire army except his closest comrades. His henchmen subsequently penetrate the palace hidden inside the dancing dragon, a Chinese Trojan Horse in mockery of the emperor's symbol.

Of course, Disney did not initiate the portrayal of the Huns as "barbarians"; the Han Chinese have historically done that. The "Frontier" genre in Tang poetry is replete with Chinese soldiers stationed near the northern border defending against the aliens on the other side of the Great Wall. Even contemporary Chinese continue to refer to China as the fusion of five races: Hans, Manchurians, Mongolians, Muslims, and Tibetans. Naming themselves after the two most glorious dynasties in Chinese history: Han (206 B.C.–A.D. 220) and Tang (A.D. 618–907), the Chinese hegemony is closely tied to the Hans. Although "The Ballad" does not allude to any specific dynasty in Chinese history, Mulan does say that she wishes only to be given a "fleet-footed camel" to take her back to her parents rather than be awarded the post of *shan-shu-lan*, a post closely associated with the Han dynasty. *Shan-shu* was created during the Ching dynasty and continued in Han.

While the Chinese have historically segregated the Hans and the Huns, Westerners, it seems, have bought into this easy distinction with their usual fervor over things Oriental. Puccini's *Turandot* opens with the conflict between Turandot—the heartless princess of Peking—and her foreign suitors. The Prince of Persia is about to be executed for failing to answer Turandot's three riddles. Calif, yet another enraptured by Turandot's icy beauty, has a name derived from the title of the secular and religious ruler of a Muslim state, hence royalty from a foreign land. Turandot in fact turns vengeful and sadistic because of her female ancestor, Princess Lou-Ling, who was ravished by "the King of the Tartars." Evidently, for Puccini, "Persia," "Muslim," and "Tartars" were all synonyms of the Huns. In splitting the Hans and the Huns, neither the Chinese nor the Westerner heeds the textual evidence within "The Ballad" suggesting that Mulan may be bicultural, if not biracial.

In "The Ballad," Mulan states, "The Khan's mustering a great army," referring to the Han Son of Heaven (*Tien-tse*) rather than the Khan of the northern nomadic tribes. Similarly, Mulan switches between "the Son of Heaven, sitting in his Luminous Hall" and "the Khan asked what Mulan desired." The fluidity of addresses points to a hybridized subjectivity of Mulan's or of her anonymous author's, or of both. The imported term "Khan," adopted side by side with the Chinese term "Son of Heaven," suggests the northern tribal origin or culture of the character in the ballad and/or of the person composing it. Indeed, a footnote in Liu and Lo's *Sunflower Splendor* (1975) attributes Mulan to "northern, i.e., non-Chinese, stock who lived during the Six Dynasties period (A.D. 220–588)" (77, n. 1). The Chinese have conveniently cleansed Mulan of her adulterated cultural and perhaps racial background, an enterprise of essentialization intensified in Kingston and in Disney for their varius ends.

Notes

This essay is drawn from my book manuscript, *The Deathly Embrace: Orientalism and Asian American Ethnicity*, which was completed with the support of the Rockefeller Foundation Fellowships, 1997–98.

1. See my "Amy Tan's *The Chinese Siamese Cat*: Chinoiserie and Ethnic Stereotype." *The Lion and the Unicorn* 23.2. Apr. 1999.
2. The site in *Mulan* is the Hall of Supreme Harmony (*Taihedian*), which, as Jeffrey F. Meyer describes it in *The Dragons of Tiananmen* (1991), the Ming and Qing emperors used to preside over "the grand audiences, the most important being New Year, the winter solstice, and the emperor's birthday" (50).
3. For clarification, please see my "Immigrant Subjectivities" in *Asian American and Asian Diaspora Literatures* (1998) and *The Deathly Embrace*.

4. The Disney portrayal of the nomadic tribes inhabiting northern China follows the implicitly derogatory description of them in *The Confucian Analects:* "*P'i-fa tso-jen*" ("loosened hair and with coats buttoned on the left side").

Works Cited

Chang, Tse-tung. *Hundred Tales of Filial Piety.* Kao City, Hopei: Mingchu, 1993.

Freud, Sigmund. "Creative Writers and Day-Dreaming." *The Freud Reader.* Ed. Peter Gay. New York: Norton, 1989. 436–43.

Hwang, David Henry. *M. Butterfly.* New York: Penguin, 1986.

Kingston, Maxine Hong. *The Woman Warrior: Memoirs of a Girlhood Among Ghosts.* New York: Knopf, 1976.

Liu, Wu-chi, and Irving Yucheng Lo, eds. *Sunflower Splendor: Three Thousand Years of Chinese Poetry.* Bloomington: Indiana UP, 1975.

Ma, Sheng-mei. *The Deathly Embrace: Orientalism and Asian American Ethnicity.* Minneapolis: U of Minnesota P, 2000.

———. *Immigrant Subjectivities in Asian American and Asian Diaspora Literatures.* Albany: State U of New York P, 1998.

Meyer, Jeffrey F. *The Dragons of Tiananmen: Beijing as a Sacred City.* Columbia: U of South Carolina P, 1991.

Mulan. Dir. Barry Cook. Animated. Voices: Ming-Na Wen, Lea Salonga, Eddie Murphy. The Walt Disney Company, 1998.

Owen, Rob. *Gen X TV:* The Brady Bunch *to* Melrose Place. New York: Syracuse UP, 1997.

Tan, Amy. *The Hundred Secret Senses.* New York: Putnam, 1995.

Waley, Arthur. *Chinese Poems.* 1946. London: George Allen and Unwin, 1962.

Part VI
Disney History

CHAPTER 12

Pocahontas: The Disney Imaginary

Pushpa Naidu Parekh

Disney's 1995 release *Pocahontas* re-creates the myth of colonial "discovery" and settlement of America in the decade referred to as that of "political correctness." The film reenacts the colonial adventure tale told from two sides of the cultural divide: the English colonists headed by John Smith and the Algonquian Indians, whose main voice is Pocahontas. Set in 1607–8 at the time of the establishment of the Jamestown Colony in Virginia, the narrative begins with Pocahontas, the beloved daughter of Chief Powhatan. The Disney film uses various available sources, both print and cinematic, in the tradition of "old West" romanticism and modern realism, in order to re-create the character of Pocahontas. Both childhood innocence and her natural love of animals reflect the "noble savage" myth so dear to Hollywood representations of the native. True to her name, Pocahontas (which in Algonquian means "Little Wanton"), is presented as frolicsome and playful, close to nature, and communing with its creatures, such as Meeko the raccoon and Flit the hummingbird, as well as the spirit of her grandmother. The sailors she encounters, however, are greedy, ignorant, and racist. Some, like John Smith, are susceptible to the beauty of the "noble savage," while others are destructive of the natives and the natural landscape they ravage in search of gold. On the other side, Powhatan, the chief of the Powhatan Confederacy, comprising thirty-two Algonquian bands and two hundred villages, and his subjects are suspicious of the white "devils" who wield the powerful guns to kill and destroy. They represent the stereotype of the "savage reactionary," explained by Michael T. Marsden and Jack Nichbar as another sentimental image that has dominated the popular imagining of the American Indian: "The Indian fitting this image is a killer because he detests the proper and manifest advancement of a white culture clearly superior to his own and often because of his own primal impulses. He must be annihilated for the good of civilization" (609). Disney perpetuates this myth, albeit comically, by depicting Powhatan as unreasonable and temperamental; fitting therefore is his practice of "savage" acts of violence, such as preparing to behead John Smith.

Pocahontas is celebrated as the heroine who bridges the gap between the two cultures. Ahistoricized and simplified, Pocahontas emerges as a new Disney heroine who remains childlike for all her wit and wisdom. Disney chooses to focus on her sprightly nature as an indication of her spiritual and creative force; this portrayal stops short of exploring her link to Mother Earth and her role in defining the continuity and completeness of life within the context of traditional Algonquian thought and the Powhatan social system. One is left with unanswered questions about the historical figure who must have commanded a certain amount of power in the political struggles and negotiations between the two factions.

In keeping with this portrayal are the pervasive visual and auditory images throughout the film. The songs, which are Disney's hallmark, of *Pocahontas* weave the affiliative aspects of cultural engagement; the "Colors of the Wind" song, in particular, embodies the magic of transformation and connection that Disney's creation of the Pocahontas myth signifies. The song carries the message of understanding and accepting the diversity and variety of things and people. While Pocahontas shares with Smith the Indian gestures of "hello" and "goodbye," John Smith allows Meeko to play with his compass. Perhaps nowhere is this theme of cultural contact emphasized more clearly than at the glade, where they hear the voice of Grandmother Willow and understand that they must create the first ripple of peace between the antagonistic factions. However, there are constant reminders, through constant contestations from both sides, as well as characters like the greedy, wily John Ratcliffe on the English side and the bravest but domineering warrior, Kocoum, in the Powhatan tribe, that this transformation is short-lived and, for the most part, illusory. Pocahontas negotiates the warring space and sustains the dream, and becomes an overly sentimentalized icon of the self-sacrificing Indian who saves the life of a white captain. Disney perpetuates the simplistic assumptions about Indian women, who are seen either as "undifferentiated mass of workers" or as heroines who help the white army "against [their] own people" (Allen, "Teaching" 134).

The shifts in subject positions from Pocahontas to the English colonists are negotiated with a conscious awareness of the racism and parochial selfishness that marked the white settlers' attitude toward the Native Americans they encountered. Pocahontas confronts John Smith's unconscious racism in using the term "savage" to describe the people who are different from Europeans. She teaches him by exposing his and his people's ethnocentrism, but the question remains: Isn't her subjectivity merely an instrument for enlightening the narrow-minded English settlers? In broadening John Smith's mind, Pocahontas gains the status of a subject in present-day "multicultural" discourses. Disturbingly, this rewrite is merely a reinscription of an old colonial practice; utilizing the "Other" in the business of spiritual awakening of the European, who still dominates the American continent. The heroines from the cultures that have been traditionally marginalized and that gain popular sympathy and recognition are often the ones who helped or tried to make peace with the white settlers, even at the cost of betraying their own tribe; for example, Malintzin, during the era of Cortes. Martin Green discusses the effect of W. H. Prescott's *Conquest of Mexico* (1843) and the creation of the Cortes myth whose romantic appeal is dependent upon the creation of the the Malintzin myth: "Malintze, or Marina, given to Cortes as a slave by a Tabascan Chief," of noble birth like Pocahontas, becomes his mistress. She eventually persuades Montezuma, the Aztec emperor, to yield himself to the "protection of the Spaniards, which event broke the back of any possible Aztec resistance" (29).

The telling of American history is the narration of cultural contact and conflict, of transplantation and displacement, forged constantly by violence and violation. Revisionist historiographers, cultural anthropologists, and theorists are revisiting this history-as-narration that articulates cultural en-counter and difference in terms of sequentiality and polarity (past/present, they/us). Powerful myths that emerge out of these narratives engage, at af-fective levels, in reinscribing or revising notions of identity and difference within the circumscribed realms of hegemonic control and authority. These dynamics are at work in the Disney film *Pocahontas*.

The central event in the adventure tale focuses on how Pocahontas saves the life of John Smith, who is about to be beheaded by the Powhatan tribe. This climactic moment is included in practically all print versions of the story, with slight variations, such as Marie Abrams Lawson's *Pocahontas and Captain John Smith: The Story of the Virginia Colony* (1950), Frances Carpenter's *Pocahontas and Her World* (1957), and later, Katherine Elliott Wilkie's *Pocahontas, Indian Princess* (1969), Philip L. Barbour's *Pocahon-tas and Her World, a Chronicle of America's First Settlement* (1970), and Kate Jassem's *Pocahontas, Girl of Jamestown* (1979). In Disney's film ver-sion, Pocahontas' expression of loyalty to John Smith above that to her own tribe plays a significant role in the development of the romantic turn that Disney gives to the relationship, just as Prescott did to the Cortes-Malintzin story. Pocahontas, according to the book accounts, is supposed to have been a child of eleven or twelve when John Smith, at the age of twenty-seven, sailed to America. These details predicate a different kind of relationship, if any, between John Smith and Pocahontas. Their age difference and Pocahon-tas' prepubescence parallel or reflect unlikely romantic bonding between the English and the natives. The book versions mentioned above also reveal elements left out in the film version: the constant tensions and conflicts that continued between the Native Americans and the English settlers, the abduction of Pocahontas by the settlers to the Jamestown colony, her meeting with John Rolfe and their eventual marriage, Pocahontas being renamed "Rebecca," her visit to London, and her early death at the age of twenty-one. These omissions fabricate the myth of reconciliation and cultural affiliation on which Disney's version seems to focus.

Historic inauthenticity is of course no major flaw in fabulist re-creations for which Disney's films are known. But in dealing with topics that have both a historical basis as well as a mythical force, Disney films reflect and unfortunately promote a certain frame of imperialist ideology that pervades modern or even postmodern thinking, an ideology that rationalizes the appropriation and often blatant misrepresentation of the history of the Other.

Martin Green underscores the politics that underlie similar colonial adventure stories of "mythic self-identification" (28). For one, he discusses Prescott's *Conquest of Mexico* and the creation of Cortes (who landed in Mexico in 1519), as a "romantic character" within a tale that "involves an extraordinary concatenation of the motifs of the adventure tale to come; notably the treasure, the exotic landscape, and the love of a native princess" (29). This adventure narrative is grounded in an ideological ethos and a system of political expansionism that not only justifies but also romanticizes colonial practice. The same paradigm operates in Disney's romantic adventure tale of John Smith and Pocahontas. In his endnotes, Martin Green considers this narrative to be "archetypical in a loose sense; in that it corresponds to a structure of feelings that recur in many times and places.... The story turns up, in fiction but also perhaps in fact, whenever thoughts of conquest stir men's minds" (348). The telling of this fiction is underlined by a glorification of the white English male whose arrival on native soil (whether Native America, Africa, or India) is given epic proportions through the devices of oracles and omens. The "gratification in the voices of historians who repeat the story" of how the natives welcomed the "white men" as gods or superhuman creatures (even "devils" have powers to be respected and feared) reflects the psychological dependency of the native and colonizer in the colonized space that Frantz Fanon talks about in *The Wretched of the Earth*, and Abdul R. JanMohamed elaborates in *Manichean Aesthetics*:

> For while he [the colonialist] sees the native as the quintessence of evil and therefore avoids all contact because he fears contamination, he is at the same time absolutely dependent upon the colonized people not only for his privileged social and material status but also his sense of moral superiority and, therefore, ultimately for his very identity. (4)

In the process of this "mythic self-identification," Caliban in Shakespeare's

The Tempest represents the depraved native who, however unwillingly, admires the "white gods" while cursing them. Kurtz in Joseph Conrad's *The Heart of Darkness* represents the colonizer gone native who is worshiped by the natives. It is interesting how the native women have been portrayed in both Conrad's and Disney's project of colonialist self-glorification through the Other. The Other in such myths is either absent or, if present, falls victim to the "primitive" culture's savage treatment of women. Such is the fate of the native black woman who bemoans inarticulately the loss of Kurtz but has no native counterpart in Conrad's narrative.

Pocahontas in Disney's film has a native suitor in Kocoum, but he consistently proves to be less attractive, compared with John Smith, as a romantic partner for Pocahontas. The native female becomes the object of the Western male fantasy, both in terms of being saved and of saving the hero whose life is threatened by the native male. She is the signifier of the colonized: the "savage" who must be civilized and proselytized, and who makes it possible for the colonizer to survive and conquer the savage and "savagehood." There are elements of heroism, chivalry, and adventure in these stories that powerfully depict the exoticizing sensibility of the colonialist enterprise.

Perhaps even more pervasive is the enfolding of the Christianizing mission rhetoric (the growth of evangelicalism with its emphasis on notions of "saving" and "being saved" was an influential response to the expressions of religious doubt in England, from the mid-nineteenth century) within the fabric of historical romance narratives that also function as cultural transmitters of nation-foundation myths.

Pocahontas becomes one such icon of the colonialist imaginary that is reimaged in Disney's version, perhaps for children who must encounter neo-colonialism in all its corrosively beneficent forms in today's "multicultural" societies. For example, today children are taught to embrace the notions of racial, gender, and even cultural equality to some extent; however, they rarely realize their participation in the commodification of this ideal through the consumption of Disney paraphernalia, like Pocahontas toys, and beach towels. Not less confusing is the invitation for our children as Disney viewers (across cultures and blurring territorial borders) to engage in an apparent "appreciation" of marginalized subjects (Pocahontas is no submissive "squaw" nor is her race mere "savages") whose humanity is still validated on conditional terms.

Pocahontas gains heroine status not because she represents the power and wisdom of Powhatan women, as subject-agents in specific historical processes, to influence and mediate in matters of political and economic importance, but because she loves John Smith, and, rising above tribal-colonial conflicts, she effects a supposedly equitable cross-cultural exchange. One

Web listserv respondent, Jim Postema, in the "Pocahontas" NatChat mailing list, regarding views on an "Open Letter from Russell Means," contests the assessment of *Pocahontas* by the former AIM (American Indian Movement) activist as "a beautiful love story about two people who wish to promote cultural understanding" (1). Postema poses valid questions regarding representation in the film:

> But whose values are shaping this "positive" image? The fact that some of the movie may be positive is not in itself the problem, but that it's culturally inaccurate, depicting one culture according to norms devised by another culture's needs or wishes regarding the depicted (image-ined) culture. Perhaps an instructive question to ask would be this: How would Indian filmmakers portray the accounts of Pocahontas' experiences with John Smith? What things would their films emphasize, de-emphasize, etc., from the way Disney has portrayed the story, or the way the story has been told in white history texts? (1)

Pocahontas, therefore, emerges as a heroine whose heroism is more problematic than Disney would have us believe.

Notions of "heroism" previously measured in terms of the supposedly "universal" standard of the hegemonic power structures have been shown, by cultural critics and theorists such as Appadurai, to be imbricated in "the plurality of imagined worlds" created by "electronic mediation and mass migration," "the new order of instability in the production of modern subjectivities," as well as "diasporic public spheres, phenomena that confound theories that depend on the continued salience of the nation-state as the key arbiter of important social changes" (Appadurai 4). That is, at a time when mass migration, border crossing, computer language, and global economics erase as much as reconfigure clear-cut notions of geopolitical and identarian boundaries, Disney asks us to forget the "ethnic" (racial) cleansing that has been the reality of U.S. history, through the unfolding magic of romantic adventure tale. Disney's "politics of innocence" through "pedagogical policing of memory" (Giroux 43–48) reduces the violence of colonialism to petty individual acts of greed and intolerance. Giroux reveals "the discourse of innocence and 'fun' that lies at the heart of the Disney company's worldview" and "how such representations mobilize popular memory to incorporate not only a particular view of...'nostalgic imperialism' but also a politics of forgetting in producing a particular view of history, racial identity, and nationalism" (48).

The multiple and contested sites at which the performative and electronic media of Disney's modern myth/fairy tale *Pocahontas* interrogate as well as participate in the deployment of the imaginary are grounded in this very "politics of innocence," what Fredric Jameson, in *The Political Uncon-*

scious, refers to as "wish-fulfillments" and "Utopian fantasies" (86). The subject of economic contingencies of navigational explorations, in the form of search for raw materials, and the subsequent politics of land appropriation are constantly deferred through the discourse of "discovery," "romance," and "adventure." Film, in general, has the power to commodify dominant ideology as well as subvert it through foregrounding questions of liminal spatiality "in-between the designations of identity" (Appadurai 4). A particular characteristic of Disney films is a refusal to explore this "in-between" space. That is, Disney provides us with a version of modernity that is closely aligned with new forms of colonizing, mental and ideological.

The cinematic portrayal of cultural politics in Disney's films has been examined from diverse critical positions. In his enlightening and relevant analysis, Jack Zipes, in "Breaking the Disney Spell," recounts the stages by which oral fairy tales gained institutionalized status through literary medium, which "violated the forms and concerns of non-literate, essentially peasant communities and set new standards of taste, production, and reception" (24). Displacing the community-centered discourse, the literary fairy tale celebrated "individualism, subjectivity and reflection" (30) through "domestication of the imagination" (25). The shift from print to cinematic technology saw the emergence of Disney's animated film, which introduced a new standard: "the spectacle of technical inventions, of the magical talents of the animator as demigod" (31). Zipes notes that while Disney returns the fairy tale to the majority of the people (as popular medium), Disney's animated versions tend to replace all versions (32). This is so not only because cinema has become a medium most "accessible to the public at large" but because Disney systematically mastered the use of technology, what Zipes calls "trickery" of animation (33) as "domestication of imagination" to conceal his control and manipulation of material. Zipes cautions,

> The domestication is related to colonization insofar as the ideas and types are portrayed as models of behavior to be emulated. Exported through the screen as models, the "American" fairy tale colonizes other national audiences. What is good for Disney is good for the world, and what is good in a Disney fairy tale is good in the rest of the world. (40)

In Disney's recent films (after Disney's death), the techniques of "automatization and trickery" (33) focus not so much on "self-figuration" but on "othering" difference, especially cultural difference. For example, *The Jungle Book* is after all a colonial's (Kipling's) representation of native culture. Disney's recent films foster history as simplistic spectacle in the name of offering "the pleasure of scopophilia and inundate(s) the viewer with delightful images, humorous figures, and erotic signs" (Zipes 33).

"American mythologizing of cultural histories" retains both patriarchal and imperialistic codes, often framing the female-centered narratives from white male discourses of gender/cultural Other in terms of domestication and essentialization.

In *Pocahontas*, the story of the most celebrated American Indian woman is shaped by this ideological framework: Pocahontas is first of all packaged as a beautiful young woman (transformed from a prepubescent girl of history textbooks) who is on the verge of being married off to a cheerless native man until she meets John Smith, who saves her from a loveless marriage. Frolicking with the tribal women and comical creatures of the wild, such as Meeko and Flit, Pocahontas fits the picture of simple, nature-loving natives; ultimately, the narrative closes with the women bringing corn to the English settlers, confirming their own domesticated status. This white-male framing dilutes what it conceives of as threateningly different: the native culture's celebration of the woman as a matriarchal force. Richard Schickel points out the implication of this mythologizing: "He [Disney] came always as a conqueror, never as a servant. It is a trait, as many have observed, that many Americans share when they venture into foreign lands hoping to do good but equipped only with know-how instead of sympathy and respect for alien traditions" (227). It is through this mythologizing that Disney films today reinscribe dominant ideologies. In particular, Disney's *Pocahontas* violates at one level the forms and concerns of Native American storytelling traditions, through displacing its woman-centered orientation, what Paula Gunn Allen refers to as expressive of "gynarchical, egalitarian, and sacred traditions" ("Kochinnenako" 223–24). This orientation is quite distinct from the Western norms in that it delineates the nature of Indian ethos, experience, and aesthetics as interrelated. For example, as Allen explains, "Right relationship or right kinship is fundamental to Native aesthetics. Right relationship is dictated by custom within a given tribal or cultural grouping, but everywhere it is characterized by considerations of proportion, harmony, balance, and communality" (*Spider* ix). Moreover, the experience of Indian women who are "ever aware that (we) are occupied peoples who have no military power on earth ready to liberate (us)" is a given in their narratives (ix).

At another level, Disney appropriates representation of Native American and European struggles through a prescriptive discourse of civility. Disney's version not only domesticates and sanitizes the narrative of cultural conflict but also commodifies it. Perhaps nothing is more representative of this commodification than the production of video sequels, such as *Pocahontas II: Journey to a New World* (1998). While the film reverses the colonial travel narrative genre and has the potential for subverting the dominant paradigm of spectator/spectacle binarism, its fabulist mode itself becomes a spectacle, a form of "swindle of fulfillment" (Giroux 58). Advertising the promise of "plenty of thrills and laughter for everyone," the sequel rejects any historical grounding, while adding many obviously unbelievable situations. Pocahontas meets and falls in love with John Rolfe; John Smith becomes a figure of the past until a magical moment reinstates him as a competing figure in a possible love triangle. Teamed with John Rolfe, he is resurrected as the savior of Pocahontas. Moreover, of all incongruous events, Pocahontas is jailed in the Tower of London. The sequel is in many ways technically much inferior to the original film; however it perpetuates the continuation and proliferation of Disney's brand of historical forgetting.

Henry Giroux addresses just such an issue. By erasing the political and ethical considerations that make history a site of struggle, Disney has produced a filmic version of popular culture through a pedagogy that rewrites history as inheritance and human agency as a condition for adapting to existing sites of injustice. Electronically mediated images, especially television and film, represent one of the most potent arms of cultural hegemony in the twenty-first century. These representations, when directed to an audience of children, have the potential to impact a whole generation that feeds on the Disney worldview as its referent. Constituted as a public sphere with an enormous global reach, the power of the electronic media reinforces Stuart Hall's claim that "there is no politics outside of representation" (qtd. in Giroux 57–8).

The electronic medium, through the various Web sites on *Pocahontas*, with multiple mailing lists, records the reception of the film and the sequel. Ranging from the "Save Our Smith" home page to the one on the Powhatan Renape Nation's counterresponse to the Disney film, through a play *The One Called Pocahontas*, there is quite a mixture of outrage at Disney's artistic license and distortion of the historical details and a steady support of Disney fans. The page on "Pocahontas Myth" by Chief Roy Crazy Horse of the Powhatan Renape Nation expresses disagreement with Roy Disney's claim that the Disney film is "responsible, accurate, and respectful": "It is unfortunate that this sad story, which Euro-Americans should find embarrassing, Disney makes 'entertainment' and perpetuates a dishonest and self-serving myth at the expense of the Powhatan Nation" (3).

Brookie Craig, in her reply to the "Pocahontas" Native-L listserv, comments on "the blatant sexism and perverted attempts to manipulate our cultural sacredness simply for the making of a buck" through the commercialism of "Pocahontas candy," "Fruit of the Loom underwear," Mattel's new toy line of "Suncolors Pocahontas, Nakoma, and Kocoum," and the "image of Nakoma...[which] includes an earthen pot and campfire that lights up in the sunlight," as well as a "river rowing Pocahontas" (1).

Perhaps the edifice of the Disney industry and its artifacts are beginning to be challenged at the "diasporic public spheres" (Appadurai 4) and domains. However, the disturbing nature of this phenomenon is that the electronic media constructs and controls knowledge through technological, not necessarily critical, engagement. The Disney imaginary is a topos where "Distory" and Audio-Animatronics construct and contain an "envelope of experience" (Fernandez 239). The true challenge would have to be located among the audience Disney targets the most, the children, through pedagogies that allow them to distinguish between life experience and virtual reality. One way would be through curriculum transformation from elementary to university level.

Allen clarifies the link between this transformation and reworking of course designs to "integrate American Indian literary traditions into the study of American literature at every level" (*Spider* viii). Cautioning against "taking a paternalistic attitude toward the materials and the people they reflect," Allen further offers several reasons for avoiding "an overly romantic response to Indians, their values, and their traditions":

> First, instructors should present these literatures as they were intended to appear to the primary audiences, so that the student or reader can enter into the universe in which the material belongs. Second, exercises in literary colonialism are dangerous to the Indian people, for they can lead to intellectual confusion, self-hatred, or rejection of the education such study is designed to further. And third, interpreting Indian cultures and artifacts as examples of unalloyed primitivism or nobility can lead to feelings of contempt for American Indians, feelings that can often result in political action against them. (*Spider* xii)

In light of Allen's recommendations, the task of educators, especially at the elementary level, should include a careful and responsible use of Native American materials, as well as an active development of methodologies and vocabularies that critique the Disney conglomerate by identifying specific ways in which its entertainment business relates to pedagogy.

As Elizabeth Bell et al. argue, this need is all the more urgent at a time when Disney has become a "'blueprint' for education and enterprise" (6). They also clarify the various ways in which Disney has entered the field of education: Disney's purchase of Childcraft, "a succesful maker of educational toys" in 1988; Disney's sponsoring of "'Teacher of the Year' awards and 'Doer and Dreamer' scholarship awards to US high school students"; and its offering of "free admission programs to Florida school children during the slow season in its Florida theme parks" (7). In an increasingly complex world where children are bombarded with multisensory images of geopolitical contestations in the form of video games, the urgency to involve our children as critical thinkers is immediate. They must become visually literate in order to connect what they see, what they think, and what they feel to how these sights, thoughts, and feelings are molded by public culture. They must be empowered to define the construction of their imaginary landscape instead of becoming passive spectators of the Disney imaginary.

Works Cited

Allen, Paula Gunn. Introduction. *Spider Woman's Granddaughters: Traditional Tales and Contemporary Writing by Native American Women*. Ed. Paula Gunn Allen. New York: Fawcett Columbine, 1989. i–xxv.

——. "Kochinnenako in Academe: Three Approaches to Interpreting a Keres Indian Tale." *The Sacred Hoop: Recovering the Feminine in American Indian Traditions*. Boston: Beacon P, 1986. 224–244.

——. "Teaching American Indian Women's Literature." *Studies in American Indian Literature: Critical Essays and Course Designs*. New York: The Modern Language Association of America, 1983. 134–144.

Appadurai, Arjun. *Modernity at Large: Cultural Dimensions of Globalization*. Minneapolis: U of Minnesota P, 1997.

Barbour, Philip A. *Pocahontas and Her World, a Chronicle of America's First Settlement*. Boston: Houghton Mifflin, 1970.

Bell, Elizabeth. Introduction. Bell, Haas, and Sells 1–17.

Bell, Elizabeth, Lynda Haas, and Laura Sells, eds. *From Mouse to Mermaid: The Politics of Film, Gender, and Culture*. Eds. Elizabeth Bell, Lynda Haas, and Laura Sells. Bloomington: Indiana UP, 1995.

Carpenter, Frances. *Pocahontas and Her World*. New York: Knopf, 1957.

Chief Roy Crazy Horse. *Pocahontas Myth*. 17 Jan. 1998. <http://www.powhatan.org/pocc.html>.

Craig, Brookie. "Pocahontas" Native-L (July 1995). NATCHAT mailing list. 17 Jan. 1998. <http://nativenet.uthscsa.edu/ natchat/archive/nc/9507/0197.html>.

Fanon, Frantz. *The Wretched of the Earth*. Trans. Constance Farrington. New York: Grove Weidenfeld, 1963.

Fernandez, Ramona. "Pachuco Mickey." Bell, Haas, and Sells 236–53.

Giroux, Henry A. "Memory and Pedagogy in the 'Wonderful World of Disney': Beyond the Politics of Innocence." Bell, Haas, and Sells 43–61.

Green, Martin. *Dreams of Adventure, Deeds of Empire*. New York: Basic Books, 1979.

Jameson, Fredric. *The Political Unconscious: Narrative as a Socially Symbolic Act*. Ithaca: Cornell UP, 1981.

JanMohamed, Abdul R. *Manichean Aesthetics: The Politics of Literature in Colonial Africa*. Amherst: U of Massachusetts P, 1983.

Jassem, Kate. *Pocahontas, Girl of Jamestown*. Mahwah, NJ: Troll Associates, 1979.

Lawson, Marie Abrams. *Pocahontas and Captain John Smith: The Story of the Virginia Colony*. New York: Random, 1950.

Marsden, Michael T. and Jack Nichbar. "The Indian in the Movies." *Handbook of North American Indians: History of Indian-White Relations*. Vol. 4. Ed. Wilcomb E. Washburn.

178

Washington: Smithsonian Institution, 1988.

Pocahontas. Dirs. Mike Gabriel, Eric Goldberg. Animated. Voices: Irene Bedard, Judy Kuhn, Mel Gibson, David Ogden Stiers. Walt Disney Pictures, 1995.

Pocahontas II: Journey to a New World. Dirs. Tom Ellery, Bradley Raymond. Animated Voices: Irene Bedard, Judy Kuhn, Billy Zane, Donal Gibson, David Ogden Stiers. Walt Disney Home Video, 1998.

Postema, Jim. "Re: *Pocahontas*: open letter from Russell Means." NATCHAT mailing list. 7 July 1995. 5 Nov. 1998. <http://nativenet.uthscsa.edu/natchat/archive/nc/9507/0021.html>.

Schickel, Richard. *The Disney Version*. New York: Simon and Schuster, 1968.

Smith, Peter. *Handicapped in Walt Disney World: A Guide for Everyone*. Dallas: Southpark, 1993.

Wilkie, Katherine Elliott. *Pocahontas, Indian Princess*. Champaign, Illinois: Gerrard, 1969.

Zipes, Jack. "Breaking the Disney Spell." Bell, Haas, and Sells 21–42.

Chapter 13

The Politics of Vision:
Disney, *Aladdin*, and the Gulf War

Dianne Sachko Macleod

Fulfilling Disney Studios' wildest dreams, *Aladdin* has grossed over $500 million since its release in late 1992. Most reviewers attribute the animated feature's blockbuster success to the appeal of its Tom Cruise look-alike hero, the brilliantly comedic performance of Robin Williams as the Genie, or the big show tunes of Tim Rice, whose lyrical skills contributed to Andrew Lloyd Webber's meteoric rise. Fewer critics, however, have credited *Aladdin*'s success to another media event: the televised staging of the Gulf War that was taking place while the film was in production at Disney Studios. Mirroring and magnifying popular stereotypes of Arab culture, *Aladdin* played to an audience already primed by the media.

It is not too much of a stretch, geographically or intellectually, to segue from *Aladdin*'s revival of British and French colonial stereotypes of Arab traders, fanatics, and beauties to the high-tech fantasies of *Star Wars*; to the military space defense program of the same name initiated by California's former governor Ronald Reagan when he reached the Oval Office, which was deployed by his successor George Bush in Operation Desert Storm; and, finally, to the marketing of the American dream by Disney CEO and chairman Michael Eisner, who is headquartered in Orange County, California, a stronghold of Republican values. Eisner's global ambitions, unanticipated economic needs, fear of failure, and reliance on special effects to bolster the illusion of success are not only responsible for *Aladdin*, but also parallel the causes and unfolding of the Gulf War.

Even though the connection was clear to me, there were many reasons *not* to write about it. An art historian who wrote about Disney lost his job at Harvard in 1942 due to our discipline's long-standing bias against popular culture.[1] Moreover the London *Sunday Times* classified those who dared to desecrate Disney as "cultural studies commies."[2] Finally, there was the legendary paranoia of the Disney corporation, which jealously guards the copyright of its images and is notoriously uncooperative with writers who are critical of its enterprise. Routledge, for instance, decided to omit an essay about imperialist images in Disney's comic books from its volume *Disney Discourse: Producing the Magic Kingdom* (Smoodin 1994) rather than risk the hazards of copyright clearance.[3]

Trained in the art of formal analysis, how could I, an art historian, write about something I could not illustrate? What tipped the scale was my realization that *Aladdin* perpetuated the iconographic and stylistic devices of nineteenth-century Orientalist painting, which was something I could write about. Like the ethnographic artists who catered to popular tastes by exaggerating the sensuality and savageness of their colonial subjects, Disney's cartoon characters magnified the least desirable traits of contemporary Middle Easterners.

Timing was everything: George Bush and Michael Eisner each desperately needed a media hit to restore confidence in their ailing empires. Suffering because of their respective imperialist interventions—Iran-Contra in Bush's case and in Eisner's, the financially troubled Euro Disney theme park—it is no coincidence that *Aladdin*'s rise in popularity paralleled Bush's ascent in the polls. This was not the first time that Disney and the U.S. government had adopted similar strategies. Walt Disney was commissioned to produce propaganda short subjects during World War II and went on to serve as a spy for the FBI in its hunt for communists in Hollywood in the 1950s, even testifying in the hearings that resulted in the infamous black list of Hollywood personnel (Eliot 165 and 238). While there was no evidence of collaboration between Eisner and the Pentagon, both relied on the same storehouse of racial and cultural images.

I shall argue that both *Aladdin* and Operation Desert Storm contrived to achieve their goals semiotically, by playing up stereotypes of the Orientalist Other; ideologically, by privileging the American myths of freedom and innocence at a time of nationalist fervor; stylistically, by naturalizing the violence of their terrifying night spectacles through an erasure of the creative hand; and technologically, by depending on digitally enhanced electronic effects to win over their audiences.

Orientalism Once Again

In his seminal work on Orientalism, Edward Said reflects that "there was (and is) a linguistic Orient, a Freudian Orient, a Spenglerian Orient, a Darwinian Orient, a racist Orient—and so on" (22). I informed Said (who had not seen *Aladdin*) in a conversation during his visit to California in February 1994 that he could now add a Disneyian Orient to his list, one which stems from the "corporate" version of Orientalism which he describes in his book

(3). No longer simply a producer of animated cartoons, the Disney conglomerate has far-flung transnational interests to protect in the amusement, retail,
video, television, and general and children's film markets.[4] Like the institutions of the past, the Disney corporation makes unilateral statements, authorizes views, and describes and influences its subjects.

Aladdin communicates this position through a semiotic typology of racial
images that are informed by Hollywood and American prejudices, and not
the indigenous cultures of the Middle East. From cartoon Bedouins astride
camels to thieves in the bazaar, the film borrows from the conventions popularized by French and English Orientalist painters. Artists such as Jean-Léon
Gérôme anticipated Disney in discovering that there was a fortune to be
made in providing popular audiences with convincing images of exotic creatures and habits from the perspective of Western superiority. Art historian
Linda Nochlin persuasively argues that such representations are based on
"absences" (35–36). We as viewers are excluded from the scene, but are
compensated by the superior position we occupy outside the action from
where we can comfortably pass judgment on what is taking place. Tied to
the notion of exclusion is the absence of history itself.

Gérôme's *Prayer in the Mosque of 'Amr*, painted c. 1872, is just as time-
less and devoid of contemporary referents as Disney's 1992 *Aladdin*. In both
instances, architecture, fashion, and custom are static. There are no signs of
wear and tear or exhaustion or any evidence of the decay that was documented at this Egyptian mosque by 1868 (Stevens 142). The same can be
said about *Aladdin*'s pristine architectural settings, precise detail, and generically turbaned characters. Gérôme's crisply robed Muslim supplicants
stand in organized rows punctuated by the irregular presence of a loin-
clothed holy man who represents the irrational excesses of the Muslim faith.
Such condescending attitudes justified the French occupation of Egypt as an
act of paternal beneficence toward a society which practiced a misguided
faith. It is this nineteenth-century Orientalist construction of the Arab world
which is reproduced in *Aladdin*, where shady street peddlers vie with dusky
figures on camels for center stage. Despite the advances made by affirmative
action, there has been little change in the West's visual representations of
the Middle East.

Another visually striking similarity occurs between Gérôme's objectifica-
tion of woman in his portrait of a *Young Egyptian Girl*, c. 1867, and the rendition of Princess Jasmine in *Aladdin*. Both representations subscribe to
Western standards of beauty designed to appeal to the male gaze: dark doe-
like eyes and artificially diminished noses offset by pale skin. Garbed in the
exotic costumes and heavy gold jewelry of male fantasy rather than the
modest robes of reality, these images devalue and sexualize the Middle

Eastern female. Jasmine's bare midriff is ridiculously at odds with her character as a princess. Nevertheless the precision of her image persuasively suggests her authenticity in a manner that replicates the embellishments of Gérôme's *Young Egyptian Girl*. Even though he made eleven journeys to the Middle East, Gérôme disregarded historical fact for the sake of offering his European patrons a double conquest: the colonization of the Orient and the colonization of the female body. Disney's artists follow in his footsteps by adopting his hypnotic attention to detail to signal the "truthfulness" of their depictions of this locale and its primitive sexuality.

Nor did Disney concern itself with questions of origin. "Aladdin and the Magic Lamp" is frequently associated with the tales of *The Arabian Nights*; however, it is not one of the original stories. Its source is Chinese, not Arabic, although it had entered the oral tradition of Middle Eastern storytelling by the fifteenth century. According to Husain Haddawy, the earliest Western textual translations of "Aladdin and the Magic Lamp" were based on Arab forgeries of French texts made in Paris in the eighteenth century (xiii).

Fidelity was not foremost in the minds of the screenwriters who decided against locating *Aladdin* in the Persia of Arabian legend in favor of the fictional city of Agrabah, an approximate anagram of the more newsworthy Baghdad. Disney then proceeded to rid Aladdin of his widowed mother and the evil African magician who is intent on claiming the magic lamp for himself. These changes were made by former studio chairman Jeffrey Katzenberg, a notoriously hands-on executive (Flower 172). Peter Schneider, president of feature animation at Disney, explained, "We made sure [Aladdin] was hunky. Basically we made him Tom Cruise. Oh, and M. C. Hammer. He was another inspiration—the baggy pants."[5] By sexualizing the Aladdin character and transferring the despicable qualities of the magician to the villain Jafar, the stage was set for a plot which offered something for everyone: a sexy hero with a love interest and a Machiavellian miscreant who combined the worst traits of two real-life Arabs, the Ayatollah Khomeini and Saddam Hussein.

In light of positive reviews by critics who praised the film for its non-white heroes, it should be stressed that the M. C. Hammer model was cosmetic, not racial. Although Disney went so far as to tinge the skin tones of Aladdin and Jasmine with a light ocher, it deepened the shade of Jafar's skin. Likewise, it distinguished between the "good" characters and the "bad" by giving the former American accents and the latter clipped British or vaguely foreign intonations. This typecasting raised the ire of Arab Americans. Yousef Salem, spokesman for the South Bay Islamic Association, complained:

All the bad guys have beards and large, bulbous noses, sinister eyes and heavy accents, and they're wielding swords constantly. Aladdin doesn't have a big nose; he
has a small nose. He doesn't have a beard or a turban. He doesn't have an accent.
What makes him nice is they've given him this American character. They've done
everything but put him into a suit and tie.[6]

Salem enumerates the stereotypical traits which have long plagued Arabs
throughout the world, but which have assumed an increasingly sinister cast
since the energy crisis of the 1970s, the overthrow of the Shah of Iran and
most recently, the events of September 11, 2001, in New York City, Washington, D.C., and Somerset County, Pennsylvania. Jack Shaheen in his study
The TV Arab concludes that the media perpetuates four basic myths about
Arabs: They are fabulously wealthy, they are barbaric, they are sex maniacs,
and they revel in acts of terrorism (4). When questioned by the *Washington
Post* about *Aladdin*, he classified it as another in the long series of depictions
of stereotypically sinister "Ay-rab lands."[7]

Conservative critics, on the other hand, questioned what the fuss was all
about. Julie Burchill, writing in the London *Sunday Times* when *Aladdin*
previewed there a year after its American release, disingenuously observed,
"It's not racist at all; it's Disney, which is a foreign country where there are
a million stories and every one's the same."[8] As naive as these remarks
might appear to be to the readers of this essay, Burchill is not alone in believing that Disney's animated features belong in a separate and innocent
category. I tested this hypothesis in the upper-division art history class in
which my project originated in the fall of 1993.

Fully expecting to spark a discussion of the arguments raised by Said and
Nochlin, which had been assigned reading, I was surprised when almost half
of the students professed that animated cartoons did not influence their daily
lives. They maintained that their views of Arabs were unaffected by Disney's simplifications. When I asked if they thought that the same was true
for children, the students reasoned that the adults who accompanied them to
Aladdin would naturally correct the film's biases by discussing these points
with their wards. Playing devil's advocate, I inquired whether anyone who
had been to see the film had actually overheard an adult telling a child that
Arabs would not cut off a thief's hand for stealing an apple, or that Arab
women did not wear the costumes of belly dancers at home, or that racial
stereotypes in general were misleading. None had. Clearly, cultural typology
was a vague intellectual concept which posed little threat to the middle-class
American students in my class.

Homi Bhabha nevertheless is optimistic about the strides made by a de-
constructionist exposé, such as the one I attempted, in unsettling this attitude
of indifference. He believes that

> it is one of the salutary features of postmodern theory to suggest that it is the disjunc-
> tive, fragmented, displaced agency of those who have suffered the sentence of his-
> tory—subjugation, domination, diaspora, displacement—that forces one to think out-
> side the certainty of the sententious. (56)

It is one thing, however, to spar with students at the university level and quite another to expose children to misleading cultural models.

It stands to reason that young children are susceptible to the values represented in films and television, particularly those of Disney, which has specifically targeted children as a consumer market. Yet remarkably little research has been undertaken in this area due to the television and movie industries' insistence that their productions do not affect behavior (a state of
denial that is rivaled only by that of the tobacco companies). In July 1992,
television executives did finally admit that TV violence contributes to social
problems. Reporting on a 1993 investigation into the scientific evidence for
the influence of violence on young people commissioned by the American
Psychological Association, *The Chronicle of Higher Education* called for
scholars to close the education gap by doing more research into the influence
of the media.[9] Also belatedly recognizing the need for parental guidance, the
New York Times inaugurated a bimonthly column on April 17, 1994, to as-
sess current films for violence, sex, and profanity, as well as provide a
"footnote" section on racial and sexual stereotyping. The *San Francisco
Chronicle* cast its net even wider after reviewing the research compiled by
Stanford University on the traumatic impact on one thousand schoolchildren
in California, Oregon, and Utah of the Polly Klaas kidnapping case—it rec-
ommended that parents prevent young children from watching the 6 O'clock
News.[10]

Despite this mounting evidence, Disney continues to insist that its animations are fantasies that have nothing to do with life today. This position was
reiterated when members of the American-Arab Anti-Discrimination Committee complained about the lyrics in *Aladdin*'s opening song, "Arabian
Nights." The film's offending stanza originally went:

> Oh, I come from a land,
> From a faraway place,
> Where the caravan camels roam
> Where they cut off your ear
> If they don't like your face.
> It's barbaric, but hey, it's home.

Disney's rebuttal, voiced by Howard Green, was to dismiss charges of racism as irrelevant and inconsequential. Green, when contacted by the *Washington Post*, attempted to rationalize away the criticism. He argued:

> It's certainly coming from a small minority because most people are very happy with it. All the characters are Arabs, the good guys and the bad guys, and the accents don't really connote anything, I don't think....As for the song, it's talking about a different time and a different place. It's a certain license that they're taking, but it's certainly not meant to reflect on the culture of today. It's a fictitious place. This seems kind of nit-picky.[11]

Resorting to the animations-are-fantasies defense that has worked so well for them, Disney stalled when Arab Americans requested a change in the lyrics, claiming that because songwriter collaborator Howard Ashman had died (from AIDS), it had no right to alter his verse. When angry activists persisted in voicing their objections, the studio reluctantly changed only the penultimate line of the stanza to: "Where it's flat and immense / And the heat is intense," in the subsequent video and worldwide film release, but not on the popular CD. Defending the decision to maintain the demeaning final line, Disney distribution president Dick Cook insisted that "barbaric" referred to the land and the heat, and not to the people.[12]

"Barbaric," however, was still a highly charged term in the months following Disney's release of *Aladdin*. How often had it been used on the nightly news during the previous three years to describe Saddam Hussein and his fellow Iraqis? Just as the giant Disney corporation defended its right to free speech, so did the United States government justify its right to intervene in Middle Eastern politics. The rationale behind both disputes centered around the iconicity of the Orientalist Other.

Operation Desert Storm

Jürgen Link has described the importance of "enemy images"— photographs, films, caricatures, and verbal metaphors—in constructing national identities. Arguing that the persuasive power of these images rests less in their ability to capture certain characteristics of a particular group and more in the assumptions they trigger, Link illustrated his point by discussing representations of Saddam Hussein (46–49). First depicted in the media as a benign presence in a Westernized, Basque cap during his period of opposition to the Ayatollah Khomeini, Hussein's character was expeditiously rewritten by newscasters into a telos of terrorism after he invaded Kuwait. Political cartoonists, however, faced more of a challenge, since they had to downplay or eliminate Hussein's headgear to accord with his disloyalty to the West.

The most common solution was to emphasize Hussein's facial features by playing on his superficial resemblance to Hitler. Paradoxically, this new image of Hussein also resembled posters advertising Hitler's archetypal Jewish Other, *Jud Süss*, the notoriously anti-Semitic hate film produced by the National Socialists in 1940 (Schulte-Sasse 85–88). The common signifiers in these "enemy images" of Nazi, Arab, and Jew are the bristly mustache, intense stare, and coarse skin. Taken independently, none signifies a particular value, but combined, they signal a range of semiotically contradictory meanings, depending on the spectator's ideological persuasions.

This "enemy image" of Saddam Hussein was given such wide currency in the media between Desert Strike in the summer of 1990 and Desert Storm in January and February of 1991 that it would have been surprising if the producers of *Aladdin*, who were hunched over the storyboards during this time, had not incorporated it into their characterization of the villain Jafar. Like Hussein, Jafar is mustachioed and dark skinned, but his appearance also owes a debt to political cartoons that reduced Khomeini to a turbaned and robed silhouette. In both cases the stereotype of the evil Orientalist Other has been collapsed into the enemy image. Musing about the source of creative ideas, art historian Ernst Gombrich contends that "the familiar will always remain the likely starting point for the rendering of the unfamiliar; an existing representation will always exert its spell over the artist" (82). That Jafar's character is more closely modeled on Hussein than on Khomeini becomes evident as the film progresses: The fictional villain is a devious plotter and untrustworthy ally who pretends loyalty to his benevolent master while scheming to seize his possessions. It was this personification of Hussein-the-betrayer that was beamed from satellite dishes around the world in 1990–91.

Both phases of the Gulf War were presented to the American public as media events, but Desert Storm, in particular, was a carefully constructed photomontage of sound bites and media clips designed to rivet viewers with short attention spans by simplifying the difference between good and evil and by keeping them entertained with nocturnal close-ups of exotic locales, terrifying scenes of destruction, and a dazzling display of technology. So did *Aladdin*. It matched the drama of the televised miniseries on the Gulf War with its own fire-eaters, underground bunkers, and son-et-lumières in the desert, most notably the frightening scenes set in the cave that showcased Disney's talent for necromancy.

Stylistically, both productions relied on conjury to engross their audiences, as one image effortlessly metamorphosed into the next. Neither revealed the telltale marks of the maker's hand. Just as Gérôme masked his brushstrokes with a high degree of finish under a smooth veneer to persuade his patrons of the authenticity of his vision of the Orient, Disney's animators sacrificed personal expression for corporate unity. Likewise the media strategists in the Pentagon's war room anonymously packaged their satellite-enhanced pyrotechnics for the nightly news. Nochlin's claim that Orientalist painters took great pains to make their viewers forget that their representations were produced by Western interlopers applies to Disney and the Gulf War as well (36–37). Like *Aladdin*'s Genie, both skillfully made their handicraft disappear.

In comparing Operation Desert Storm with World War II and the United States' engagements in Korea and Vietnam, John Kenneth Galbraith caustically observed that "technology had made war a clean, ascetic event, except perhaps for those under the bombs."[13] Television and technology had succeeded in naturalizing violence. Broadcasts of the Gulf War were beamed into the homes of spectators accustomed to adopting a passive position in front of their television sets or VCRs, where they routinely witnessed actors or cartoon characters reappear after suffering mortal wounds. Nor did death seem any more imminent in the televised specials on the war in the Middle East which diverted the viewer's attention from human targets to Iraqi Scud missiles. Moreover, the air-to-air Sparrow and Sidewinder missiles engaged in dogfights, and the air-to-ground Maverick missiles bore an uncanny visual similarity to weaponry launched and controlled by Sega's and Nintendo's joysticks. So striking was this affinity that General Norman Schwartzkopf found it necessary to issue a disclaimer stating, "It is not a Nintendo game. It is a tough battlefield where people are risking lives."[14] But at the time these words were uttered, the Pentagon's involvement in the entertainment industry had already become a matter of public record.

The Pentagon turned to Hollywood and Silicon Valley for hardware and software to expedite its "technowar." The Air Force realized that the movie industry's methods of electronically storing photographs would allow its spy planes immediate access to data on computer screens. A more telling contract was forged with a computer company which had developed software for a flight simulation game. The Pentagon, with its typical disregard for costs, decided to transform the $69.95 game into a $300,000 training simulator for the F-16.[15] Having realized since the Gulf War how easy it is to dazzle a media-ready public with electronic gadgetry, the Pentagon has now gone into the business of financing it. It announced a $1 billion ten-year program to develop flat-panel displays for use in laptop computers, aircraft cockpit displays, and goggles for virtual reality video games.[16]

The danger in this growing symbiosis between the Pentagon and the entertainment industry is that violence will become more abstracted, fulfilling the prophecies made over fifty years ago by Walter Benjamin and Theodor Adorno. Their fears about the sadomasochistic trend in mass culture were awakened by the antics of Mickey Mouse. Miriam Hansen contends that the two theorists saw the Disney syndrome as perched on the threshold to fascism: for Benjamin, a dialectical image of the utopian possibilities of technology in an age of technological warfare; for Adorno, a sociogram of the psychic deformations that linked the liberal-capitalist culture industry to its *völkisch* counterpart (54). Benjamin's concern has been borne out by the worldwide success achieved by Disney and other purveyors of domesticated violence, while Adorno's cause for anxiety has materialized in the enormous profits that have been reaped by captains of the culture industry who profess to have the good of the people at heart.

Still applicable today, this argument accounts for why Disney's top executives can be generous contributors to liberal Democratic causes and still double the deductible on employee health insurance at a time when quarterly profits had increased by 159 percent (Flower 257).

Disney's animation staff, in particular, has complained of layoffs, noncompetitive wages, and lack of individual recognition. Supposedly resolved after a 1941 strike (Schickel 254), these issues continue to fester, causing Disney's in-house dissidents to resort to subversive means. Its animators claimed credit for morphing Nancy Reagan's bony features onto Jafar's,[17] for turning an undersea tower into a phallus in *The Little Mermaid*, and for including Eisner's home phone number in the graffiti on a men's room wall in the laser disc version of *Who Framed Roger Rabbit?*[18] Even Robin Williams felt exploited when he discovered, after he had agreed to be paid at standard union scale for playing the Genie, that his voice was being used in commercials to promote *Aladdin*'s spin-off products.[19]

When Eisner was brought in to restructure Disney, he continued to operate on the defensive, staging daily battles with stockholders, critics, and disgruntled employees. Tension escalated in 1992 as the losses incurred at Euro Disney approached the $1 billion mark. The reasons are similar to those that alienated much of *Aladdin*'s public: the stereotypical treatment of non-Americans. Euro Disney's executives did not bother to research the habits of the French people—their dislike of long lines, their expectation of alcohol with lunch, and their preference for dining between 1:00 and 3:00 P.M. rather than "grazing" all day. Like the United States' attitude to the Middle East, the assumption was that foreigners should have to adjust to its standards.

The Ailing Empires

The corporate giant and the richest country in the world share the same paradoxical goal of international control based on the principles of freedom and family values. It is instrumental to their success that they project benevolent images while doing whatever they deem necessary to maintain their hegemonic positions. Disney works very hard to ensure that its name is synonymous with wholesome entertainment by producing a steady stream of animated features which result in new cartoon characters for it to promote at its theme parks and on lunch pails, T-shirts, and the dozens of other retail items it merchandises worldwide which keep its identification with "pixie dust" at the fore. Yet, at the same time, Eisner produces R-rated films under the Miramax, Hollywood Pictures, and Touchstone labels. Ever since Walt Disney was at the helm, the company has promoted the American myth of freedom, such as in *Aladdin* when the Genie wistfully aspires "to be free, to be my own master." That was, of course, the ostensible raison d'être for the Gulf War—to protect the "freedom" of Kuwatis and Saudis. Less was said about corporate America's interest in the oil fields or Saudi Arabia's mega-investment in America, which, if withdrawn, would have precipitated an economic crisis. Both empires, then, had a vested interest in perpetuating the illusion of guilelessness.

Mythmaking has always been central to the American agenda, yet even today, many politicians do not like to be reminded about the part it played in the development of this country. An exhibition at the National Museum of American Art in 1991 which attempted to illustrate how the concept of Manifest Destiny had been used by landscape artists to justify the appropriation of Western land was chastised in the Senate as "perverted" (Wallis 27), thus proving the point of its curator, William Truettner, that myth continually intersects with ideology to justify itself (40). According to Roland Barthes, myth becomes even more powerful when it assumes visual form. He contends that "pictures, to be sure, are more imperative than writing; they impose meaning at one stroke, without analyzing or diluting it" (110). As objectionable as that may seem to some of our elected officials, the military has rediscovered the potency of historical images.

Hoping to recoup the stature it lost after Vietnam, the Pentagon's teledrama of the Gulf War drew on apocalyptic myths deeply embedded in visual culture: the annihilation of the evil descendants of the Assyrian hordes on the sands of Mesopotamia. Symbolically casting out the forces of darkness with the phosphorescent light of its infrared scopes and laser-guided missiles, the victor claimed the spoils. Yet it was a hollow victory. The wicked Orientalist refused to be cowed and remains a continuous threat.

Disney, on the other hand, has rescued its empire from the taint of failure. Despite a series of setbacks in 1995 including the death of president Frank Wells, quadruple-bypass surgery for Eisner, the acrimonious departure of Katzenberg, and public opposition to a proposed Civil War theme park in Virginia, the company managed to stem its losses at Euro Disney by cutting costs and bringing in outside investors. It has even managed to placate its disgruntled Genie: Robin Williams agreed to star in Disney's hugely successful takeoff on *Aladdin, Aladdin and the King of Thieves*, which was released as a home video in the summer of 1996. Disney is stronger than ever. Its acquisition of Capital Cities/ABC for $19 billion makes it the largest entertainment company in the world. In addition to local TV stations, Disney now owns the cable sports channel ESPN, interests in the Lifetime and Arts & Entertainment cable networks, and newspapers and magazines.[20]

Its "infotainment" monopoly stretches from Latin America to Asia and Australia. Disney's global reach is cause for alarm: What mythic version of American values will it beam across its empire of Others? Nonetheless, Eisner staunchly maintains that "the most exportable form of TV entertainment are sports and children's programming because they have universal appeal and offend no political position."[21] Disney, like the Orientalist artists of the nineteenth century, is relying on the illusion of innocence to shield its controlling gaze.

Notes

I am indebted to my former student Kristina Lindell who sketched out the parallels between Aladdin and Orientalism in a term paper she wrote for my undergraduate course "Art in the Age of Revolutions." She subsequently proved to be an enthusiastic and dedicated research assistant when I decided to reconfigure this notion from semiotic and ideological perspectives and to situate it in the context of the Gulf War.

1. *The Chronicle of Higher Education,* 16 Feb. 1994.
2. 21 Nov. 1993.
3. The article in question was by David Kunzle. Stephen Fjellman was also forced to substitute a drawing instead of a photograph of the Magic Castle on the cover of his *Vinyl Leaves: Walt Disney World and America.* See Scott Heller.
4. *New York Times* 28 April 1994.
5. London *Sunday Times* 21 Nov. 1993.
6. *Washington Post* 10 Jan. 1993.
7. 10 Jan. 1993.
8. 21 Nov. 1993.
9. 5 Jan. 1994.

10. 27 April 1994. See also Keisha L. Hoerrner, "Gender Roles in Disney Films: Analyzing Behaviors from Snow White to Simba," *Women's Studies in Communication* 19. Summer 1996: 213–28.
11. 10 Jan. 1993.
12. *Los Angeles Times* 10 July 1993.
13. *Los Angeles Times* 10 Feb. 1991.
14. *Washington Post* 28 Feb. 1991.
15. *Washington Post* 27 Jan. 1991.
16. *New York Times* 1 May 1994.
17. *New York Times* 11 Nov. 1992.
18. *San Francisco Chronicle* 18 Feb. 1994.
19. *New York Times* 11 Nov. 1992.
20. *New York Times* 6 Aug. 1985.
21. *New York Times* 6 Aug. 1985.

Works Cited

Aladdin. Dirs. Ron Clements, John Musker. Animated. Voices: Scott Weinger, Robin Williams, Linda Larkin. The Walt Disney Company, 1992.

Aladdin and the King of Thieves. Dir. Tad Stones. Animated. Voices: Scott Weinger, Robin Williams, Linda Larkin. Walt Disney Home Video, 1996.

Barthes, Roland. *Mythologies*. Trans. Annette Lavers. New York: Hill and Wang, 1972.

Bhabha, Homi K. "Postcolonial Authority and Postmodern Guilt." Eds. Laurence Grossberg, C. Nelson, and P. Treichler. *Cultural Studies*. New York: Routledge, 1992. 56–68.

Eliot, Marc. *Walt Disney: Hollywood's Dark Prince*. New York: Birch Lane, 1993.

Fjellman, Stephen. *Vinyl Leaves: Walt Disney World and America*. Boulder, Colorado: Westview, 1992.

Flower, Joe. *Prince of the Magic Kingdom: Michael Eisner and the Re-Making of Disney*. New York: John Wiley, 1991.

Gombrich, Ernst. *Art and Illusion: A Study in the Psychology of Pictorial Representation*. Princeton UP, 1960.

Haddawy, Husain. Introduction. *The Arabian Nights*. Trans. Husain Haddawy. New York: Norton, 1990.

Hansen, Miriam. "Of Mice and Ducks: Benjamin and Adorno on Disney." *South Atlantic Quarterly* 92 (1993): 28–61.

Heller, Scott. "Dissecting Disney: Scholars Examine the Entertainment Empire's Contribution to Popular Culture." *The Chronicle of Higher Education* 16 Feb. 1994.

Link, Jürgen. "Fanatics, Fundamentalists, Lunatics, and Drug Traffickers—The New Southern Enemy Image." *Cultural Critique*. Fall 1991: 33–53.

Nochlin, Linda. "The Imaginary Orient." *The Politics of Vision: Essays on Nineteenth-Century Art and Society*. New York: Harper, 1989. 33–59.

Said, Edward W. *Orientalism*. New York: Vintage, 1979.

Schickel, Richard. *The Disney Version*. New York: Touchstone, 1985.

Schulte-Sasse, Jochen, and Linda Schulte-Sasse. "War, Otherness, and Illusionary Identifications with the State." *Cultural Critique*. Fall 1991: 67–95.

Shaheen, Jack. *The TV Arab*. Bowling Green, Ohio: Bowling Green State U Popular P, 1984.

Smoodin, Eric, ed. *Disney Discourse: Producing the Magic Kingdom*. New York: Routledge, 1994.

Stevens, MaryAnne, ed. *The Orientalists: Delacroix to Matisse*. London: Royal Academy of Arts, 1984.

Truettner, William H., ed. *The West As America*. Washington, DC: Smithsonian Inst. P, 1991.

Wallis, Brian. "Senators Attack Smithsonian Show." *Art in America* July 1991: 27.

EPILOGUE

I have often felt guilty about participating in this project and even more so for being its leader. Disney has been a constant in my life, as hardly anything else has. It was Disney's *Snow White* that probably introduced me to clear concepts of good and evil in ways, to a child, that Sunday School and the King James' did not. It also taught me an important lesson: If you disobey, if you do something you were told not to do—like speak to strangers or, worse, accept something to eat from strangers—something awful will happen to you. And yes, as I discussed in chapter 3, I learned a few things from *Snow White* as well as from other Disney movies that I have had to unlearn.

But it was at a Disney attraction at the 1964 World's Fair where I heard, again probably for the first time, that diversity of cultures was what made the world so wonderful. "It's a Small World," in the Pesi-Cola pavillion, did not just celebrate the universal innocence of childhood; it celebrated multiculturalism, and said that regardless of race, gender, ethnicity, and nationality, people are the same everywhere. This was a revolutionary statement made during the heat of the Cold War, the Civil Rights riots, and the anti-Woman's Movement in the sixties.

Another attraction at that fair presented by Disney, in the General Electric pavillion, was the Carousel of Progress. As Audio-Animatronic figures demonstrated the technological changes since the turn of the century, the audience was invited to sing along: "There's a great, big, beautiful tomorrow shining at the end of every day." The optimism of harmony in the world possible through scientific invention is the mantra of Epcot Center today, as it was at the World's Fair nearly three decades—an entire generation—before.

Elsewhere in theme parks resonate songs like "Colors of the Wind" and "Circle of Life" with similar messages of hope. In *Hunchback*, children are told that God loves the outcast; in *Beauty*, one should see what is on the inside of people; in *Mermaid*, one may be born in a world of limitation, but one need not stay there; in *Pocahontas*, one must live in harmony with the land; in *The Lion King*, *hakuna matata* ("no worries"), but you must take responsibility; in *Mulan*, the preservation of honor is not the domain of only one gender. In all of the film animations are sociomoral messages that, if regarded by children of today, will indeed make the world a better place tomorrow.

Regardless, as argued by each contributor to this collection, there are problems with these messages. Disney is insidious, especially because the company's animated and live-action films seem innocuous and are geared primarily to an audience of children. Disney is seductive. Recently I spent six days at the theme parks in Orlando and was seduced over and over by the goodness of Disney. After all, as I took the boat ride through "It's a Small World," I wanted to "remember the magic," as the song goes and goes in the 3 o'clock parade through the Magic Kingdom. I wanted to return to the inno-cent pleasure of my own faded childhood, a pleasure that indeed millions of children enjoy at Disneyworld and at a Disney movie. Regardless of contra-dictory messages in any given Disney film, being told "When you wish upon a star / makes no difference who you are / your dreams will come true" is not a bad thing. It is true that the heavyset octopus in *The Little Mermaid*, and the jealous stepmothers, and the second-born Scar, and all of the other vil-lains have their own stories to tell that are not told by Disney. Nevertheless, is it not good to be told by Disney that if you show kindness to other people and animals, even if it costs you your life, that this is right to do, and to do the opposite is wrong?

Besides, regardless of the agency or instrument, no man, no corporation, no film will ever depict a morality that is politically correct and acceptable to all of us short of the golden rule, Do unto others as you would have done unto you. When I went to Disneyworld, I went alone and was very much aware of how different I was from nearly everyone else. People in wheel-chairs, the elderly, those of all manner of skin and dress—all seemed to be with someone else. Family, heterosexual marriage, children—this was what I saw and heard everywhere, even if some of the performers were homosexual. The shows and attractions reiterated the message that people must form nu-clear families.

While jostled by the maddening crowd, I was thinking that someone ought to make it a requirement of marriage that honeymoons be taken at Dis-neyworld. Ironically, it would persuade anyone, I would think, to practice birth control. I am not referring to just the multitude of little people there seems to be in this world, and of course, you would find a concentrated amount at Disneyworld, which was a shock to this person, who rarely sees children in the academic world in which I live. I am not referring to just quantity; I am referring to quality. I heard children scream at their parents in every language possible. And I heard parents scream at their kids in every language possible and then some. We expect these theme parks and the entire Disney operation to return all of us to happy, sweet childhood. But we must not blame Disney for our obnoxious, self-centered, mean-spirited, childish behavior. Although many detractors have decried the commercialization of Disney, let us not blame Disney for all of our woes. I think that he was a man with a vision, and because of him, much goodness and virtue continue to be urged by sometimes a lone voice in a world that otherwise clamors with maliciousness.

Christmas 2000, I took my nieces to see *The Emperor's New Groove* (which was when I got the idea for this book's title). Throughout that movie, I was ecstatic that Disney was finally saying something that needed to be said, and said emphatically, to an entire generation of children: If you grow up to be self-centered and self-absorbed, you will make yourself and everyone around you miserable.

Let us keep taking our children and ourselves to Disney movies and theme parks and come away feeling uplifted and motivated to be better human beings. However, the Disney ideology—the Emperor's old groove—is fraught with colonizing messages that continue to advocate white, Anglo-Saxon, middle-class, Protestant, heterosexual, patriarchal American superiority. This process—this Disneyfication of our children—should not be overlooked in favor of cuteness and promises of happy endings. On the other hand, since we live in a world that is conflicted with multiple perceptions that are largely not respected from culture to culture, let us remember that that is the real world in which we live and must change, and that Disney's is a magic kingdom that cannot fix our problems with just the sweep of a magical wand.

Brenda Ayres

CONTRIBUTORS

MARK AXELROD is Professor of Comparative Literature and Film and Television at Chapman University, Orange, California. His doctorate came from the University of Minnesota; and his master's, from Indiana University in Comparative Literature. He has taught in Cuba, Chile, Scotland, Argentina, England, and Denmark as well as the United States, earning numerous awards for both his fiction and film writing.

BRENDA AYRES is Associate Professor of English at Middle Georgia College in Cochran, Georgia. Her PhD, from the University of Southern Mississippi, is in Nineteenth-century British Literature. She is the author of *Dissenting Women in Dickens' Novels: Subversion of Domestic Ideology* (Greenwood, 1998), and the editor of *Frances Trollope and the Novel of Social Change* (Greenwood, 2002), *Silent Voices: Forgotten Novels by Victorian Women Writers* (Greenwood, 2003), and *The Emperor's Old Groove.*

KELLIE BEAN is Associate Professor at Marshall University in Huntington, West Virginia. She received her PhD from the University of Delaware and writes on British drama and feminism.

STEPHEN M. BUHLER is Professor of English at the University of Nebraska–Lincoln, where he teaches courses in Renaissance literature, early modern culture, and contemporary stories/storytelling. He received his doctorate from the University of California at Los Angeles. His most recent publications include: *Shakespeare in the Cinema: Ocular Proof* (Albany: State University of New York P, 2002); "Reviving Juliet, Repackaging Romeo: Transformations of Character in Pop and Post-Pop Music," in *Shakespeare after Mass Media*, ed. Richard Burt (New York: Palgrave, 2002); and "To Challenge Ghostly Fathers: Teaching *Hamlet* and Its Interpretations Through Film and Video," in *Approaches to Teaching Shakespeare's* Hamlet, ed. Bernice W. Kliman (New York: MLA, 2001).

RICHARD FINKELSTEIN is Professor and Chair of English at the State University of New York College at Geneseo. He holds a PhD from the University of Chicago. His articles and book reviews on Shakespeare, Jonson, and other Renaissance dramatists have appeared in *The Journal of Medieval and Renaissance Studies, Comparative Drama, Renaissance and Reformation,* and *Modern Philology.*

SUSAN HINES is the Director of Instructional Design at the Savannah College of Art and Design. She received her PhD in English from Georgia State University and has published with *Educause Online, Syllabus, H-Net, Extrapolation, The Victorian Newsletter, The Priest, Contemporary Poets,* and *Studies in Browning and His Circle.* This project—then "Decolonizing Disney," now *The Emperor's Old Groove*—was her brainchild, and she participated in its early editing as well as in co-writing the introduction.

SHENG-MEI MA is Associate Professor of English at Michigan State University, specializing in Asian American studies and Holocaust/genocide studies. He wrote *Immigrant Subjectivities in Asian American and Asian Diaspora Literatures* (State U of New York P, 1998). Completed under the auspices of the Rockefeller Fellowship for 1997–98, his second book, *The Deathly Embrace: Orientalism and Asian American Ethnicity,* was published by the University of Minnesota P, 2000.

DIANNE SACHKO MACLEOD is Professor of Art History at the University of California at Davis. She received her doctorate from the University of California at Berkeley. Her *Art and the Victorian Middle Class: Money and the Making of Cultural Identity* was published by Cambridge University Press in 1996 and was awarded the Jacques Barzun Prize in Cultural History by the American Philosophical Society. She also coedited a volume of essays titled *Colonialism Transposed: The Impact of the Colonies on Great Britain* (Ashgate, 1998).

KATHLEEN E. B. MANLEY is Professor Emeritus at the University of Northern Colorado, having taught in the honors and women's studies programs as well as in the English Department. She earned her PhD in folklore from Indiana University. Some recent publications include "The Woman in Process in Angela Carter's 'The Bloody Chamber'" in *Angela Carter and the Fairy Tale,* ed. Danielle M. Roemer and Cristina Bacchilega; "Native American Writing," in the *Encyclopedia of Folkore and Literature,* ed. Mary Ellen Brown and Bruce Rosenberg; and "Atwood's Reconstruction of Folktales: *The Handmaid's Tale* and 'Bluebeard's Egg'" in *Approaches to Teaching Atwood's* The Handmaid's Tale *and Other Works,* ed. Sharon R. Wilson, Thomas B. Friedman, and Shannon Hengen.

PUSHPA NAIDU PAREKH, a native of India, is Associate Professor of the English Department and Director of the Honors Program at Spelman College, Atlanta. She teaches Postcolonial Women's Literature, Women in Non-Western Literatures (including Native American literatures), Contemporary African Literature, African Diaspora and the World, Immigrant Women's Literature, and Victorian and Modern British Literature. She has published several essay chapters and articles on postcolonial writers and is coeditor of the sourcebook *Postcolonial African Writers* (Greenwood, 1998) and author of a book-length critical study of selected nineteenth- and twentieth-century British poets, *Response to Failure* (Peter Lang, 1998).

CHRISTIANE STANINGER has worked most recently at the University of San Diego and Palomar College, teaching Literature in Translation, German, and Composition. She received her undergraduate degrees in literature and linguistics from the University of Goettingen in Germany and completed her master's and doctorate in literature at the University of California, San Diego. Recent publications include essays on the poetry of Paul Celan and E.T.A. Hoffmann's *The Sandman* as criticism of the Enlightenment.

BRIAN E. SZUMSKY teaches writing at Robert Morris College. He works and lives with his family in the Chicago area. His other writings have appeared in *Lion and the Unicorn, Marvels and Tales*, and *In Posse* on the *Web Del Sol* Web site.

CHRISTOPHER WISE is currently an Associate Professor in Islamic and American Studies at the University of Jordan in Amman. In 1996–97 he taught at L'Université d'Ouagadougou on a Fulbright. Besides authoring some thirty scholarly articles, many of them dealing with postcolonialism, he recently edited *The Desert Shore: Literatures of the Sahel* and *Yambo Ouologuem: Postcolonial Writer, Islamic Militant.*

INDEX